new classic family dinners

new classic family dinners

mark peel

WITH MARTHA ROSE SHULMAN
PHOTOGRAPHY BY LUCY SCHAEFFER

WILEY

JOHN WILEY & SONS, INC.

[ACKNOWLEDGMENTS]

To Martha Rose Shulman, for her talent, taste, and perseverance.

To photographer Lucy Schaeffer, for her eye, and also to food stylist Anne Disrude for the same.

To my editor Justin Schwartz and my agent Janis Donnaud.

To Jay Perrin, our General Manager at Campanile, the man who keeps the lights on.

To Erica Lins, our Chef de Cuisine.

To Fernando Salazar, our pastry chef.

To Jack Stumpf, my farmers' market companion and helper, who never misses a Monday Night Family Dinner.

To the entire staff at Campanile.

This book is printed on acid-free paper.

For general information on our other products and services or for technical support, please contact our Customer Care Department within the United States at (800) 762-2974, outside the United States at (317) 572-3993 or fax (317) 572-4002.

Wiley also publishes its books in a variety of electronic formats. Some content that appears in print may not be available in electronic books. For more information about Wiley products, visit our web site at www.wiley.com.

Prop Styling by Dani Fisher
Food Styling by Anne Disrude

Library of Congress Cataloging-in-Publication Data:
Peel, Mark.
New Classic Family Dinners / Mark Peel, with Martha Rose Shulman;
photography by Lucy Schaeffer.
p. cm.
Includes index.
ISBN 978-0-470-38247-9 (cloth)
1. Cookery. 2. Cookery, International. 3. Campanile (Restaurant) I. Shulman, Martha Rose. II. Title.

TX714.P4393 2009
641.59– dc22
2008049901

Printed in China

10 9 8 7 6 5 4 3 2 1

To Daphne, who has made my life whole.

[CONTENTS]

[INTRODUCTION]

This collection of recipes, drawn from many years of Campanile Monday Night Family Dinner menus, is the reference book I'd like to have on my shelf right now. It's a cheat sheet with a cross section of basic and classic material, everything from garlic mayonnaise, Russian dressing, and Caesar salad to pot roast, spaghetti and meatballs, and Boston cream pie. These comforting dishes are simple enough to make at home for anyone who cooks, classic enough to become family standards, and easily adaptable for dinner parties.

I started serving family dinners at Campanile as a way to make a habitually quiet night at the restaurant more interesting. Mondays can be slow, which is why many restaurants are closed on that night. The idea was to offer a reasonably priced three-course meal, served family style, with a suggested wine by the glass or bottle. The dinners evolved into a weekly event, attracting regular customers who have been coming back every Monday night for years. They come because they love the food and the relaxed ambiance at the restaurant, and it's a great deal.

Like our regular Campanile menus, Monday Night Family Dinner menus are seasonal. Sometimes they revolve around a holiday, sometimes around an ingredient that's in season for a short time, sometimes around a type of food, such as shellfish. My inspiration for the menu is usually an idea for the main dish, and this sets the tone for the meal. Some menus are thematic—a New England clambake, Southern fried chicken, meat and three. Often I'll have a craving for a comforting American or European family dish, like pot au feu, coq au vin, roast beef, seven-hour leg of lamb, or a more lowbrow comfort food classic like tuna noodle casserole (but we make it with homemade tuna confit, creamy béchamel sauce, and the highest quality Gruyère cheese).

More than anything, I love to evoke a particular era in American gastronomy, circa 1950. I'm intrigued by dishes known collectively as "continental classics," such as veal piccata, lobster Newburg, spaghetti with clam sauce, and peach melba. These dishes were extremely popular in America in the 1950s and '60s, but eventually they became clichés and fell out of favor. They were done by too many restaurants, usually badly with lousy ingredients and lots of shortcuts. But a dish doesn't end up on thousands of menus if it doesn't have some kind of core value. I've made it my mission to find those core values and bring these dishes back to life, and you'll find the results in the pages that follow.

[FROM RESTAURANT TO HOME KITCHEN]

Since beginning work on this book I've cooked more at home than ever before, and in so doing I've learned a lot more about the demands of home cooking. I've also learned a lot from my wife Daphne Brogdon, who did not grow up in a cooking household and has never been particularly comfortable at the stove.

As I developed recipes for the book, I would often ask myself the question: "Would Daphne do this?" It's a rhetorical question, but the point here is that this is not a chef cookbook. The recipes aren't difficult, the food isn't fancy, and you won't require a kitchen staff to succeed.

When professional chefs cook at home we face the same challenges you do, and in some cases we're at a disadvantage. Yes, we can chop faster and we're not afraid of turning the heat up high (though we often forget to turn on the fan, only to have our smoke alarms go off); but we also make a bigger mess, because we're used to having dishwashers scooping up dirty dishes and coming through the work area with a broom and mop. I never think twice about using two or three pans and more than one strainer for different steps when I'm testing a dish in the Campanile kitchen, but at home I have only one strainer, a limited number of pots and pans, and nobody to clean up after me, so I've learned to consolidate some of those steps. In a restaurant, cooking is segmented; nobody makes a dish from beginning to the end. When I begin a chicken fricassee, somebody has already chopped the onions and peeled the garlic, skimmed the chicken broth and cleaned the mushrooms. After a few too many late-night dinners when my daughter Vivien was too tired and cranky to eat, I've finally learned what the experienced home cook knows: Shopping, preparing the ingredients, and cooking a dish, even an easy dish, take time. So, planning is essential.

I do want you to take time with these recipes. My cooking is all about drawing out the maximum flavor from good ingredients, and sometimes ingredients make you work hard and take an extra step or two to yield the extra bit of flavor that makes a dish memorable. If you make a stock with lobster shells that requires you to pound the shells, sauté them, cook them with aromatics, and strain them

twice, it's because the dish you will make with that stock will be so incredible that your reputation as a cook will be solidified forever—even if you never cook anything this complex again.

But there are plenty of easy recipes in this book. If you're not an experienced cook and/or want to cook something after work on a weeknight, make one of the roast chicken recipes on pages 151-153, or Spaghetti with Garlic, Olive Oil, and Basil (page 99), or Cornmeal-Crusted Pan-Fried Trout (page 184). If you don't feel comfortable with a kitchen knife, don't try to make a composed salad that calls for finely and precisely diced vegetables; make Butter Lettuce Salad with Stilton and Walnuts (page 16) instead. For every recipe that calls for finely diced vegetables there are two or more stews that call for a rough chop. If you do something well, do it often; become comfortable with five dishes and build from there. If you make a great meatloaf your family will love it even if they have it twice a month.

Every so often, try a more complicated recipe. But don't decide to make something like Lobster Pot Pie (page 176) plus a dessert on a whim. Some recipes, like Lasagne with Bolognese Sauce, Creamed Spinach, and Poached Egg (page 97), are really compound recipes that rely on building blocks. The lasagne requires a Bolognese sauce and a béchamel sauce for the creamed spinach, which are both time-consuming. These are not recipes to make from scratch on a weeknight. When you have some leisure time on a Sunday afternoon, make Bolognese sauce (page 91). By doing this, you'll be learning how to make a stew, and you'll end up with a freezer full of rich, complex stewed beef sauce that you can use for a number of dishes in this book. Then learn to make a béchamel sauce (it's really easy) using the recipe on page 111. With Bolognese sauce in your freezer, béchamel under your belt, and a little advance planning, the lasagna for a dinner party becomes quite simple.

The recipes in this book express how I feel about food: You can make the most common dish supremely good if your ingredients are the best and each step is done correctly. If you are making a Caesar salad, use only the hearts of the romaine, the best Parmesan, garlic croutons made from good country bread, fresh garlic crushed in a mortar and pestle, and the best extra virgin olive oil. If you're making mashed potatoes, use enough butter and cream to make them truly creamy and rich (I am convinced that most people lie about their mashed potatoes; if they're good, it's because they're full of butter and cream) and get them silky by straining them and heating them in a double boiler. A simple potato and leek soup will have great depth of flavor if you use a good chicken stock, and it will have a silky texture only if you put it through a sieve after you blend it. You can make mediocre fried chicken, or you can fry the chicken in pork lard in a cast-iron skillet after marinating it in buttermilk and it will be fantastic. Even a steak house salad that many chefs turn up their noses at, iceberg lettuce with Roquefort dressing, will make you sit up and take notice if you use a heavy head of crunchy, juicy iceberg lettuce and good-quality blue cheese. This is the crux of the book. Cooking this way will make you a better and more confident cook, and will endear you forever to your family and friends.

[MISCELLANEOUS EQUIPMENT]

This list of equipment is not for a complete batterie de cuisine. Rather, it's a short list of a few items you may not have that are useful in the recipes in this book. We rely on them at Campanile, and you can easily find them, at cookware stores and online. If you want to execute the recipes properly, I urge you to invest in these few simple items.

FOOD MILL

A food mill is a piece of equipment that purees and strains food at the same time. It consists of a bottomless bowl fitted with an interchangeable bottom screen with fine, medium, or large holes that is locked into place with a crank. The crank is fitted with a blade, and when you pour soft food into the food mill and turn the crank, the blade pushes it against the bottom and through the screen. It's very useful for pureeing soups and sauces, mashing potatoes, and pureeing cooked vegetables. In some recipes the food must be strained through a fine strainer once it has gone through the food mill.

KITCHEN SCALE

Americans aren't in the habit of using kitchen scales, but they're a great help when it comes to accuracy, especially for pastry. I recommend a digital scale with a large platform and a capacity of at least 2 pounds or 1 kilo, preferably 4 pounds.

ICE CREAM MAKER

There are many small, reasonably priced electric ice cream makers on the market. The best are the old-style ones that use ice and salt as the freezing agent. Although they're cheap and make great ice cream, they are horrifically noisy. Lock it in the garage while it's spinning.

IMMERSION BLENDER

We use these most often for soups. An immersion blender is a blender blade on a stick. You immerse it into a pot of food and blend the food right in the pot. It simplifies this task, and if you're working with a hot soup, it's much safer than using a blender or food processor. Get a strong one with a long shaft.

MANDOLIN OR JAPANESE SLICER

This piece of equipment speeds up and simplifies the task of making thin, even slices, particularly helpful if you are making a potato gratin or need fine vegetable shreds for a salad or coleslaw. The simple light green plastic Japanese Benriner slicer, which you can find online and at Japanese markets, is a much less complicated and expensive piece of equipment than a French mandoline. These machines come with a slicing guard. Use it. You don't want to know about the accidents I've seen in restaurant kitchens.

MORTAR AND PESTLE

You will need a mortar and pestle to make many of the mayonnaise-based sauces and pestos in this book. It's a piece of equipment every kitchen should have for mashing garlic, making pesto, or grinding small amounts of spices. A mortar and pestle is easy to use, fast, and easy to clean. They come in many sizes, made of different materials, including wood, granite, porcelain, and marble. Only buy a wooden one if it's made from olive wood, which is very hard and won't

absorb the aromas of the foods you grind. Get one that will hold at least 2 cups and is sturdy enough that it won't break if you pound a little too hard.

SALAD SPINNER

Herbs and lettuces need to be properly dried after washing, and this is the best tool for it. After you spin herbs, lay them on paper towels to dry completely before chopping.

ELECTRIC SPICE MILL

When spices are ground, their aromas begin to dissipate quickly, so we use whole spices and grind them as needed. An electric spice mill is the same piece of equipment as a coffee grinder. But don't use your coffee grinder for spices or your coffee will smell like spice and your spices will smell like coffee. (I don't care what anyone says: Spiced coffee is not good.) Label your coffee mill and your spice mill.

RUBBER SPATULA

The rubber spatula is your friend. You may have one, but it is underutilized. Get the heat-resistant kind, and use it to fold and stir ingredients together and to stir sauces on the stove to prevent scorching. Use it to scrape out the last bit of food from a bowl, a pan, a pot, or a blender, to push food through a strainer, and to scrape the food that sticks to the outside. We save hundreds of dollars in potentially lost servings every year in the restaurant just by using the spatula.

STRAINERS (SIEVES)

Strainers or sieves are important in many of the recipes in this book. The ultimate texture of a dish often depends on them. There are several types. If you are going to have only one, get a medium wire-mesh strainer, the kind you can find in a supermarket. If you need finer holes, you can always line it with cheesecloth. For large quantities of soup and sauce (such as Bolognese sauce, page 91), it's very useful to have a chinois, a large conical strainer, either metal with small holes or wire mesh with a wooden pestle to push the food through. Just make sure you have a deep pot to set it into to catch the puree that comes through the sides. A flat, fine strainer stretched in a round wooden or metal frame, called a tamis, is useful for mashed potatoes and other purees, and it makes a good sifter, but it's not essential.

THERMOMETER

A digital thermometer is essential for gauging the doneness of meat, for deep frying, and for many pastry procedures, such as making caramel or custard sauce. These are cheap and available everywhere. Make sure you get the kind that goes up to 400°F (a regular meat thermometer will not go high enough for deep frying and caramel).

TONGS

Tongs are much more useful than spoons or spatulas for cooking and manipulating meat and many other types of food, especially when you're searing items on top of the stove or removing foods, such as just opened mussels or clams, from a hot pan or pot. You will encounter the phrase "Using tongs" in many of the recipes in this book. I keep a pair next to the stove at all times.

ZESTER OR MICROPLANE®

When a recipe calls for the zest of citrus fruit, you want the outer layer of peel but none of the bitter white pith. The zester is a special tool you use for this that removes the zest in long, thin strands (which then require chopping). You can also use a Microplane zester, the kitchen version of a rasp. The Microplane zester grates zest very fine so that it requires no chopping. This tool can also be used to grate ginger and nutmeg.

[NOTES ON A FEW INGREDIENTS]

I've been specific about this in the ingredients list for each recipe, but I want you to know this in advance.

- Salt is Diamond Crystal kosher salt. Except in pastry, I always use kosher salt. Because of its crystalline structure, kosher salt is not as salty as regular table salt or fine sea salt.
- Milk is whole milk.
- Butter is unsalted butter.
- Olive oil is extra virgin olive oil.
- Eggs (and egg yolks) are large or extra-large eggs.

[1]

SALADS AND WARM STARTERS

All of the recipes in this chapter have been served as first courses on our Monday Night Family Dinner menus and were selected to complement the main dish. Although the dinners almost always derive their names from the entrée (when you ask "what's for dinner," you're not thinking about the salad), the salad or starter is a crucial part of the menu; many times it's what you remember most about a meal.

There are several things to consider when you're planning dinner. The first course should go with the main dish thematically and balance out its flavors. If you're serving a French classic like pot au feu, which is a time-consuming dish, you'd look to other French family classics, but easy ones like Leeks Vinaigrette. A dish from the American South like fried chicken calls for a starter that evokes the same region, like a green and red tomato salad. Sometimes our theme revolves around a type of food, like "Mollusks and Crustaceans"; that meal could start with Grilled Squid, Potato, and Asparagus Salad, and feature Lobster Newburg as the main dish. The first course should have flavors and textures that contrast with the main dish. If your entrée is a rich ragout or a stew, for example, don't serve a soup or a ragout for the appetizer; serve something light instead, like a salad with firm, crunchy textures. There's a reason that crunchy, simple salads like iceberg lettuce with blue cheese dressing are on steak house menus; when you're getting a big juicy steak as your main dish, you don't want to overload before it arrives.

Though we normally serve these as first courses at Campanile, you can certainly make a delicious meal out of some of the substantial dishes here. The vegetarian dishes here make great entrées. You can also make a meal serving two or three of these at a time; they're informal and look beautiful presented on platters.

There are recipes here, such as Caesar Salad and Chef's Salad, that are variations on dishes I've tasted over and over throughout my life. I want to restore them to their former glory. Most of the work is in the preparation, with easy final assembly. Use the best ingredients you can find and prepare them with care. I'm not sure if the whole is greater than the sum of its parts, but if the parts are not of high quality, the sum won't amount to much.

butter lettuce salad with stilton and walnuts [makes 4 servings]

This simple, elegant salad is almost like a cheese course; all you need is some Port to go with the Stilton and walnuts. Arrange it on a large platter. If you toss it in a bowl the heavy ingredients (the nuts and cheese) will fall to the bottom of the bowl, whereas on the platter you can scatter them over the lettuce and they'll stay there, where they belong. The dressing here is the lemon vinaigrette we use every day at Campanile on any basic green salad, especially the tender ones. If Campanile were a baseball team, this dressing would be our utility infielder. The recipe makes more than you'll need for this salad, but it will keep in the refrigerator for a couple of days.

[BASIC LEMON VINAIGRETTE]

	Zest of ½ large lemon
1	small or ½ medium shallot, minced, rinsed with cold water, and drained on paper towels
2	tablespoons strained freshly squeezed lemon juice
1½	teaspoons white wine vinegar or champagne vinegar
¼	teaspoon kosher salt
⅛	teaspoon cracked black peppercorns
¼	cup canola oil
¼	cup extra virgin olive oil

[SALAD]

2	small heads Bibb lettuce, leaves separated, washed and dried
3	ounces Stilton cheese
16	walnut halves (8 whole walnuts), very lightly toasted and broken up into smaller pieces
1	teaspoon Dijon mustard
½	teaspoon mild honey, such as clover
1	tablespoon plus 1 teaspoon chopped chives

1. Make the dressing: Bring a small pan of water to a boil and add the lemon zest. Blanch for 45 seconds, drain, and dry on paper towels. Chop fine and transfer to a medium bowl, along with the shallot. (Blanching reduces the bitterness in the lemon zest, which is important here, but not in other recipes.)

2. Pour the lemon juice over the shallot and lemon peel. Add the vinegar, salt, and pepper. Stir together. Whisk in the canola oil and the olive oil. Taste by dipping a piece of lettuce into the dressing, and adjust the seasoning. Set aside ⅓ cup in a bowl, measuring cup, or jar, and refrigerate the rest of the dressing in a covered jar.

3. Make the salad: Arrange the lettuce leaves on a large platter (or 2 smaller platters). Sprinkle on the cheese and the walnuts.

4. Whisk the mustard and honey into the ⅓ cup dressing and drizzle over the salad. Top with the chives and serve.

[NOTE] I prefer to use white wine vinegar—champagne vinegar with 7 percent acidity, to be exact—in most of my salad dressings. High-quality red wine vinegar would be good too, though white wine or champagne vinegar has greater clarity. I find sherry vinegar too sweet for some dressings, and balsamic unacceptably so.

[HOW TO TOAST NUTS]
Preheat the oven to 350°F. There is a very small margin of time between the moment when nuts are toasted and the moment they begin to burn and become bitter, so you must watch carefully. Put the nuts into a small ovenproof pan or on a baking sheet and place in the oven. Check after 4 minutes; they usually take around 5 to 6 minutes. They should have a toasty, popcorn aroma. Transfer immediately to a bowl to cool. You can also toast them in a pan over medium heat, shaking the pan constantly, or in a toaster oven.

almost classic caesar salad [makes 6 servings]

As simple as a Caesar salad is, it may have more variations than any other American salad. I've had incredible Caesars and horrible ones. They're truly deserving of their popularity if you follow certain rules: Use only the hearts of the romaine and don't chop them up; make fresh dressing and use the best Parmesan you can find. If it weren't for the attractive, irregularly shaped garlic croutons, this would be a classic Caesar salad (though it isn't made tableside by a waiter in an ill-fitting vest).

[DRESSING]

1	fat garlic clove, halved, green shoot removed
¼	teaspoon kosher salt
¼	cup plus 1 teaspoon canola oil
2	anchovy fillets, soaked, drained, and patted dry (page 131)
	Zest of 1 lemon
1	tablespoon red wine vinegar
1½	teaspoons strained freshly squeezed lemon juice
1	large egg yolk (coddle for 3 minutes if desired; see page 29)
⅓	cup extra virgin olive oil
⅓	teaspoon cracked black peppercorns
3	tablespoons freshly grated Parmesan cheese

[SALAD]

⅓	cup finely diced red onion
3	cups garlic croutons (page 29)
3	romaine hearts, leaves separated, washed and dried
3	ounces Parmesan cheese, shaved
	Cracked black peppercorns to taste

KOSHER SALT

There are two types of kosher salt: Diamond Crystal salt and flaked kosher salt. Diamond Crystal is made up of several salt crystals stuck together, and each grain has a larger surface area than each grain of flaky kosher salt. Because the grains are bigger, there is actually less of it per measure than there is of the flaky type. So a teaspoon of Diamond Crystal salt will not be as salty as the same measure of flaky kosher salt. With the exception of pastry, I use Diamond Crystal kosher salt in virtually all of my cooking.

1. Make the dressing: In a mortar and pestle, mash the garlic clove with the salt and 1 teaspoon of the canola oil until smooth. Add the anchovies and continue to mash together until the mixture is very smooth.

2. Bring a small pan of water to a boil and add the lemon zest. Blanch for 45 seconds, drain, and dry on paper towels. Chop fine and add to the garlic mixture. Add the vinegar and lemon juice and mix together. Stir in the egg yolk.

3. Slowly whisk in the ¼ cup canola oil, then the olive oil (it's important to whisk in the canola oil first, because it stabilizes the dressing). Whisk in the pepper and the Parmesan. If the dressing seems too thick, thin with a tablespoon or two of water. Refrigerate and allow the dressing to mellow for an hour or more before serving.

4. Make the salad: Place the diced red onion in a strainer and set the strainer in a small bowl. Cover with cold water and let sit for approximately 5 minutes. Swish the onion around in the water, then lift the strainer out of the water and rinse the onion with cold water. Dry on paper towels.

5. In a large bowl, toss the garlic croutons with 3 tablespoons of the salad dressing to soften them slightly. Add the romaine and the remaining dressing and toss together with the croutons. Arrange on a platter or on plates. Top with the shaved Parmesan, sprinkle on the red onion, add 2 to 3 pinches of cracked pepper, and serve.

garlic croutons [makes about 4 cups]

Croutons can be very oily. These are not. Rather than cut even squares, I tear pieces from a country-style loaf, one with an open-hole structure such as a ciabatta, and toss them with only a tablespoon of olive oil before baking in the oven until crisp. When I pull them from the oven I toss them with minced fresh garlic and leave them to cool. We use these for any salad that requires croutons (they're essential for Caesar salad), as a garnish for many of our soups, and as a starting point for delicious bread crumbs.

¼ pound bread, preferably a ciabatta
or similar bread with a loose crumb
and open-hole structure
1 tablespoon extra virgin olive oil
1 fat garlic clove, halved, green shoot
removed, very finely minced
1 teaspoon minced fresh flat-leaf parsley
¼ teaspoon kosher salt

1. Preheat the oven to 325°F. Cut the crusts off the bread and tear the bread into approximately 1-inch pieces. They should be irregularly shaped. Place in a large bowl and toss with the olive oil until the bread is evenly coated.

2. Spread the bread in an even layer on a baking sheet. Bake 25 to 30 minutes, until crisp. Remove from the oven, transfer back to the bowl, and toss at once with the minced garlic, the parsley, and the salt. Allow to cool. With your hands, lift the croutons from the bowl, allowing much of the garlic to fall to the bottom of the bowl. Transfer the croutons to an airtight container and discard the garlic left in the bowl.

[HERBED GARLIC BREAD CRUMBS, makes 2 cups]
To the above recipe add:

2 tablespoons minced fresh flat-leaf parsley
2 tablespoons minced celery leaves

1. Make the garlic croutons as directed above, but omit the teaspoon of parsley.

2. Once the croutons have cooled completely (this is critical), lift from the bowl, leaving much of the garlic behind, and transfer to a food processor fitted with the steel blade. Pulse until the bread has broken down into bread crumbs that are somewhere between coarse and fine. Toss with the herbs in a wide bowl.

[NOTE] If you want to store these for any length of time, omit the herbs. In a sealed jar, the toasted crumbs can be a staple in your refrigerator. Add herbs when you use the bread crumbs.

iceberg lettuce salad with roquefort-buttermilk dressing

[makes 6 servings]

Many salads are really about the dressing, and some more than others. That would certainly apply here. The blue cheese is the source of 95 percent of this salad's flavor and at least 90 percent of its calories. But the salad is also about texture, and that comes from the crunchy, juicy, thirst-quenching lettuce. Many chefs turn their noses up at iceberg lettuce, but I welcome it in this classic steak house salad. Look for a large head of iceberg lettuce that is dense for its size, or you'll be disappointed when you cut it into wedges and find very little lettuce and a lot of air. I've heard people say that you shouldn't waste good blue cheese on a salad dressing, but I disagree. You should definitely use the best Roquefort you can get to make the best possible dressing. Making the dressing a day ahead of time and letting it sit overnight allows the garlic to mellow and the mixture to thicken. Make sure to rub the thyme leaves between your fingers when you add them to the top of the salad; rubbing the leaves releases their aroma and flavor.

[ROQUEFORT-BUTTERMILK DRESSING]
- 1 small garlic clove, halved, green shoot removed
   Pinch of kosher salt
- 2 teaspoons chopped fresh thyme leaves
- ¾ cup buttermilk
- 4 ounces Roquefort cheese, crumbled (½ cup tightly packed)
- ½ teaspoon cracked black peppercorns

[SALAD]
- 1 large dense head of iceberg lettuce
   Freshly ground black pepper
- 3 ounces Roquefort cheese, crumbled (about ⅓ cup)
- 1 tablespoon thyme leaves
- 2 tablespoons finely chopped fresh flat-leaf parsley

1. Make the dressing: Place the garlic, salt, and thyme in a mortar and pestle with 1 teaspoon of the buttermilk, and grind the garlic to a paste. Using a fork, whisk in the Roquefort, remaining buttermilk, and the pepper. Cover and let sit overnight. Stir together before serving.

2. Make the salad: Strip off the dark outer leaves of the lettuce. Cut the lettuce through the core into 6 wedges. Don't cut away the core, because the core holds the wedge together.

3. Place each wedge on a salad plate or a platter, and spoon on 2 to 4 tablespoons Roquefort-buttermilk dressing (to taste). Grind on some pepper and top each wedge with a tablespoon of crumbled Roquefort; ½ teaspoon of rubbed thyme leaves, and a teaspoon of parsley. Serve cold.

[NOTE] Fresh garlic only! Pre-minced garlic in olive oil is never a useful alternative to freshly minced garlic because it's bitter. Using this product is a good way to mess up a perfectly good recipe. It isn't even permitted for use in restaurants by the health department because it's susceptible to botulism.

frisée salad aux lardons with warm bacon vinaigrette

[makes 4 servings]

This is a classic French salad, but in fact, it's very American—bacon and eggs with a French twist! In the classic version, the eggs are poached. I like to fry the eggs in the same bacon fat/oil combination I use for the vinaigrette. Good-quality slab or thick-cut bacon is essential for this. The dressing makes a delicious counterpoint to bitter lettuces like frisée as well as greens like spinach and rapini (see recipes on pages 227-228). In order to render enough fat and become crispy on the edges, the piece of slab bacon you use has to have enough fat. It shouldn't look like steak.

[WARM BACON VINAIGRETTE]
- 4 ounces slab bacon or thick-cut bacon strips
- ¼ cup plus 1 teaspoon water
- 4 tablespoons canola oil, or 2 tablespoons extra virgin olive oil and 2 tablespoons canola oil
- 2 tablespoons minced shallot
- 1 teaspoon fresh thyme leaves, roughly chopped
- 2 tablespoons plus 2 teaspoons sherry vinegar
- 1 to 2 teaspoons Dijon mustard, to taste
- ¼ teaspoon kosher salt
- ¼ teaspoon ground black pepper

[SALAD]
- 4 large eggs
- 2 heads frisée, trimmed and roughly chopped
- 1 cup garlic croutons (page 18; optional)

CROUTONS

Although the croutons are always present in the traditional frisée salad aux lardons, they're optional here. Sometimes an element that is time-consuming can be eliminated when making a classic dish at home, and your dish will be no less delicious. You save an enormous amount of time when you cut down on restaurant-type garnishes.

1. Make the warm bacon vinaigrette: Cut slab bacon into ¼-inch-thick slices, then cut the slices on the diagonal into strips about ¼ inch wide by 1½ inches long. Place the bacon in a small frying pan or saucepan with ¼ cup water. It should be in a single layer. Bring to a simmer over medium-low heat and simmer until the water disappears, about 10 minutes (this step renders out some of the fat without overbrowning the bacon).

2. Add the canola oil (or olive oil and canola oil) to the pan and cook the bacon for 3 to 5 more minutes, until the edges are crisp but the bacon is still supple and the oil is nicely infused. Using a slotted spoon, remove the bacon from the pan and drain on paper towels. Remove 1 tablespoon of the fat from the pan and set aside.

3. Add the shallot and thyme to the pan and cook until the shallot is tender, about 2 minutes. Remove the pan from the heat and immediately add the sherry vinegar; stir and scrape the pan to deglaze. Whisk in the mustard and add a pinch of salt. Whisk in 1 teaspoon water and the pepper. Keep warm.

4. Make the salad: Heat the tablespoon of fat you set aside in a medium skillet above medium heat and fry the eggs until the whites are set but the yolks are still runny, about 3 to 4 minutes. Remove from the pan and set aside.

5. Set aside 2 teaspoons of the warm vinaigrette and toss the frisée, croutons, and bacon with the remaining dressing. Divide among 4 plates. Top each serving with a fried egg, drizzle ½ teaspoon vinaigrette over each egg, and serve.

green bean salad with walnuts [makes 6 servings]

Green beans and walnuts are a heavenly match, but you should only make this salad if you can get really firm fresh beans. Spongy, woody green beans can be used for the long-cooked beans on page 231. Also, make sure you use an excellent fresh walnut oil for this. If yours is stale or less than fragrant, use extra virgin olive oil instead. Walnut oil can go rancid very quickly, so buy small amounts (a cheap quart is not a bargain), and keep it well sealed in the refrigerator. Smell it before you use it to make sure it smells fresh; luckily it's no secret when walnut oil goes rancid.

1	pound green beans
12	walnuts in the shells
2	teaspoons coarse mustard
¼	cup Basic Lemon Vinaigrette (page 16)
1	tablespoon walnut oil
1	tablespoon chopped chives
	Fleur de sel

FLEUR DE SEL

Fleur de sel is a rarefied French salt that crystallizes on top of salt ponds. It has a light, crystalline structure (it means "salt flower" in French) and because of its structure it is salty and crunchy but not overly salty. It's very expensive and should only be used to accent or garnish dishes.

1. Pick over the beans, but don't trim them until after they've been blanched. Bring a large pot of generously salted water to a boil and add the beans. Boil for 4 to 5 minutes and transfer to a bowl of ice water. Cool in the ice water, then drain and dry on paper towels. Trim off the stem ends.

2. Crack the walnuts, holding the seamed sides against the nutcracker. Remove the meat from the shells, trying to keep the halves intact. If you crack the shell on the rounded side (as opposed to the seamed side), you might crush the walnut meat and you won't be able to extract neat halves. Toast the nuts lightly in a 350°F oven, or in a pan on the stove, for 4 to 5 minutes (page 16). Remove from the heat. Separate out 6 halves and set aside. Coarsely chop the rest.

3. Whisk the mustard into the lemon vinaigrette. Set aside 1 teaspoon of the dressing. Make sure the beans are dry, and toss with the remaining vinaigrette and the chopped walnuts. Toss the whole halves with the teaspoon you set aside. Arrange the beans on a platter or in a wide bowl. Arrange the walnut halves over the top. Drizzle on the walnut oil and sprinkle with the chives. Sprinkle a few pinches of fleur de sel over the top and serve.

[NOTE] The reason you don't trim the beans until after you blanch them is that, like cut flowers, they will absorb water at the broken or cut ends. They'll have a better texture and a more vivid flavor if left intact until after they've been cooked.

green and red tomato salad with russian dressing [makes 4 to 6 servings]

I made this dish after seeing the movie *Fried Green Tomatoes*. It's a perfect salad to make at the end of summer or the middle of fall (depending on where you live), that time of year when the last of the tomatoes have come in and the green ones that are still growing on your vines will never fully ripen. Tomatoes with Russian dressing is one of my favorite steak house combos. This rendition with green and red tomatoes is a great study in contrasts—creamy and chunky (dressing and tomatoes), sweet (red) and sharp (green), crisp (green) and juicy (red). I use beefsteak tomatoes for this; they're perfect for any all-tomato salad. They slice well and have a great firm texture.

[RUSSIAN DRESSING]

1	large egg, hard-boiled (below)
½	recipe Garlic Mayonnaise (below)
½	teaspoon white wine vinegar or champagne vinegar
1	teaspoon freshly squeezed lemon juice
3	tablespoons Heinz ketchup
½	teaspoon Lee & Perrins Worcestershire sauce
¼	teaspoon Tabasco sauce (more to taste)
2	tablespoons finely chopped red onion, soaked in cold water for 5 minutes, drained, rinsed, and dried on paper towels (page 17)
1½	teaspoons (packed) grated fresh or prepared horseradish
1	tablespoon finely chopped fresh flat-leaf parsley Salt
⅛	teaspoon ground black pepper

[SALAD]

1¾	pounds mixed green and red tomatoes, sliced ¼ inch thick
	Kosher salt and freshly ground black pepper to taste
1	hard-boiled egg, finely chopped
1	teaspoon finely chopped fresh flat-leaf parsley
½	red onion, sliced very thin in half-moons, soaked in cold water for 5 minutes, drained, rinsed, and dried on paper towels (page 17)

[HARD-BOILED EGGS]

Place the eggs in a medium saucepan, cover with cold water, and bring to a boil. Cover the pot tightly and turn off the heat. Meanwhile, fill a bowl with ice and water. Let sit for 10 minutes for a dark, very slightly soft yolk, 12 minutes for a lighter, thoroughly hard-boiled but still very tender yolk. Drain and chill in the ice bath for several minutes, then peel.

1. Make the Russian Dressing: Peel the hard-boiled eggs, cut in half (or break the eggs in half and scoop out the yolks and whites), and remove the yolks from the whites. Chop the whites very fine. Separately, chop the yolks very fine and mix with a tablespoon of the mayonnaise. They should almost be a puree (and indeed, you can puree them through a sieve instead of chopping them). Set aside.

2. Place the rest of the garlic mayonnaise in a bowl. Stir in the vinegar, lemon juice, ketchup, Worcestershire, Tabasco, onion, horseradish, and parsley. Season to taste with about ¼ teaspoon salt and the pepper. Stir in the minced hard-cooked egg whites and the yolks. Taste and adjust the seasonings. Transfer to a covered container and refrigerate. It will keep for about 5 days in the refrigerator.

3. Make the salad: Line an oval or round platter with the tomato slices, overlapping them slightly and alternating red and green. Season with salt and pepper and let sit for 10 minutes.

4. Spoon the dressing over the tomatoes. Sprinkle on the chopped egg and the parsley, and if you wish, top with the onion slices. Serve.

VARIATION / THOUSAND ISLAND DRESSING

Substitute ¼ cup finely chopped cornichons for the horseradish.

[GARLIC MAYONNAISE, makes 1¼ cups]

This isn't as garlicky as Provençal aïoli but it's garlicky nonetheless. We use it as a starting point for Russian Dressing (above) and Remoulade (page 34). The bread, blended as it is with the egg yolk, makes for a tighter mayo.

¼ cup diced baguette, without crusts
2 teaspoons white wine vinegar
1 to 2 fat garlic cloves (to taste), halved,
    green shoot removed, quartered
½ teaspoon kosher salt (more to taste)
½ cup plus 1 teaspoon canola oil, at room temperature
1 large egg yolk
1 tablespoon warm water
1 level teaspoon Dijon mustard
½ cup extra virgin olive oil, at room temperature
1 teaspoon freshly squeezed lemon juice

1. Place the diced bread in a small bowl and toss with the vinegar until saturated. Squeeze the bread over the bowl, extracting as much vinegar as you can (you may not be able to squeeze out any at all), and set the bread aside.

2. Place the garlic, salt, and 1 teaspoon of canola oil in a mortar and mash to a paste; don't pound the garlic, but grind it against the sides and bottom of the bowl. Add the bread and continue to mash until the mixture is smooth. Add the egg yolk, water, 1 teaspoon of the vinegar squeezed from the bread, and the mustard and mix together thoroughly. Slowly begin to drizzle in the remaining canola oil, stirring constantly with the pestle. When you've added about a third of the canola oil and the mixture has begun to emulsify, scrape the mixture into a medium bowl. Wet a dish towel and wrap it around the base of the bowl so the bowl doesn't move around while you whisk. Switch to a wire whisk.

3. Very slowly drizzle in the remaining canola oil while whisking constantly. When all of the canola oil has been added, drizzle in the olive oil, whisking all the while. Once the mixture has emulsified you can add the oil a little more quickly. Add the remaining vinegar and the lemon juice. Taste and adjust the seasoning, adding more vinegar or lemon juice or salt if desired. Scrape into a jar or small bowl, cover tightly, and refrigerate until ready to use.

[MASHING GARLIC AND OTHER INGREDIENTS IN A MORTAR AND PESTLE]

When a recipe instructs you to mash garlic to a paste, it means to mash by grinding, not by pounding. The movement of the pestle should not be up and down but circular. If you pound the garlic, you'll release too many volatile oils and your puree will be too pungent. Also, you risk breaking your mortar. It's just as easy to get a smooth puree by slowly but firmly grinding the garlic against the sides and bottom of the mortar.

HEINZ KETCHUP, LEE & PERRIN'S WORCESTERSHIRE SAUCE, AND TABASCO

Some commercial brands of food have their place in gastronomy, and the above-named are three of them. You can rely on their quality and consistency when you use them to season dishes. This point was brought home to me when I was a young chef, training at the 3-star French chef Roger Vergé's restaurant Moulin de Mougins in the south of France. One afternoon between the lunch and dinner service, Chef Vergé came into the kitchen to prepare a late lunch of steak tartare for his friends. He grabbed a superb piece of sirloin and I watched as he hand-chopped it with impressive skill. He seasoned the meat, then reached into a cabinet and pulled out some Heinz Ketchup to mix into the tartare. I couldn't believe my eyes, but it was at that moment I realized that a good product is a good product, worthy of even a 3-star kitchen.

beefsteak tomatoes with cumin-oregano vinaigrette and feta

[makes 4 servings]

This is an easy cross between a Greek salad and a classic steak house salad (though a steak house salad would probably use blue cheese instead of feta). The dish, like Greek salad, tastes best if made during tomato season, July through October. Make the dressing at least 30 minutes before you serve the salad so the cumin and oregano can steep. Because it doesn't contain fresh herbs, the dressing is a good keeper; you can refrigerate it for a few days. If you can find Greek dried oregano, still on the branch (available at some Greek markets), it's the best to use.

[CUMIN-OREGANO VINAIGRETTE]
- I   teaspoon cumin seeds
- ½   teaspoon cracked black peppercorns
- I   teaspoon dried oregano
- I   tablespoon extra virgin olive oil
- I   small garlic clove, halved, green shoot removed, finely minced
- I   tablespoon plus I teaspoon red wine vinegar
        Kosher salt to taste
- ¼   cup canola oil or extra virgin olive oil (to taste)

[SALAD]
- 3   beefsteak tomatoes, sliced in ½-inch-thick rounds
        Kosher salt or fleur de sel and freshly ground black pepper
- 2   ounces feta cheese
- ½   to I teaspoon dried oregano, preferably Greek oregano on the branch, to taste
- I   tablespoon chopped fresh flat-leaf parsley

1. Make the dressing: Heat a small skillet over medium heat and add the cumin seeds and pepper. Heat in the pan until the spices smell toasty, like popcorn, a couple of minutes. Transfer to a small bowl and cool for 5 minutes, then grind in a spice mill. Transfer to the small bowl.

2. Rub the oregano between the palms of your (clean) hands to draw out the aroma, and add to the bowl with the cumin and pepper.

3. Heat I tablespoon olive oil and the garlic in a small pan over medium-low heat until the garlic is just fragrant and simmering. Pour over the spices. Stir in the vinegar and salt to taste. Whisk in the remaining oil. Measure ⅛ cup dressing for the salad. Let sit for 30 minutes before using.

4. Make the salad: Arrange the tomato slices on a platter. Just before serving, season lightly with fleur de sel or kosher salt and freshly ground pepper. Drizzle on the vinaigrette and crumble on the feta. Rub the dried oregano between the palms of your hands or between your fingertips and sprinkle over the feta. Top with the parsley and serve.

VARIATION / BEEFSTEAK TOMATOES WITH ROQUEFORT
Substitute ½ cup Roquefort-Buttermilk Dressing (page 19) for the Cumin-Oregano Vinaigrette and I ounce blue cheese for the feta. Substitute fresh thyme leaves for the oregano and proceed with the recipe.

spinach and mushroom salad with warm bacon vinaigrette

[makes 4 servings]

I have taste memories of this classic café salad that date back to 1974 during my college days at the University of California at Santa Barbara. It was on the menu at a hippie café in Isla Vista, and I never forgot it. I've refined the dish since then. This version includes thinly sliced celery, which completes the salad in a delicious and unexpected way. Elements that complete a dish don't have to be exotic or expensive. Celery, for example, despite its bad rap for being flavorless, is actually full of flavor and texture. The tough, woody outer stalks are altogether too flavorful, so use the inner stalks here.

1	recipe Warm Bacon Vinaigrette (page 20)
2	celery hearts, thinly sliced on the diagonal
¼	pound white mushrooms, washed, trimmed, and thinly sliced (6 medium mushrooms)
6	ounces baby spinach
	Freshly ground black pepper

1. Make the vinaigrette, but after you remove the bacon from the oil and before you add the shallots, add the celery and cook for 1 minute, until slightly softened. Remove from the oil with a slotted spoon and drain on paper towels. Continue making the vinaigrette as directed and keep warm.

2. Place the mushrooms, spinach, bacon, and celery in a bowl and toss gently with the warm vinaigrette and freshly ground pepper to taste. Divide among 4 wide soup bowls or salad plates and serve.

[CLEANING MUSHROOMS]
Always wash the mushrooms before you trim the ends so they won't absorb water. Place in a bowl of water, swish them around, and lift out of the water. Do not soak. Rinse 2 to 3 times, depending on how sandy they are, then dry with paper towels.

baby artichoke, fennel, and mushroom salad [makes 4 to 6 servings]

We get artichokes throughout the year in California, but in the spring they're particularly tender, so tender that you can slice them very thin and serve them uncooked, as the Italians do, in salads. You need to slice everything paper thin for this salad and serve it quickly before the artichokes discolor. If you don't have a mandoline, make sure your knife is very sharp.

3	tablespoons freshly squeezed lemon juice, plus the juice of I lemon
5	tablespoons extra virgin olive oil
8	baby artichokes, trimmed (see below)
I	pound fennel, thick outer layer removed, sliced very thin lengthwise (on a mandoline if possible)
4	ounces white mushrooms, rinsed (page 25), trimmed, and sliced very thin
½	teaspoon kosher salt (more to taste)
¼	teaspoon cracked black peppercorns
½	cup whole fresh flat-leaf parsley leaves

1. Place 2 tablespoons of the lemon juice and the olive oil in a large bowl. Cut the artichokes in half, then lay them on the cut side and slice very thin. Toss with the lemon juice and olive oil as you go.

2. Add the fennel, mushrooms, the remaining tablespoon of lemon juice, the salt, pepper, and parsley to the bowl, and toss together. Serve at once.

[TRIMMING BABY ARTICHOKES]

When you trim baby artichokes, you remove the tough outer green leaves and fibers so you can eat the entire artichoke. With baby artichokes you don't have to worry about the chokes, which have to be removed from the hearts of mature artichokes.

Before you begin, fill a large bowl (2-quart or bigger) two-thirds full with water and add the juice of I lemon.

Break off all the tough outer leaves until you reach the lighter, more tender leaves at the center. Using a paring knife, trim the "shoulders," or bottom of the bulb, right above the stem by holding the knife almost parallel to the artichoke and cutting around the artichoke. You can also use a vegetable peeler for this. Cut the tops off; if you have removed the tough leaves, your knife should cut right through. Peel the stems. Place in the bowl of acidulated water. Don't let them sit in the water for too long or the flavor will leach out and they'll taste like lemon water.

chef's salad [makes 6 generous servings]

There was a time when chef's salad was on the menu of every restaurant in the country, and it got to be pretty boring and predictable. A good chef's salad should be a composed salad, with shredded lettuce on the bottom and meats, cheeses, and vegetables layered across the top in neat ribbons. It can be a "festival of leftovers" salad that you put together with odds and ends in your refrigerator, but they have to be good odds and ends. What you don't want here is a landfill, with everything tossed together. I use two different dressings, a lemon vinaigrette to lightly dress the lettuce and Russian dressing spooned over the top to enhance the meats and vegetables. This salad can make a lunch or light supper.

3	ounces Italian provolone cheese, cut in julienne (¾ cup)
3	ounces medium-sharp, artisanal cheddar cheese, cut in julienne (¾ cup)
2	ounces thinly sliced ham, cut in julienne (½ cup)
1½	ounces thinly sliced dry-cured salami, cut in julienne (⅓ cup)
2	ounces cooked chicken breast, cut in ¼-inch-thick julienne (½ cup)
3	ounces haricots verts or Blue Lake green beans, cooked
3	ounces thin asparagus, boiled for 3 minutes and refreshed with cold water, or roasted (page 100)
4	ounces baby artichokes, cooked, or good-quality jarred artichoke hearts, halved
9	cherry tomatoes, halved
½	head iceberg or romaine lettuce, cut in chiffonade
½	cup Basic Lemon Vinaigrette (page 22)
2	hard-boiled eggs (page 22), quartered
½	cup Russian Dressing (page 22)

1. Prepare all of the cheeses, meats, and vegetables and keep in separate containers or dishes.

2. Toss the lettuce with ¼ cup of the lemon vinaigrette and pile onto a large platter or wide shallow bowl. Separately, toss the beans with 1 teaspoon of the vinaigrette, toss the tomatoes with another teaspoon or 2 of the vinaigrette, and do the same with the asparagus.

3. Arrange the artichokes, cut side up, over the lettuce at both ends. Make a ribbon of the beans next to the artichokes at one end, then arrange ribbons of the meats and cheeses. Arrange the asparagus spears over the top, and dot with the egg wedges and halved cherry tomatoes. Drizzle another 2 tablespoons vinaigrette over the top, and spoon on ⅓ cup of the Russian dressing. Serve, passing the additional Russian dressing for people to add to their salad if they wish.

waldorf salad with curried mayonnaise dressing [makes 6 servings]

I call this a grown-up Waldorf salad. It's more interesting and less gloppy than the traditional Waldorf; the curried mayonnaise adds a nice accent to the apple and raisins. Waldorf salad is all about texture, and this one has that, plus the added value of flavor. The original version was made with apples, celery, and mayonnaise only, and the inventor was not happy when walnuts were added to the mix. But I think the walnuts are an improvement. I added fennel, which is in the same family as celery, because I think they work well together, and endive for the bitter/sharp edge that contrasts nicely with the apples and raisins.

[DRESSING]

½	to ⅔ cup mayonnaise (page 29), to taste
¾	teaspoon curry powder
¼	teaspoon powdered ginger
1	tablespoon plus 1 teaspoon freshly squeezed lemon juice (more to taste)

[SALAD]

1	crisp, sweet apple, such as a Fuji
1	teaspoon freshly squeezed lemon juice
2	ounces walnut halves, preferably fresh from the shell, lightly toasted (page 16) and broken in half (heaping ½ cup)
1	cup sliced celery, from the heart of the celery, sliced on the diagonal
½	small fennel bulb, finely diced
	Scant ⅓ cup raisins (1½ ounces)
1	Belgian endive, outer broken leaves removed, cut in chiffonade
4	romaine lettuce leaves, from the hearts, cut in chiffonade
¼	cup celery leaves from the heart, coarsely chopped
4	radishes, cut in half lengthwise and thinly sliced
1	tablespoon chopped fresh flat-leaf parsley
¼	teaspoon cracked black peppercorns (optional)
1	tablespoon minced fresh chives

1. Mix together the mayonnaise, curry powder, ginger, and lemon juice. Set aside.

2. Peel the apple and cut into 12 wedges. Cut away the core, and slice each wedge into thin crosswise slices. Toss in a large bowl with 1 teaspoon lemon juice. Add the remaining ingredients, except the chives, and toss together.

3. Shortly before serving toss the salad with the mayonnaise. Garnish with chives, and serve.

hand-made mayonnaise [makes 1⅔ cups]

Making mayonnaise by hand is surprisingly easy, and yields a mayonnaise that is smoother and silkier than mayonnaise made in a food processor. It's worth trying this to see the miracle that happens when an egg yolk emulsifies with oil. Warm water helps the process along, and you must add the oil very slowly at first, until you see that the oil and egg have emulsified—that is, when you have a homogenous, thick mixture. Then you can add the oil in a a stream rather than a drizzle.

1	extra large egg yolk, straight from the refrigerator
1	level teaspoon Dijon mustard
2	teaspoons white wine vinegar
1	tablespoon warm water
½	teaspoon kosher salt
1	cup canola oil, at room temperature
½	cup extra virgin olive oil, at room temperature
1	teaspoon fresh lemon juice

1. Set a medium bowl on a work surface. Wet a dish towel and wrap it around the base of the bowl so that the bowl does not move when you whisk.

2. Place the egg yolk, mustard, 1 teaspoon of the vinegar, the water, and the salt in the bowl and whisk together until thoroughly combined.

3. Very slowly begin to drizzle in the canola oil while whisking constantly. When all of the canola oil has been added, drizzle in the olive oil, whisking all the while. Add the remaining teaspoon of vinegar and the lemon juice. Scrape into a jar or small bowl, cover tightly, and refrigerate until ready to use.

VARIATION / CODDLED EGG YOLK MAYONNAISE

There really is very little risk of food poisoning from raw egg yolks. But if you wish, you can coddle the egg yolk first. Bring a small pot of water to a boil, slowly add the egg in its shell, and cook for 3½ minutes. Transfer to a bowl of ice water, then carefully crack the egg and remove the yolk. Proceed with the recipe above.

VARIATION / FOOD PROCESSOR MAYONNAISE

Mayonnaise that is made in the food processor is tighter than hand-made mayonnaise, and the texture, for some reason, is oilier. You do save a little time and elbow grease, though.

Place the egg yolk, water, mustard, salt, and 1 teaspoon of the vinegar in the bowl of a food processor fitted with the steel blade. Turn on the food processor and begin drizzling in the canola oil. Add all of the canola oil, then slowly stream in the olive oil. Add the remaining vinegar and lemon juice. Stop the processor and scrape the mayonnaise into a container. Cover and chill.

[WHAT TO DO IF MAYONNAISE "BREAKS"]

When a mayonnaise "breaks," the oil separates. This can happen if it becomes too tight—thick and stiff—or if you beat it too much, which can happen when you use a food processor. Often you can rectify the problem simply by whisking in a tablespoon or 2 of warm water. If this doesn't work, break a whole egg into the bowl of a food processor fitted with the steel blade. Turn on the processor and slowly drizzle in the broken mayonnaise.

shrimp louis [makes 4 servings]

Both Shrimp Louis and Crab Louis are West Coast classics. Crab Louis was the original, then people began making it with bay shrimp. I use medium shrimp, which I poach gently in a court bouillon, then split in half. The dish is a simple combination of shrimp dressed with Thousand Island Dressing or Russian Dressing (page 22), embellished with avocado, hard-cooked egg, and tomatoes and set on a bed of shredded lettuce.

[COURT BOUILLON]

1	tablespoon canola oil
½	cup chopped onion
⅓	cup chopped celery
¼	cup chopped fennel bulb (you can use the coarse outer layer for this)
	The green part of 1 small leek (optional)
2	fat garlic cloves, coarsely chopped
	A few sprigs parsley
1	bay leaf
1	chile
½	cup dry white wine
2	tablespoons white wine vinegar
2	cups water
1	teaspoon kosher salt

[SALAD]

16	medium shrimp, with shells on
1	Japanese cucumber, cut in half lengthwise, seeded, and cut on the diagonal in ¼-inch-thick slices
¼	teaspoon kosher salt
¼	cup minced red onion, soaked in cold water for 5 minutes, drained, rinsed, and dried on paper towels (page 17)
1	head Boston lettuce, outer leaves removed, inner leaves cut in chiffonade
¼	small head radicchio, cut in chiffonade
1	small or ½ large avocado, sliced
1	medium tomato, quartered, seeds and seed pods cut away, and sliced lengthwise in thin strips (about ⅛ inch thick)
2	extra-large eggs, hard-boiled (see below), quartered
	Fleur de Sel
⅔	cup Russian Dressing (page 22) or Thousand Island Dressing (page 22)
2	teaspoons minced chives

1. Make the court bouillon: Heat the canola oil in a medium saucepan over medium heat and add the onion, celery, fennel, leek green, and garlic. Cook gently until the vegetables soften, about 5 minutes, and add the parsley, bay leaf, chile pepper, wine, and vinegar. Bring to a boil, reduce the heat, simmer 1 minute, and add the water and salt. Bring to a simmer and simmer 10 minutes. Remove from the heat and allow to cool (you can do this quickly by setting the pot in an ice bath). Strain into a bowl, pressing the ingredients against the strainer. Return to the pot.

2. Make the salad: Bring the court bouillon to a simmer and add the shrimp. Turn off the heat, cover, and let cool in the court bouillon. Peel the shrimp and devein if necessary.

3. Toss the cucumber with ¼ teaspoon salt. Let sit for 15 minutes, then rinse and dry on paper towels. Toss with the onion, the shredded inner leaves of the lettuce, and the radicchio. Add 2 tablespoons of the dressing and toss again.

4. Line a large platter with the whole lettuce leaves. Place the shredded lettuce mixture on top. Arrange half the avocado slices on one side, fanning them over the lettuce, and the other half on the other side. Arrange half the tomato slices and half the egg wedges on one side and the other half on the other side. Sprinkle with fleur de sel and drizzle with ¼ cup of the dressing. Toss the shrimp with the remaining dressing and arrange over the shredded lettuce. Sprinkle with the chives, and serve.

[NOTE] I like the eggs just under hard-boiled for this. Place in a saucepan and cover with cold water. Bring to a rolling boil, cover and turn off the heat. Let stand 8 minutes, then drain and transfer to an ice bath.

sweet corn and crab salad [makes 6 servings]

The French would call this a *salade composée*, a "composed salad," that begins with a beautiful *mise-en-place*, everything separate and cut just so and tossed together one minute before serving. All of the ingredients have great inherent flavor (providing the corn you use really is sweet), so the dressing is very simple, just lemon and olive oil. In that sense it has the spirit of an Italian salad. As the saying goes, the French make a dressing, then use it for a salad; the Italians make a salad, then season it.

I like to use peeky-toe crabmeat from Maine for this. I love Dungeness crab, but I find that it has more bits of broken shell mixed in when you buy the crabmeat. Also, with the Maine crabmeat, you don't get as much water, so pound for pound it's a better buy.

2	ears sweet corn
1	tablespoon canola oil
½	medium fennel bulb (about 3 ounces), cut in fine dice Kosher salt
4	ounces sweet red pepper (1 small), cut in fine dice (page 44), rinsed with cold water, and drained on paper towels
	Scant ½ cup finely diced red onion, soaked in cold water for 5 minutes, drained, rinsed, and dried on paper towels (page 17)
1	tablespoon finely chopped fresh tarragon
2	tablespoons finely chopped fresh flat-leaf parsley
½	teaspoon finely chopped lemon zest Freshly ground pepper
1	heart of romaine lettuce
2	tablespoons freshly squeezed lemon juice
6	tablespoons extra virgin olive oil
8	ounces crabmeat (peeky-toe from Maine if available), picked over for shells
4	sprigs chervil, for garnish
1	avocado, sliced, for garnish

MISE-EN-PLACE

The eye affects how you taste a dish. A composed salad can be pretty, or it can be a mish-mash. The amount of care you put into preparing the ingredients really does matter. A beautiful *mise-en-place* results in a beautiful dish. For this salad, I make the smallest dice possible, and arrange all of the ingredients on a platter before I toss everything together.

1. Steam or boil the corn for 4 to 5 minutes, until tender. Transfer to a bowl of cold water to cool for 5 minutes, then drain. Cut away the kernels; cut just deep enough into the cob so that you don't get resistance from it, but you get all of the tasty kernel without fibrous pieces of cob. Place in a large bowl.

2. Heat the canola oil over medium heat in a small frying pan and add the fennel with a pinch of kosher salt. Cook, stirring, until tender and translucent, 4 to 5 minutes. Remove from the heat and transfer to a plate. Allow to cool for 10 minutes.

3. Toss together the corn, fennel, red pepper, onion, tarragon, parsley, and lemon zest in a bowl. Season to taste with salt and pepper. Remove the outer leaves of the romaine heart and arrange them on a platter. Cut the inner leaves crosswise into thin ribbons (chiffonade), and set aside.

4. Whisk together the lemon juice, ¼ to ½ teaspoon salt (to taste), the olive oil, and ¼ teaspoon ground pepper. Pour onto the vegetable mixture. Add the lettuce chiffonade and the crabmeat and toss well. Mound over the lettuce leaves on the platter, garnish the top with chervil sprigs and the optional avocado slices, and serve.

radish and cucumber salad in yogurt vinaigrette [makes 4 servings]

Cucumbers and radishes are equally at home in a Mediterranean or northern European setting. This clean-tasting, bright salad has North African flavors and cooling, crisp, luscious textures. There's a nice combination here of juicy and sweet, sharp and sour. I use a mandoline to slice the radishes paper thin. You can buy simple and inexpensive plastic Japanese mandolines that are very easy to use and do the job just fine (but be very careful with your fingertips and use the finger guard!). I prefer to use Japanese cucumbers for this; they have the sweetest, most vivid flavor of any of the cucumbers available to me (Persian, hothouse, regular). If you can't find Japanese cucumbers, use Persian or the long European hothouse variety. If you can find the large, multi-colored radishes called Easter radishes at your farmers' market, they'll add even more color to the salad.

[SALAD]

¾	pound thin Japanese cucumbers
1	tablespoon kosher salt
5	ounces radishes (about 1 bunch), trimmed and sliced paper thin on a mandoline
½	small finely diced red onion (about 6 ounces), soaked in cold water for 5 minutes, drained, rinsed, and dried on paper towels (page 17)
1	tablespoon minced chives, for garnish

[DRESSING]

½	teaspoon cumin seeds
¼	teaspoon cracked black peppercorns
⅓	cup plain yogurt
	Pinch of turmeric (optional)
1	small garlic clove, halved, green shoot removed, and finely minced
1	tablespoon freshly squeezed lemon juice
	Kosher salt to taste

1. Cut the cucumbers in half lengthwise and scoop out the seeds (a demitasse spoon or a grapefruit spoon is a good tool for this). Lay them cut side down on your work surface and slice on the diagonal into thin half-moon–shaped slices, about 2 inches long by ⅛ inch thick. You should have about 4 cups of sliced cucumbers. Place in a bowl and toss with ¾ teaspoon kosher salt. Set aside to wilt for 10 minutes.

2. Meanwhile, make the dressing: Heat the cumin seeds with the cracked peppercorns in a small skillet over medium heat, shaking the skillet constantly so the spices will move around and toast before they burn. When the cumin smells toasty and fragrant, remove both spices from the heat and transfer to a spice mill. Allow to cool for 5 minutes. Grind the spices and stir into the yogurt with the turmeric, if using. Add the garlic, lemon juice, and salt to taste. Set aside.

3. When the cucumbers have wilted, after about 10 minutes, cover them with cold water, swish them around, drain, and repeat. Taste for salt. If they still taste too salty, rinse once more and drain. Wrap in a clean kitchen towel.

4. In a large bowl, toss together the sliced cucumbers, radishes, and onion. Make sure the sliced radishes are separated. Add the dressing and toss again. Taste and adjust the seasoning. Mound on salad plates, sprinkle each portion with chives, and serve.

[NOTE] Don't use your coffee mill for spices or your spice mill for coffee. Buy two; they're not expensive.

[CUTTING RADISHES ON THE MANDOLINE]
To avoid catching the skin and tearing the radish on the mandoline, each time you slice, turn the radish a quarter turn.

[TOASTING SPICES]
Toasting spices brings out their volatile aromas. Toast them in a dry skillet over medium heat and watch them carefully, because once they smell toasty, like popcorn, they will quickly begin to burn. Remove them from the pan immediately and allow to cool for 5 minutes before you grind them.

coleslaw [makes 6 servings]

Coleslaw is one of the most underrated and well-loved salads in America. It can be so much more than the industrialized salad you get in five-gallon drums at package stores. It's worth it to take the time to make the remoulade sauce, and to look for good crisp lettuces and firm cabbage. I think caraway is an important ingredient here, but if you don't like it you can leave it out; the salad will still be good. Serve this with any barbecue and any sandwich.

¼	medium head green cabbage
⅛	medium head red cabbage
1	medium carrot, peeled and cut in fine julienne, preferably on a mandoline (use the protective glove!), or shredded using the shredding attachment of a food processor
1	Belgian endive, outer leaves discarded if discolored, halved and cut crosswise into thin slivers
1	teaspoon kosher salt
½	teaspoon caraway seeds (optional)
½	cup Remoulade Sauce (recipe follows)
2	tablespoons white wine vinegar
1	tablespoon Dijon mustard (optional)
¼	cup parsley leaves, tightly packed, cut in chiffonade

1. Core both the green and red cabbages, then slice crosswise in thin slivers.

2. Toss together the vegetables and salt, and let sit for 1 hour. Rinse and spin dry in a salad spinner. Toss with the caraway seeds, remoulade sauce, vinegar, and mustard (for a hot coleslaw), season to taste, and let sit for 1 hour or preferably longer in the refrigerator. Add the parsley and toss again before serving.

VARIATION / CELERY REMOULADE
Omit the carrot and endive. Substitute 1 good-size celery root for half the cabbage. Cut the celery root in fine julienne on a mandoline (use the protective glove!) or grate on the shredding blade of a food processor, and toss with ½ teaspoon salt. Let sit for 30 minutes, then rinse thoroughly in a bowl of cold water. Drain and rinse again, then drain on paper towels or spin dry in a salad spinner. Add the optional 1 tablespoon Dijon mustard to the remoulade sauce.

[REMOULADE SAUCE, makes 1½ cups]
To me, this mayonnaise-based sauce doesn't stand alone; it evokes a whole class of dishes that call for it, such as the crab cakes we serve at Campanile, Oyster Po'Boys (page 198), and Coleslaw. I also like to serve it with Braised Baby Artichokes (page 38). It's both spicy and soothing at the same time.

1	anchovy fillet, soaked in water for 15 minutes (30 minutes if salted), rinsed, and dried on paper towels
1½	teaspoons capers or caper berries, rinsed and finely chopped (if using salt-packed caper berries, rinse and soak in water for 30 minutes, then rinse again before chopping)
1	tablespoon Dijon mustard
3	tablespoons chopped gherkins
1	tablespoon finely chopped fresh flat-leaf parsley
1½	teaspoons finely chopped tarragon
1	tablespoon finely chopped chervil
1	tablespoon minced shallot, rinsed and dried on paper towels
1	recipe Garlic Mayonnaise (page 22)
	Kosher salt to taste

In a mortar and pestle, grind the anchovy fillet and the capers to a paste. Add the remaining ingredients and stir together. Taste and adjust the seasoning. Cover and refrigerate. The remoulade will keep for 3 or 4 days in the refrigerator.

VARIATION / TARTAR SAUCE
Add 1 hard-boiled egg, yolk and white separated and finely chopped, to the remoulade sauce.

leeks vinaigrette [makes 4 servings]

For some reason, Americans don't use leeks as much as Europeans do. This classic French bistro dish may change your habits. Leeks are sweet, tender, and only mildly oniony; I love their gentle flavor and their pale, translucent green color. This works best if you have a baking pan that the leeks fit snugly into in a single layer. It will keep for several days in the refrigerator, but give it time to come back to room temperature before you serve it or the flavors will be muted.

[LEEKS]
2	pounds leeks, white and light green parts only
½	cup dry white wine
1	teaspoon kosher salt
¼	teaspoon freshly ground black pepper
½	cup extra virgin olive oil
¼	lemon, cut in paper-thin slices, seeds removed
3	or 4 fresh flat-leaf parsley sprigs

[TOPPING]
1	tablespoon white wine vinegar or champagne vinegar
1	teaspoon freshly squeezed lemon juice
¼	teaspoon kosher salt
3	tablespoons extra virgin olive oil
2	hard-boiled eggs (page 22)
2	teaspoons chopped fresh flat-leaf parsley

1. Preheat the oven to 400°F. Cut the leeks in half lengthwise and trim away all but ⅛ inch of the root, so that they hold together in one piece. Place in a bowl of cold water and swish to loosen the dirt, then run cold water over them, fanning the layers to wash away any dirt that may linger in between. Lay the leeks side by side, cut side up, in a baking dish. They should fit in one snug layer. Pour on the wine and sprinkle with the salt and pepper. Drizzle on the olive oil and place the lemon slices over the leeks. Top with the parsley sprigs.

2. Cover the baking dish tightly with foil and place in the oven. Roast for 30 minutes. Uncover, raise the heat to 450°F, and return to the oven for another 15 minutes, until the leeks are tender but not mushy and are beginning to color very lightly. Remove from the heat and allow to cool.

3. Using tongs, remove the leeks from the baking pan and arrange in a gratin dish or in a wide bowl or platter. Pour the liquid in the pan into a bowl and whisk in the vinegar, lemon juice, salt, and olive oil. Pour over the leeks. Allow to cool, or if serving the next day, cover and chill. For best results, refrigerate overnight. Bring back to room temperature before serving.

4. Press the hard-cooked eggs through a sieve or chop them very fine, and season with salt and pepper. Arrange over the leeks, sprinkle with parsley, and serve.

braised baby artichokes [makes 4 first-course servings or 8 hors d'oeuvre servings]

In France they would call these braised, marinated artichokes "artichokes à la barigoule." You can serve them warm, as a side dish, or cold or at room temperature as a starter. At the restaurant we serve them with a Remoulade Sauce (page 34) as an appetizer. They're double dipped this way, from the marinade to the remoulade.

¾	cup extra virgin olive oil
2	pounds baby artichokes (about 16), trimmed (page 26)
1	small onion, sliced
3	fresh flat-leaf parsley sprigs
	Leaves from 1 stalk celery, coarsely chopped
1	generous bunch basil (about 12 sprigs)
3	medium garlic cloves, lightly crushed
½	teaspoon kosher salt (more to taste)
½	teaspoon cracked black peppercorns
1	small or ½ large dried chile (preferably Japanese)
¼	cup dry white wine
½	cup water
	Remoulade Sauce (page 34), for serving

1. In a medium saucepan, heat ¼ cup of the olive oil over medium-high heat until very hot but not smoking. Add the trimmed artichokes and cook until very slightly colored, moving them around in the pan and flipping them over from time to time, 5 to 10 minutes. Turn the heat down to medium.

2. Add the onion, parsley, celery leaves, basil, garlic, salt, pepper, and chile, and cook, stirring, for about 3 to 5 minutes, until the onion softens slightly. Add the remaining 2 tablespoons olive oil, the white wine, and the water, and bring to a simmer. Reduce the heat to low.

3. Cover and simmer for 15 to 20 minutes, until the artichokes are tender. To check, pierce the middle of an artichoke with the tip of a paring knife. It should slip in easily. Remove from the heat and allow the artichokes to cool in the liquid. Remove and discard the parsley and basil sprigs.

4. Transfer to a bowl or a container, pour the juice and seasonings over the artichokes, cover, and chill.

5. To serve, cut the artichokes in half and arrange on a platter with some of the cooked onion. Drizzle on some of the juice, and serve with remoulade sauce on the side.

VARIATION
If you can't get baby artichokes, you can use small globe artichokes. Trim, halve or quarter (depending on the size), and cut away the chokes. Proceed with the recipe.

warm german potato salad [makes 6 servings]

Is this really German, or do we think it's German because of the pork and potatoes? Whatever the answer, the comforting, vinegary salad is delicious. Serve it with anything that goes well with mashed potatoes; it fills the same flavor niche and it's easier to make.

2 to 2¼ pounds Yukon Gold potatoes
2 ounces sliced bacon, cut in ¼ x 1-inch slivers
1 large or 2 small leeks, white and light green
    parts only, chopped and cleaned
⅓ cup white wine vinegar
1 teaspoon kosher salt (more to taste)
¼ teaspoon freshly ground black pepper
2 tablespoons chopped fresh flat-leaf parsley

1. Steam the potatoes until tender, about 25 minutes. Remove from the heat and allow to cool for 10 minutes. Steadying them with a kitchen towel, peel and cut in 1-inch dice.

2. Cook the bacon in a large skillet over medium heat until just crisp on the edges. Remove with a slotted spoon and drain on paper towels. Add the leeks to the skillet and cook until they soften, 2 to 3 minutes.

3. Add the cooked diced potatoes, vinegar, salt, and pepper to the pan and gently toss together. Scrape the bottom of the skillet with a wooden spoon to loosen the glaze from the bacon. Turn off the heat. Taste and adjust the seasonings. Stir in the parsley and serve warm.

grilled insalata tricolore [makes 4 servings]

Twenty years ago there wasn't an Italian restaurant that didn't have this salad, named for the three colors in the Italian flag: red (radicchio), white (endive), and green (arugula). This is a twist on the classic. Do not overcook the lettuces. They are bitter to begin with, and if they get charred they'll be really bitter. So cook on the cooler part of the grill.

2 Belgian endive, cut in half lengthwise
1 small radicchio, cut in half through the core
¼ cup extra virgin olive oil
    Kosher salt
2 teaspoons red wine vinegar or sherry vinegar
¼ teaspoon freshly squeezed lemon juice
2 cups tightly packed baby arugula
1 ounce Parmesan cheese, shaved

1. Prepare a medium-hot grill (if your grill is ashen white, it's too hot). Toss the endives and radicchio with 2 tablespoons olive oil until thoroughly coated, and sprinkle with ¼ teaspoon salt. Place, cut side down, on the medium-hot part of the grill, and grill just until the edges have colored slightly,

about 2 minutes. Turn over and move to the edge of the grill, out of direct contact with the heat and with the butt ends toward the heat. Cover, making sure to open the vents of your grill cover. Leave for 10 minutes. Remove from the grill and allow to cool.

2. Cut the radicchio halves into thirds and separate the leaves. Discard the cores. Break off the endive leaves and cut the outer leaves into large pieces. Leave the inner leaves whole. Discard the cores. Toss in a bowl with the vinegar, lemon juice, 1/4 teaspoon salt, and 2 tablespoons olive oil. Add the arugula leaves and toss again. Top with the shaved Parmesan and serve.

braised hearts of celery vinaigrette [makes 4 servings]

Celery is a much maligned vegetable. The hearts, in particular, are delicious. Once you've tasted this, you'll buy celery for the tender hearts (fill the outer ribs with peanut butter and let the kids have them). You can serve this dish hot or cold. Some supermarkets sell packaged celery hearts, without the tough outer stalks. If you can't find them, buy bunches and remove the tough outer ribs until you get to the pale green tender ribs; those are the celery heart.

3	celery hearts, cut in half lengthwise, ends trimmed
¼	cup extra virgin olive oil
½	medium onion, sliced
	Kosher salt
4	garlic cloves, halved, green shoots removed, and sliced
1	cup Chicken Stock (page 66, or commercial)
¼	teaspoon freshly ground black pepper
1	lemon, sliced
	A few sprigs fresh thyme
	Fleur de sel and freshly ground pepper
½	cup Basic Lemon Vinaigrette (page 16; optional)
1	tablespoon finely chopped flat-leaf parsley

1. Preheat the oven to 400°F. Bring a large pot of generously salted water to a boil and drop in the celery. Boil until partially cooked, about 3 minutes. Drain, pat dry, and lay side by side, cut side up, in a baking dish.

2. Heat 2 tablespoons of the olive oil in a medium skillet over medium heat and add the onion and ½ teaspoon salt. Cook, stirring, until the onion softens, about 5 minutes, and add the garlic. Stir together for a minute, until fragrant, and add the chicken stock. Bring to a simmer on top of the stove and pour over the celery. Season the celery with ½ teaspoon salt and the pepper. Lay the lemon slices and thyme sprigs over the celery. Cover tightly and place in the oven. Braise for 40 minutes, or until the celery is thoroughly tender but still holds its shape, and the liquid has reduced by half. Remove from the heat and allow the celery to cool for 15 minutes in the liquid.

3. Using tongs, remove the celery from the dish and cut the halved bunches lengthwise in half. Transfer to a platter. Sprinkle with fleur de sel and freshly ground pepper. Drizzle on the vinaigrette, if using, or just drizzle on some of the braising liquid, sprinkle on the parsley, and serve. Or, refrigerate and serve cold (but not too cold) or at room temperature.

giant tuna or salmon tartare [makes 4 servings]

If a dish has the word *tartare* in the name, there is a protein in it that isn't cooked. The name comes from the Tartars, ferocious fighters who never stopped to cook their meat when they were on the rampage. Classic tartare is made with beef (though the Tartars ate mainly horsemeat), but contemporary tartars are often made with fish. If you are using tuna for this, make sure to get center-cut tuna (the belly is good because it's fatty and tender); the tail will be too stringy. Dishes like this are partly about appearance, so be careful to cut the ingredients into fine, even dice.

1	Japanese cucumber (about 4 ounces), cut in half lengthwise, seeds scraped out with a small spoon, cut in ¼-inch dice (about ½ cup)
	Kosher salt
½	cup finely diced red onion (¼-inch dice), soaked in cold water for 5 minutes, drained, rinsed, and dried on paper towels (page 17)
¾	pound center-cut albacore or salmon fillet, cut in ½-inch dice (or a little smaller)
2	tablespoons finely chopped fresh dill
1	tablespoon plus 1 teaspoon fresh lime juice
2	tablespoons extra virgin olive oil
	Pinch of cayenne
	Lettuce or endive leaves and toasted croutons for serving

1. Sprinkle the cucumber with salt and let sit for 15 minutes while you prepare the remaining ingredients. Rinse and drain on paper towels.

2. In a medium bowl, gently toss the cucumber, fish, onion, and dill with the lime juice and olive oil. Season with about ½ teaspoon salt and a pinch of cayenne. Taste and adjust seasonings. Chill until ready to serve. Serve on lettuce or endive leaves, with toasted croutons.

[NOTE] If you are worried about eating raw fish because of parasites, use frozen fish. Freezing kills the parasites; many sushi chefs use fish that has been previously frozen for this reason.

grilled squid, potato, and asparagus salad [makes 4 servings]

This wonderful charcoal-flavored combo is a salad for a summer night, when you've got the grill going. The ingredients—even the lettuce—are grilled and tossed at once with a gingery vinaigrette. Use the larger (East Coast) squid for this, as they're much easier to grill; they should be at least 4 ounces each.

¾   pound fingerling, White Rose, or Red Rose potatoes, cooked (steamed, boiled, or roasted)
12   thick stalks asparagus, woody ends broken off
¾   pound large Eastern squid, cleaned, heads and bodies separated
3   tablespoons extra virgin olive oil
¾   teaspoon kosher salt
¼   teaspoon freshly ground black pepper
I   heart of romaine lettuce, cut in half lengthwise

[DRESSING]
I   teaspoon finely minced fresh ginger
½   teaspoon finely minced garlic
I   tablespoon plus I teaspoon minced shallot
2   tablespoons champagne vinegar
¼   to ½ teaspoon kosher salt (to taste)
¼   teaspoon cracked black peppercorns
I   teaspoon freshly squeezed lemon juice
⅓   cup extra virgin olive oil
I   tablespoon chopped fresh flat-leaf parsley
    Fleur de sel, for sprinkling

1. Prepare a medium-hot grill. Meanwhile, make the dressing: In a large bowl, mix together the ginger, garlic, shallot, and vinegar. Add the salt, pepper, and lemon juice. Whisk in the olive oil and stir in the parsley. Taste and adjust the seasoning. Set aside.

2. Cut the potatoes in half lengthwise. Fingerlings look pretty if halved on the diagonal. Toss the halved potatoes, the asparagus, and the squid with 2 tablespoons of the oil, the salt, and the pepper. Drizzle the other tablespoon of oil over the cut side of the romaine lettuce.

3. Place the vegetables and squid separately on the hot grill. The squid and asparagus should be on the hotter part, the romaine and the potatoes away from the direct heat. Grill the asparagus for 3 to 5 minutes, or until lightly charred and softened, turning every minute. Grill the squid bodies for 2 minutes on each side, and the tentacles for about 5 minutes total, turning often. Grill the potatoes for about 5 minutes, turning once, until grill marks appear. Grill the lettuce for 2 to 3 minutes, until lightly charred. As each food is finished, transfer to the bowl with the salad dressing. Cut the romaine lengthwise into thirds. Cut the squid bodies into ½-inch-wide rings and cut the tentacles in half through the center. When all of the squid and vegetables are done, toss together with the dressing and arrange on a large platter. Sprinkle with fleur de sel and serve.

tuna ceviche [makes 4 servings]

You can use bigeye or yellowfin for this ceviche, but make sure to get the center cut and not the tail, which is too stringy and tough. When you make ceviche with tuna, you don't marinate the fish for a long time in the lime juice, as you would in a Mexican-style ceviche. Otherwise the fish will cook through, and you want it to remain rare and tender. The vegetables are diced very small so they look like confetti. If you don't have wild fennel, serve without.

12	ounces big eye or yellowfin tuna, cut in ½-inch dice
3	tablespoons finely diced sweet red pepper (⅛-inch dice)
3	tablespoons finely diced red onion (⅛-inch dice), soaked in cold water for 5 minutes, drained, rinsed, and dried on paper towels (page 17)
3	tablespoons finely diced fennel bulb (⅛-inch dice)
½	large ripe but firm avocado, cut in ¼ x ½-inch dice
1	to 2 tablespoons finely diced jalapeño, depending on your taste
3	tablespoons freshly squeezed lime juice
1	tablespoon white wine vinegar
1	teaspoon kosher salt (more to taste)
¼	cup extra virgin olive oil
½	teaspoon freshly ground black pepper
¼	cup roughly chopped cilantro
	Bibb lettuce leaves, for serving
1	tablespoon plus 1 teaspoon chopped wild fennel fronds (optional)
1	tablespoon pumpkin seeds, toasted and coarsely chopped (optional)

1. Dice the tuna and store, covered, in the refrigerator while you prepare the other ingredients.

2. Place the diced red pepper in a bowl, cover with water, and let sit for a couple of minutes. Drain and dry on paper towels (you soak the pepper so that its red color doesn't bleed into the salad). Set aside.

3. Toss together the onion, fennel, avocado, jalapeño, and tuna in a medium bowl.

4. Mix together the lime juice, vinegar, salt, olive oil, and pepper. Toss with the fish mixture. Cover and refrigerate for 15 to 30 minutes. Remove from the refrigerator, add the diced red pepper and cilantro, and toss together. Taste and adjust the seasonings.

5. Line plates with Bibb lettuce leaves and top with the ceviche. Sprinkle each portion with chopped wild fennel and chopped toasted pumpkin seeds, and serve.

[NOTE] Look for fat fennel bulbs and use the inner layers; they're more tender than flat bulbs.

[NOTE] Prepare the red pepper. To get really fine dice, cut the top and bottom off the pepper and cut into lengthwise quarters. Lay a quarter down on your cutting board. Using a sharp, thin-bladed knife held parallel to the cutting board, slice in half (as if you were slicing a side of smoked salmon), so you have a thin sheet, about ⅛ inch thick, of pepper. Dice the half with the skin on.

bagna cauda with fennel, endive, rapini, and asparagus

[makes 8 to 10 servings]

We use the Italian name of this pungent, garlicky anchovy dip because the literal English translation ("hot bath") is not as delicious sounding. It makes a nice winter hors d'oeuvre; you can make a batch, rewarm it any time, and serve it with various vegetables. Don't use a strong green olive oil for this; it should not overwhelm the butter and anchovies. The vegetables listed here work well with bagna cauda, but so do other vegetables. Let the market be your guide when it comes to choosing.

[BAGNA CAUDA]

½ cup (1 stick) unsalted butter
6 fat garlic cloves, halved, green shoots removed, and thinly sliced, plus 1 clove, minced
5 whole salted anchovies, boned, soaked, rinsed, and mashed (page 131); or 5 oil-packed anchovy fillets, soaked, rinsed, and mashed (1½ ounces fillets)
¼ teaspoon finely chopped lemon zest
1 teaspoon freshly squeezed lemon juice
¼ teaspoon kosher salt
¼ teaspoon freshly ground black pepper
1 tablespoon warm water
½ cup extra virgin olive oil

[VEGETABLES]

1 Belgian endive, brown or split outer leaves removed, cut lengthwise into 8 thin wedges
1 small fennel bulb, trimmed and cut into thin wedges
1 celery heart, broken into stalks, the wider stalks cut in half lengthwise
10 asparagus spears, woody ends broken off, blanched for 1 minute in salted boiling water, refreshed, drained, and patted dry
Leaves from 1 romaine heart
½ bunch rapini (broccoli rabe), stems trimmed, blanched for 4 minutes in salted boiling water, refreshed, drained, and patted dry

1. Melt the butter in a small earthenware pot or heavy saucepan over low heat. Add the sliced garlic and cook very slowly until the garlic is soft and fragrant but not at all colored, 3 to 4 minutes. Add the anchovies, lemon zest, lemon juice, salt, and pepper, and whisk for a minute or 2, until the anchovies are well amalgamated in the butter.

2. Add the water and slowly whisk in the oil. Continue to stir until the mixture is amalgamated. Do not allow it to boil, but keep at a bare simmer. Whisk in the minced garlic and continue to simmer for 1 minute. Transfer to a small, warm ceramic bowl and place in the middle of a large platter.

3. Arrange the vegetables on the platter and serve, making sure the bagna cauda is warm. Alternatively, give a ramekin of warm bagna cauda to each guest and pass the vegetables. Make sure to scoop up the anchovies and garlic from the bottom of the bowl or ramekin when you dip your vegetables.

scrambled eggs for two [makes 2 servings]

For this dish, 3 extra-large eggs are just the right amount for two people. One is never enough per person, and two can be too much. These are seasoned and enhanced with a little bit of bacon (one strip for two people) and parsley. I like serving this with rye toast; the tartness is a perfect counterpoint to the velvety eggs. Serve with a cup of coffee and four ounces of orange juice for a perfect start to your day, or as a light supper without the coffee and juice.

3	extra-large eggs
1	tablespoon whole milk
¼	teaspoon kosher salt
1	teaspoon chopped fresh flat-leaf parsley
1	piece thick-cut bacon, cut on the diagonal into ⅛-inch-wide slivers
2	slices rye bread
1	teaspoon unsalted butter, plus butter for the toast

1. Beat the eggs in a medium bowl with 2 teaspoons of milk, the salt, and the parsley.

2. Heat an 8- or 10-inch skillet over medium-high heat and add the bacon. Cook the bacon until it is chewy in the middle and crisp on the edges. Remove the pan from the heat, transfer the bacon to a double thickness of paper towel, and allow to cool. Cut crosswise into ⅛-inch-thick slivers. Set aside.

3. Put the rye bread in the toaster so it will be ready when the eggs are ready. Pour off most of the bacon grease from the pan, turn the heat to low, and add 1 teaspoon butter and the slivered bacon. Heat over medium-low heat and when the butter begins to sizzle, pour in the eggs. Stir slowly with a rubber spatula until the eggs are just set. Remove from the heat and stir in the remaining teaspoon of milk.

4. Remove the toast from the toaster, butter, and cut on the diagonal. Arrange on plates and pile the eggs partially over the toast. Serve at once.

spanish tortilla with jamón serrano and clams

[makes 8 starter servings or 4 main dish servings]

Every café in Spain serves tortilla española, a flat omelet that's traditionally filled with potato and onion (it has nothing to do with Mexican tortillas). The array of fillings you can use in a Spanish tortilla is only limited by the available ingredients. In this one, which I've served as a first course for a few Monday Night Family Dinners, I've added steamed clams and thinly sliced Serrano ham. I serve it with freshly made herb mayonnaise flavored with the juice from the clams. Make the tortilla ahead for a great late-night supper dish. It should be served warm or at room temperature, not hot. You can easily cut the recipe in half and cook the tortilla in a smaller pan.

3	tablespoons extra virgin olive oil
2	tablespoons minced red onion
1	pound small clams, such as Manila, purged (page 83)
¼	cup dry white wine
8	large eggs
1	small or ½ large garlic clove, green shoot removed, finely minced
⅓	cup heavy cream
1	teaspoon kosher salt
¼	teaspoon freshly ground black pepper
1	tablespoon finely chopped fresh flat-leaf parsley
1	teaspoon chopped chives
½	pound firm potatoes, such as fingerlings, Yukon Gold, Red, or White Rose, roasted or steamed and cut into ¼-inch dice
1½	ounces Serrano ham

[MAYONNAISE]

¾	cup Garlic Mayonnaise (page 22)
1	tablespoon minced fresh flat-leaf parsley
1	tablespoon minced chives
1	tablespoon minced chervil

1. Heat 1 tablespoon of olive oil over medium heat in a large saucepan or lidded skillet and add the onion. Cook, stirring, until tender, about 3 minutes. Add the clams and white wine. Bring to a boil, cover, and reduce the heat to medium. Steam 4 to 5 minutes, until the clams have opened. Remove from the heat and remove the clams from the pan.

2. Strain the cooking liquid from the clams through a cheesecloth-lined strainer and bring to a boil in a small saucepan or skillet. Boil, watching very carefully so that it doesn't burn, until reduced to a syrupy consistency, about 1 tablespoon. Set aside.

3. Remove the clams from their shells, rinse briefly, and chop coarsely. Set aside.

4. Preheat the oven to 400°F. Heat a heavy, well-seasoned 10-inch cast-iron or ovenproof nonstick skillet over high heat. Meanwhile, beat the eggs briskly in a bowl. Add the garlic, cream, salt, pepper, parsley, and chives and beat together.

5. Add the remaining 2 tablespoons of olive oil to the pan and when the oil ripples and is just short of smoking, pour in the eggs. They should begin to cook immediately. Shake the pan and tilt, lifting the edges of the omelet so the eggs run under themselves.

6. Sprinkle the diced potatoes over the eggs in an even layer, then sprinkle on the chopped clams. Turn the heat down to medium, and when the tortilla is halfway cooked, lay the ham slices in an even layer over the top. Transfer to the oven.

7. Bake the omelet until set, about 15 minutes. Remove from the heat and allow to cool to room temperature (or you can serve it warm, but not hot).

8. Meanwhile, stir the reduced clam juice into the mayonnaise. Just before serving, stir in the parsley, chives, and chervil. Taste and adjust the salt. Cut the omelet into wedges and serve with the mayonnaise on the side.

clams casino [makes 24 clams, 6 to 8 servings]

This is one of those classic American dishes that inspired me to write this book. I wanted to renew interest in some dishes that were delightful in their original incarnations, but then were overdone, often badly, to such an extent that they fell out of favor. If you make the dish this way (and this recipe is different from the classic because I don't crumble the bacon), you'll understand why it became so popular. Cut the bacon into small slabs, which protects the clams from overcooking while infusing them with its flavor. The bacon crisps up around the edges, giving you a nice contrast of chewy and crisp textures. This can be prepped ahead of time through step 4.

1	tablespoon chopped chives
1½	tablespoons chopped fresh flat-leaf parsley
1	tablespoon chopped fresh tarragon
½	small garlic clove, green shoot removed, roughly chopped
	Pinch of kosher salt
	Freshly ground black pepper to taste
4	tablespoons (½ stick) unsalted butter, softened
1½	ounces bacon (2 strips)
	Rock salt for the baking sheet (optional)
24	cherrystone clams, shucked and left on the half shell
½	lemon

1. In a mortar and pestle, mash together the herbs, garlic, salt. and pepper. Add the butter and mash together.

2. Cook the bacon until just cooked through but not crisp. Remove from the heat and cut in 1-inch pieces.

3. Preheat the oven to 400°F. Cover a baking sheet with a ½-inch-thick layer of rock salt, if using. Heat in the oven for 5 minutes. Now preheat the broiler.

4. Place the clams on top of the salt (this is just to keep them steady). Top each with about 2 drops lemon juice and ½ teaspoon of the butter mixture. Lay a piece of bacon over the top.

5. Place under the broiler for 2 to 3 minutes, until the butter is sizzling. Serve immediately.

stewed chickpea salad with feta, olives, and mint [makes 4 servings]

I'm not sure if the flavors here come from North Africa or Greece, but they're decidedly Mediterranean. It's a vegetarian dish that tastes meaty and refreshing at the same time. Good-quality feta, one that isn't too salty or dry, is essential here.

½ pound chickpeas, soaked for 6 hours or overnight
1 quart water
2 fat garlic cloves, peeled and lightly crushed
2 thyme sprigs
1 bay leaf
2 teaspoons kosher salt
½ cup kalamata olives, pitted and sliced lengthwise
2 large tomatoes, peeled, seeded, and finely diced
1 bunch scallions, trimmed and sliced thin
    on the diagonal
1 tablespoon slivered mint leaves
¼ to ½ teaspoon cracked black peppercorns (to taste)
⅓ cup Basic Lemon Vinaigrette (page 16) or
    Cumin-Oregano Vinaigrette (page 24) made
    with extra virgin olive oil
1 ounce feta, crumbled

1. Drain the chickpeas and place in a large saucepan with the water, garlic cloves, thyme sprigs, bay leaf, and salt. Bring to a simmer, cover, and cook gently for 1½ to 2 hours, until tender. Remove from the heat, uncover, and allow to cool slightly in the cooking liquid.

2. Drain the cooked chickpeas and transfer to a salad bowl. Allow to cool slightly, and while still warm toss with the olives, tomatoes, scallions, mint, pepper, and vinaigrette. Taste and adjust the seasoning. Sprinkle on the feta and serve warm.

early spring fava beans and artichokes with cumin [makes 4 servings]

We start to get fava beans in March, and they continue to come in for about three months. But only in March can you get the thin, tender pods whose beans are small and don't require skinning. When I make this I separate the larger beans and skin them, which makes for a nice color contrast. The skinned beans are bright green, and the artichokes and unskinned favas are drab. You can serve this simple vegetable ragout warm or at room temperature. It makes a great vegetarian entrée.

2 ½   pounds fava beans, preferably thin pods (thinner than your index finger) or a combination of thin and thicker pods
1¾   pounds baby artichokes, trimmed (page 26), quartered, and placed in a bowl of water acidulated with the juice of 1 lemon
3   tablespoons extra virgin olive oil
½   pound spring onions, cut in half and sliced crosswise about ¼ inch thick
1   fat garlic clove, cut in half, green shoot removed, and sliced
     Kosher salt
1   teaspoon cumin seeds, lightly toasted and crushed in a mortar and pestle or spice mill
¼   cup dry white wine
¼   cup chicken stock or water
2   tablespoons chopped fresh chervil
2   tablespoons chopped fresh tarragon
1   to 2 teaspoons freshly squeezed lemon juice (to taste)
     Bibb lettuce leaves, for serving
1   teaspoon chopped fresh flat-leaf parsley

1. Sort the beans, placing the larger pods in one pile and the thinner ones in another. Shuck them and place all the small beans that won't require peeling in one bowl and the larger beans (1¾ inch or longer) in another. Bring a small pot of water to a boil and add the larger beans. Boil 1 minute and transfer to a bowl of ice water. Allow to cool, then pop off the skins and set aside.

2. Drain the artichokes and pat dry. Heat the oil in a medium saucepan over medium-high heat and add the artichokes. Cook, stirring, for 2 minutes, until they just begin to color, and add the onions, garlic, ½ teaspoon salt, and the cumin. Turn the heat to medium-low, stir together, cover, and cook over low heat for 5 minutes.

3. Add the small, unskinned favas to the pan. Stir together, cover, and cook for 5 minutes.

4. Add the wine to the pan and bring to a boil. Add the chicken stock or water and boil uncovered for 2 minutes. Add the peeled fava beans and another ½ teaspoon salt, cover, and simmer for 5 minutes. Check to make sure the artichokes are tender. If they are not, continue to simmer for another 5 minutes, or until they are tender. Stir in the herbs and remove from the heat.

5. If serving at room temperature, transfer to a bowl and chill in an ice bath or the refrigerator. If serving warm, allow to cool slightly. Stir in the lemon juice and adjust the seasonings.

6. Line plates with lettuce leaves (if serving at room temperature) and top with a generous spoonful of the vegetables. Sprinkle with parsley and serve.

tomato and goat cheese tart [makes 6 to 8 servings]

We serve this savory tart as a starter when tomatoes are in season, but you could also make a light meal of it. When you make a tomato tart with fresh tomatoes, it's important to use tomatoes that are not too watery. Good farmers' market beefsteaks and Romas are ideal for this. Meaty heirlooms, like pineapple tomatoes, work well, too.

½	recipe Savory Flaky Dough (recipe follows) or 1 sheet puff pastry
1½	pounds firm but ripe beefsteak tomatoes, sliced ½ inch thick
	Kosher salt
2	tablespoons unsalted butter
1	pound onions, halved lengthwise and sliced across the grain
	Freshly ground black pepper
1	large or 2 small garlic cloves, thinly sliced
1	large egg, beaten
2	tablespoons whole milk
½	cup (tightly packed) goat cheese
1½	teaspoons chopped fresh thyme

ONION SLICES

If you are using sliced onions in a dish that requires cutting, like this tart, and you want the onions to fall apart easily when you bite into them, slice them across the grain. This cuts through their structure so the onion slices won't be stringy.

1. If using flaky pastry, roll out to a rectangle about 10 inches long by 8 inches wide, and make a ½-inch-high lip down the long sides. Prebake, following the directions below. If using commercial puff pastry, thaw one sheet and form a rectangle by gently rolling a lip along two opposite sides. Pre-bake following the directions below.

2. Place the tomato slices on a rack set over a baking sheet. Salt generously on both sides and leave to drain for 30 minutes.

3. Meanwhile, heat the butter in a large, heavy skillet over medium heat and add the onions. Cook, stirring often, until they begin to soften, about 5 minutes. Add ¾ teaspoon salt and ¼ teaspoon freshly ground pepper, and continue to cook for another 5 to 10 minutes, stirring often, until tender. Add the garlic, cover the pan, and continue to cook for another 15 minutes, stirring often, until the onions are very tender and golden brown.

4. Rinse the tomatoes and pat dry on both sides with paper towels.

5. Preheat the oven to 350°F. Beat the egg, the tomato juice that has accumulated in the baking sheet, and the milk together, and beat in the goat cheese. Combine until smooth. Stir in the thyme and some freshly ground pepper.

6. Layer the onions evenly over the prebaked pastry. Top with the tomatoes, overlapping them slightly. Dollop the goat cheese over the tomatoes. Bake 30 minutes, until the goat cheese mixture is just beginning to brown. Remove from the oven and serve warm or at room temperature.

[PREBAKING PUFF PASTRY]

When you prebake puff pastry, you need to weight it so it doesn't puff up too much. Preheat the oven to 425°F. Line a baking sheet with parchment and place the puff pastry on the parchment. Place another sheet of parchment over the puff pastry and top with a cooling rack. Place in the oven and bake 15 minutes. Turn the oven down to 350°F and bake for another 15 minutes. Remove from the heat.

savory flaky dough [makes two 9-inch crusts]

I use this dough for savory tarts like the Tomato and Goat Cheese Tart on page 52, or the Leek Tart with Crème Fraîche on page 54. Since this makes enough for two tart shells, you can keep one on hand in the freezer, all rolled out and ready to go. As with all pastry recipes, pay attention to the measurements; creativity in cooking is a wonderful thing, but not here.

I	cup (2 sticks) unsalted butter
2½	cups all-purpose flour
I	teaspoon salt
½	cup ice water (approximately)
½	teaspoon freshly squeezed lemon juice

I. Chop the butter into 1-inch pieces and place it in the freezer to chill for 15 minutes. Sift together the flour and the salt and place in the bowl of a standing electric mixer fitted with the paddle attachment. Add the partially frozen butter.

2. Turn the machine on low and mix for 2 minutes, until the butter is broken down to the size of a walnut (the inside of a walnut—the meat—not the whole nut in the shell). After 2 minutes, stop the machine, and by hand pinch flat any large pieces of butter and flour that remain.

3. In a small bowl, combine the ice water and lemon juice. Turn the mixer on low speed and add the water all at once. Mix just until the dough comes together, about 15 seconds. The dough should be tacky but not sticky. Add a little water if the dough seems dry.

4. Remove the dough from the bowl, divide in two, and press each half into a ½-inch-thick disk. Wrap tightly in plastic and chill the dough for at least 1 hour before use. Well-wrapped flaky dough may be kept in the refrigerator for up to 3 days or frozen for 3 weeks.

5. Roll out the dough and line two 9- or 10-inch tart pans (or roll out ½ of the pastry into a rectangle as directed above). If only using one, wrap the other airtight and freeze for another use. Chill for at least 15 minutes to help maintain the decorative shape when filling and baking.

[BLIND BAKING]

Prebaking a tart shell is known as "blind baking." The shell must be weighted to prevent it from puffing up as it bakes, so line the shell with foil, parchment paper, or coffee filters, then fill it with beans (don't use the beans that you use for blind baking for anything else; I keep some old beans around just for this). Once it is baked halfway through, remove the weights, and continue to bake without weighting it.

To blind bake, preheat the oven to 425°F with the rack in the lower third of the oven and prick the bottom of the pastry a few times with a fork. Line the pastry shell with parchment paper, aluminum foil, or coffee filters. Fill the lined shell to the rim with dried beans, and gently press the filling into the corners. Place in the oven and bake for 10 minutes, then turn the heat down to 350°F and bake for another 7 minutes. Remove from the oven and remove the beans and the lining. Return to the oven for 10 minutes, or until the center turns golden and looks dry. There should be no sign of moisture. Remove from the oven and allow to cool on a rack.

leek tart with crème fraîche [makes one 10-inch tart, 8 servings as a starter]

This is simple French food at its best. The flavor is all about leeks, enhanced with a little sage and thyme, and every time I eat it I wish I had a garden full of this underused vegetable.

2	tablespoons unsalted butter
1	pound leeks, light part only, root end cut away, sliced thin across the grain and washed in 2 to 3 changes of water (see below)
1	teaspoon kosher salt
1	fat garlic clove, cut in half, green shoot removed, sliced
2	sage leaves, chopped
½	teaspoon fresh thyme leaves
½	cup heavy cream
¼	teaspoon freshly ground black pepper
½	cup crème fraîche
1	large egg yolk, beaten
1	9-inch Savory Flaky pastry shell (page 53), or 1 sheet commercial puff pastry, prebaked (page 52)
½	cup Herbed Garlic Bread Crumbs (page 18)

1. Heat the butter in a large, heavy skillet over medium-low heat and add the leeks, salt, garlic, sage, and thyme. Cook gently, covered, until the vegetables are very tender, about 20 minutes. Do not brown. If they begin to stick and color, switch pans and add a tablespoon of water to the new pan. Add the cream and continue to cook, uncovered, until most of the cream is absorbed, about 10 minutes. Remove from the heat. Stir in the pepper.

2. Preheat the oven to 350°F. Beat together the crème fraîche and egg yolk, and spread over the bottom of the prebaked piecrust. Spoon on the leeks, then gently spread out to make a layer. Sprinkle the bread crumbs over the top in an even layer.

3. Bake 30 minutes, until the top has colored and the tart is slightly resistant to the touch. Remove from the heat and allow to sit for 10 minutes or longer before serving.

[HOW TO CLEAN LEEKS]
To clean the leeks, which are almost always sandy and often caked with mud, cut away the root end. Slice the leeks crosswise and place in a bowl. Cover with cold water and swish the leek slices around in the water. Lift from the water and place in a strainer. Drain the water, rinse the bowl, and fill with water again. Return the leeks to the water, swish around one more time, and lift out into the strainer. If the water in the bowl is sandy, repeat one more time, or until there is no longer any sand. Rinse the sliced leeks with cold water and drain on paper towels.

onion, potato, and bacon tart [makes 6 to 8 servings]

I like this tart partly because it's not limited to a particular season. Onions, potatoes, and bacon are some of the most versatile ingredients, and they're available year round. The flavors here are decidedly Alsatian. Be sure to slice the onions across the grain so that they break down easily when you slice the tart.

1	large (10-ounce) russet potato, peeled and cut in ½-inch dice
	Kosher salt
2	strips thick-cut bacon
3	tablespoons unsalted butter
2	pounds onions, cut in half lengthwise then thinly sliced across the grain
	A bouquet garni made with 1 small sprig rosemary, 1 bay leaf, and 2 juniper berries, lightly crushed (page 66)
½	cup heavy cream
2	tablespoons chopped fresh flat-leaf parsley
1	10-inch Savory Flaky pastry shell (page 53), or 1 sheet commercial puff pastry, prebaked (page 52)

1. Bring a medium saucepan full of salted water to a boil and add the diced potato. Cook until tender, about 10 minutes. Drain and set aside.

2. Heat a large, heavy frying pan over medium-high heat and cook the bacon until crisp. Remove the bacon from the pan and when cool enough to handle, crumble it and set aside. Pour off the grease from the pan.

3. Add the butter to the pan in which you cooked the bacon and heat over medium-low heat. Add the onions, the bouquet garni, and ½ teaspoon salt, and cook gently, stirring often, until caramelized and meltingly tender, about 40 minutes. Stir in the potatoes and cream and continue to cook, stirring often, until the cream has been just about all absorbed, about 10 minutes. Stir in the bacon and add salt and pepper to taste. Remove the bouquet garni, and stir in the parsley.

4. Preheat the oven to 350°F. Spread the onion filling over the pastry and place in the oven. Bake 30 minutes, until the top is beginning to brown. Remove from the heat and allow to cool for at least 10 minutes before slicing. Serve hot, warm, or room temperature.

fresh shell bean ragout [makes 6 servings]

Fresh shell beans come in many varieties at our California farmers' markets. I like the beautiful purple runner beans and cranberry beans (which do fade during the cooking), as well as fresh black-eyed peas. The trick here is to keep the beans at a very slow simmer (just trembling, as the French would say), so that they cook thoroughly but don't fall apart. These cooking times are for fresh beans; dried beans would take 1½ to 2 hours.

One of my favorite ways to eat this is cold, for a quick lunch. I drizzle on some sharp green olive oil, grind some pepper, and sprinkle some Parmesan over the top, and without heating up the kitchen I've got a delightful and hearty meal. Make this a day ahead if you can for the best flavor.

[RAGOUT]

¼ cup extra virgin olive oil
6 ounces pancetta, diced (about ¼-inch dice)
1 large onion (about 12 ounces), diced (about ½-inch dice)
Heaping ½ cup sliced celery heart
1 leek, white and light green parts only, halved, washed, and sliced across the grain
Kosher salt
Cracked black peppercorns
Bouquet garni made with 3 or 4 parsley sprigs, 3 or 4 thyme sprigs, 3 or 4 fresh sage sprigs, 2 rosemary sprigs, 1 large bay leaf, 3 outer dark leaves of the leek, and 1 celery top (page 66)
4 to 6 plump garlic cloves (to taste), halved, green shoots removed, and thinly sliced
3 cups fresh shell beans, such as purple runners, cranberry beans, black-eyed peas
4 cups water, or a mixture of chicken stock and water
1 pound fresh ripe tomatoes
1½ cups fresh soybeans (edamame; may use thawed frozen)

[SERVING]

Parsley Pesto, for garnish (page 59; optional)
Extra virgin olive oil, for drizzling
Freshly ground black pepper
⅓ cup freshly grated Parmesan cheese

1. Combine the olive oil, pancetta, onion, sliced celery heart, and white and light green parts of the leek in a large, heavy saucepan or Dutch oven and heat over medium-low heat until the mixture begins to sizzle. Add ½ teaspoon salt and ¼ teaspoon cracked black pepper, and cook slowly for 10 to 15 minutes, until the vegetables are very soft but not colored.

2. Add the bouquet garni and the garlic, stir together, and cook for a minute or 2, until the garlic smells fragrant. Add the 3 cups fresh shell beans (not the soybeans). Stir together for about 5 minutes, and add the water or chicken stock and water. Bring to a simmer and simmer gently, partially covered, for 30 minutes.

3. Meanwhile, blanch the tomatoes in boiling water for 1 minute. Transfer to a bowl of ice water, then drain and remove the skins. Cut in half across the equator, and squeeze out the juice and seeds into a strainer set over a bowl. Press the seeds and pulp against the strainer to extract as much juice as possible, then discard. Dice the tomatoes.

4. After 30 minutes, add the diced tomatoes and the juice in the bowl, and the soybeans (edamame) to the beans, along with 1 teaspoon salt. Taste and add more salt if desired. Simmer, partially covered, for another 30 minutes to an hour, until the beans are tender. Taste and adjust the seasonings. For best results, refrigerate overnight. Reheat, or serve at room temperature with a drizzle of parsley pesto or olive oil, a twist of freshly ground black pepper, and a spoonful of freshly grated Parmesan.

VARIATION / FRESH SHELL BEAN MINESTRONE

To the above recipe add:

½   pound cabbage (¼ medium head) or kale,
         cored or stemmed and cut in chiffonade
½   pound zucchini, cut in ½-inch dice
1   cup cooked tubular pasta, such as trenne or penne
1   tablespoon olive oil
½   cup basil chiffonade (leaves cut crosswise in strips)

1. Make the ragout as directed, but using 2½ quarts liquid (preferably half chicken stock, half water).

2. Add the cabbage or kale along with the tomatoes.

3. Add the zucchini when the beans are tender and simmer 10 minutes, or until tender and translucent.

4. Meanwhile, slice the cooked tubular pasta into ¼-inch-thick rounds. Heat 1 tablespoon olive oil in a medium skillet over medium-high heat and add the pasta in one layer. Cook until lightly browned, and flip the rounds over. Cook on the other side until crisp and lightly browned. This should take about 5 minutes total. Add the crisp pasta directly to the soup if serving right away, or drain on paper towels and add shortly before serving.

5. Shortly before serving, stir the basil chiffonade into the soup. Taste and adjust the seasonings.

6. Serve with a drizzle of parsley pesto or olive oil and a heaped spoonful of freshly grated Parmesan.

[NOTE] Like the ragout, it's best if you make this hearty, earthy minestrone a day ahead. Add the basil chiffonade when you reheat.

parsley pesto [makes ⅔ cup]

We use Parsley Pesto at the restaurant even more than we use Basil Pesto. I particularly like the deep emerald green color of this versatile condiment. It has a slightly bitter edge to it, which makes it more refreshing to my palate than Basil Pesto, not as sweet. It goes well with meats as well as fish and poultry, and holds its color longer than basil pesto, which oxidizes quickly. The pesto you make in a food processor will never have the depth of flavor that the mortar and pestle version has. Make sure the parsley and basil leaves are perfectly dry and that your knife is sharp.

2	garlic cloves, halved, green shoot removed, roughly chopped
½	teaspoon kosher salt
½	cup extra virgin olive oil, as needed
2	cups tightly packed fresh flat-leaf parsley leaves, coarsely chopped
1	tablespoon tightly packed mint leaves, coarsely chopped
2	tablespoons tightly packed basil leaves, coarsely chopped
2	to 6 tablespoons freshly grated Parmesan cheese, depending on what you are using the pesto for (optional)
	Freshly ground black pepper (optional)

1. In a mortar and pestle, combine the garlic, salt, and 1 teaspoon of the olive oil and grind to a paste. Add the parsley, a handful at a time, and grind to a paste, moving the pestle around in a circular motion. Add the mint leaves and the basil leaves and grind with the parsley.

2. Once the mixture is well combined, begin adding the remaining olive oil and work it in, a tablespoon or 2 at a time. Blend in the Parmesan, if using. Add pepper as desired. The pesto should be runny. Scrape into a bowl or container, cover, and refrigerate. Bring to room temperature at least an hour before using, and stir to restore the color.

VARIATION / BASIL PESTO
Substitute basil for the parsley and parsley for the basil in the above recipe.

GARLIC'S GREEN SHOOTS
As garlic bulbs mature, the cloves develop green shoots. These are bitter, and you should remove them, especially if the garlic is not going to be cooked. Cut the cloves in half lengthwise. It will be easy to lift out the green shoots that you'll find in the middle.

TOP LEFT Cut garlic cloves in half lengthwise and lift out the green shoots that you'll find in the middle.
TOP RIGHT Place the split garlic cloves in a mortar and pestle.
MIDDLE LEFT Add the salt and 1 teaspoon of the oil and gently begin to mash the garlic to a paste. Do not pound the garlic, but grind it. The movement of the pestle should be mostly circular.
MIDDLE Add the parsley a handful at a time and grind with the garlic paste, moving the pestle around in a circular motion
MIDDLE RIGHT Once the parsley is reduced almost to a paste, begin adding the olive oil and work it in a tablespoon at a time, continuing to move the pestle in a circular motion, until all of the olive oil has been added. The pesto should have a runny rather than a pastelike consistency.
BOTTOM RIGHT Blend in the Parmesan cheese, if using.

eggplant parmesan [makes 6 servings]

In my quest to give you a reliable collection of classic recipes, here is one for eggplant Parmesan, a dish for which you have no doubt seen many recipes. Eggplant Parmesan is a perfect example of the kind of dish I wanted to include in this book. We've all had perfectly abysmal versions of it—stale, greasy, mushy, rancid, burnt—pick your adjective and it's out there wrapped around eggplant Parmesan along with canned bread crumbs (you might as well use canned eggplant) and Kraft Parmesan, sometimes all of them at once. The key, as always, is the quality of your ingredients, and these are simple and easy to find. The eggplant should be firm and dense with shiny, smooth skin (think college sophomore, male or female); the bread crumbs should come from quality bread; the Parmesan should be Parmigiano-Reggiano; the tomato sauce should be homemade; and the mozzarella should be fresh. If you wilt, bread, and fry your eggplant properly, then you're there. The herbed bread crumbs in this version are particularly tasty. There are two methods you can use for the eggplant: You can salt it and fry it, or you can first roast it in a hot oven instead of salting, then drain, slice, and fry. The second method requires a little less oil than the first.

When breading an ingredient for frying, always have more bread crumbs, flour, and egg for dredging than you think you need. It makes the process easier.

	Canola oil
2	pounds eggplant (2 large)
	Kosher salt
1	cup dry bread crumbs
1	cup freshly grated Parmesan cheese
1	tablespoon finely chopped fresh flat-leaf parsley
3	large eggs
2	tablespoons whole milk
1	cup all-purpose flour
½	teaspoon freshly ground black pepper
	Extra virgin olive oil
1	recipe Simple Tomato Sauce (page 90)
½	pound fresh mozzarella cheese, thinly sliced

[PREPARE THE EGGPLANT]

1. OPTION A: Preheat the oven to 450°F. Cover a baking sheet with foil and oil the foil. Cut the eggplants in half lengthwise and cut the stem ends off. Score with the tip of a sharp knife down the middle of the cut side, almost to the skin, being careful not to cut through the skin. Place, cut side down, on the baking sheet and roast for 20 minutes, until the skin is shriveled and the eggplant is slightly softened but holds its shape when lightly pressed. Remove from the oven and place, cut side down, in a colander set in the sink or over a bowl. Allow to cool and drain for 30 minutes, then slice lengthwise about ½ inch thick and season the slices with 1 teaspoon kosher salt.

OPTION B: Slice the eggplant lengthwise in ½-inch-thick slices. Salt generously. Lay on a rack set over a baking sheet, and when you see water beading on the top surface, turn the slices over and salt the other side generously. Let sit 30 minutes, then rinse and pat dry.

2. Prepare the breading ingredients. In a wide baking dish, mix together the bread crumbs, ½ cup of the Parmesan, and the parsley. In another bowl, beat together the eggs and milk. In a wide baking dish, mix together the flour, 1 teaspoon salt, and the pepper.

3. Dip the eggplant slices first in the flour, then in the egg, then in the bread crumb and Parmesan mixture, and coat thoroughly. Transfer to a parchment-lined baking sheet and allow to sit for at least 15 minutes so that the surface of the breaded eggplant dries out.

4. Heat ¼ cup canola oil in a large, heavy frying pan over medium-high heat. When the oil is rippling, just short of smoking, fry the coated eggplant slices in batches until nicely browned on each side and soft in the middle. The roasted slices will take about 1 to 1 ½ minutes per side. The salted slices will take longer, about 1 ½ to 2 minutes per side. They should be a dark golden brown; be careful not to burn the coating. Drain the slices on a rack or on paper towels.

5. Preheat the oven to 400°F. Oil a 3-quart gratin dish with olive oil. Cover the bottom of the dish with ½ cup of the tomato sauce. Top with the eggplant slices, overlapping them in a single layer. Spread half the remaining tomato sauce down the middle of the eggplant layer, and top with the sliced mozzarella in a single layer. Top with the remaining tomato sauce, again spooning it down the middle of the casserole. Sprinkle on ½ cup Parmesan, and drizzle on a tablespoon of olive oil. Bake 30 minutes, or until browned and bubbling.

TOP With one hand, dip the eggplant slices first in the flour…
MIDDLE …then in the egg
BOTTOM …then in the bread crumb and Parmesan mixture. Using your other hand, coat thoroughly and remove to a parchment-covered tray.

spring vegetable ragout with lentils [makes 4 servings]

You could serve this dish as a first course, or as a vegetarian main dish, using the larger amount of lentils. It's a beautiful springtime ragout. You don't need to be wedded to the vegetables in this list; if you find beautiful green beans or romano beans, or different types of squash, or lovely spring carrots or turnips, use them. Let the market be your guide. Make sure to use either beluga or green Le Puy lentils for this. Brown lentils are too mushy.

¼ cup extra virgin olive oil

3 ounces wild mushrooms, such as oyster mushrooms, maitake or shiitake, washed first, stems trimmed or removed altogether if tough, cut in thick slices

¼ pound spring onions, white part only, trimmed (if large, quartered and sliced across the grain into ¼-inch slices)

1 bouquet garni made with a few sprigs each chervil, tarragon, and thyme (page 66)
Kosher salt

6 ounces baby pattypan squash, trimmed and halved

6 ounces zucchini, cut oblique (page 81)

1 garlic clove, halved, green shoot removed, and sliced

½ pound asparagus, woody stems trimmed off, cut on the diagonal into 2-inch lengths

½ cup shelled and skinned fava beans (page 51)

1 to 2 cups cooked beluga or green Le Puy lentils (below, to taste)

¼ red bell pepper, cut in very thin strips, rinsed and patted dry on paper towels
Freshly ground pepper

1 tablespoon finely chopped flat-leaf parsley or tarragon, or a combination

1. Heat the olive oil in a large, heavy saucepan or Dutch oven over medium heat and add the mushrooms. Cook until lightly colored and beginning to release moisture, about 5 minutes, and add the onions, the bouquet garni, and ½ teaspoon salt. Stir together, cover and reduce the heat. Cook gently for 8 minutes, stirring occasionally, until the onions are tender. Add the pattypan squash, the zucchini, and the garlic and continue to cook, stirring occasionally, until the squash begins to soften, about 5 minutes. Add the asparagus and favas, and stir in 1 cup water and another ½ teaspoon salt. Bring to a simmer, cover, and simmer 5 minutes.

2. Stir in the lentils and the rinsed red pepper. Add freshly ground pepper to taste and adjust salt. Simmer 3 minutes, until the pepper is just tender, and remove from the heat. Stir in the chopped parsley or tarragon. Taste, adjust seasonings, and serve.

[NOTE] It's important to cut the pepper very thin, so that it softens quickly without bleeding into the mixture.

[COOKED LENTILS, makes 4 cups]

2 to 3 fat garlic cloves (to taste), halved, green shoots removed, and sliced

2 cups beluga or Le Puy lentils, rinsed
Kosher salt

1 bay leaf
Freshly ground pepper

2 large basil sprigs

Combine the lentils, garlic, enough water to cover by 1½ inches, 1 teaspoon salt, and the bay leaf. Bring to a simmer, reduce the heat, cover and simmer over low heat until just tender, 30 to 40 minutess. Taste and adjust salt. Remove from the heat and immediatly grind in some pepper. Drain and use as needed, or serve in a bowl with the broth.

[2]

SOUPS

All restaurants, from the corner café to the three-star temple of molecular gastronomy, offer soup in one form or another. Soups often provide chefs with an outlet for an overabundance of one ingredient or another, but that's not why you should make them. Make them because they're comforting, restorative, and delicious, a way to concentrate the flavors of the season. Browse the pages of this chapter and you will have accompanied me on my weekly trips to the farmers' market. With late summer produce we make our iconic Roasted Tomato Soup (page 71) and our fresh shell bean Ribollito (page 75). As the tomato harvest winds down, leaving us with green tomatoes that will never ripen, we make a popular Green Tomato Soup with Bacon (page 72). Fall and winter markets provide the dense, sumptuous squash we use for Roasted Winter Squash Soup (page 69). Our spring soups show off the market's bounty of English peas, green garlic, and spring onions that are so sweet and fleeting.

Not all of the soups here are restricted by the seasonality of our produce. The mother of all of our soups is a classic pureed potato and leek soup that you can make at any time of year. Master this and you will have a formula for any number of similar potato-thickened purees that begin with a sautéed flavor base of onions, celery, garlic, and leeks. From this base you can progress to a host of new flavors, colors, and textures.

You'll also find dense hearty soups here, like the Wild Mushroom and Farro Soup (page 76) and the Clam, Corn, and Potato Chowder (page 82). They make substantial meals, needing little more than a salad and some good crusty bread to complete the menu.

If you're going to take the time to make soup, you should make it right and make a good quantity, so you can have it on hand in the refrigerator or freezer. The recipes here make large batches, but you can never have too much. Most soups keep well for at least three or four days in the refrigerator and freeze well for a few months. Once made, they're convenience food. Take some out of the refrigerator and ladle into a bowl, heat in the microwave, and dinner is done.

chicken stock [makes 4 to 5 quarts]

You have the option of using canned chicken stock or broth in these soup recipes, but homemade stock will always taste better. The stock should simmer very slowly over low heat for about 4 hours, never boiling, and you need to skim the top regularly. A rapidly boiling stock won't cook the chicken bones faster, it will just churn the ingredients and cause them to break up, clouding the stock and mucking up the pure flavor of chicken a good stock should have. This makes a lot of stock and requires a large stockpot. If you're going to spend the time, you might as well make a large quantity; it freezes well, and you'll be glad to have it on hand.

4½	to 5 pounds chicken backs, bones, and wings, trimmed of fat
4	to 5 quarts water, as needed
2	tablespoons canola oil
1	medium onion, coarsely chopped
1	large leek, sliced and cleaned
2	stalks celery, sliced
1	medium carrot, sliced
6	fat garlic cloves, halved, green shoots removed
2	teaspoons kosher salt
	A bouquet garni made with 4 sprigs each of thyme and parsley, 2 bay leaves, and ½ teaspoon cracked black peppercorns

[HOW TO MAKE A BOUQUET GARNI]

A bouquet garni is a bouquet of herbs and other seasonings that go into soups and stews to add flavor. I usually tie the ingredients into a piece of cheesecloth, but if your bouquet garni consists only of herb sprigs and a bay leaf, you can tie them together with kitchen string. To tie them into cheesecloth, cut a square of cheesecloth approximately 8 x 8 inches. Place the ingredients on the cheesecloth about 2 inches in from the bottom edge. Fold the ends of the cheesecloth in over the ends of the herb sprigs, then fold the bottom edge over and roll up the cheesecloth. Tie up with a piece of kitchen string, wrapping the string from one end to the other and back to make sure the packet is secure.

Another way to make a bouquet garni is to use the dark green ends of leek greens instead of cheesecloth. Wash the greens and cut two 8-inch lengths. Lay them overlapping, and place the ingredients on top. Fold the sides up and the ends in over the ingredients, then tie up with kitchen string.

1. Combine all the chicken and bones with the water and bring to a simmer over medium-high heat. Using a ladle, skim off any foam that rises, turn the heat to low, and simmer 3 hours. Skim off the foam from time to time.

2. Heat the canola oil in a large skillet over medium heat and add the onion, leek, celery, carrot, garlic, and 1 teaspoon salt. Cook gently until the vegetables soften slightly, 5 to 10 minutes. Scrape into the pot with the chicken and add the bouquet garni and remaining teaspoon of salt. Continue to simmer for 1 hour.

3. Strain the stock into a large bowl or pot through a cheesecloth-lined strainer. Refrigerate overnight and lift off the fat from the surface. Transfer to smaller containers and refrigerate or freeze.

pureed potato and leek soup [makes 8 servings]

We make soup all the time in the restaurant, and this classic French potage is often a starting point, a "mother soup" that can be transformed into myriad other soups (see below), depending on what other ingredients we have on hand. Everybody loves this combination, and the soup can be vegetarian if you substitute water for the chicken broth. It's important to strain the soup after you puree it to get a nice smooth texture, so don't omit that step.

4	tablespoons (½ stick) unsalted butter
1	pound leeks, both white and light green parts, sliced ½ inch thick across the grain and washed (page 54)
1	stalk celery, from the tender heart, diced
½	medium onion, chopped
1	tablespoon salt
1¼	pounds russet potatoes, peeled and cut in 1-inch chunks
8	garlic cloves, cut in half, green shoots removed
	A bouquet garni made with a handful of parsley sprigs, 1 bay leaf, 2 thyme sprigs, and ½ teaspoon cracked peppercorns (page 66)
1	quart Chicken Stock (page 66), or 2 cups canned chicken broth and 2 cups water
1	quart water
	Freshly ground pepper to taste

[GARNISH]

3	tablespoons crème fraîche whisked with 1 tablespoon cream until fluffy
	Chopped fresh chives

1. Heat the butter in a heavy 4-quart soup pot over medium-low heat and add the leeks, celery, and onion. Cook gently, stirring, for about 20 minutes, until very tender. Add ¼ teaspoon salt after the first 10 minutes, and make sure that the vegetables do not color.

2. Add the potatoes, garlic, and bouquet garni. Stir together and add the chicken stock and the water. Bring to a simmer, add the remaining salt, cover, and simmer over low heat for 30 to 40 minutes, until the potatoes are falling apart and the broth is very fragrant. Remove from the heat.

3. Remove the bouquet garni from the soup. Using an immersion blender or a food mill fitted with the fine screen, puree the soup, or working in 1½-cup batches, ladle into a blender. Cover the blender, placing a towel over the cover and pulling it down tightly to prevent splashing. Blend each batch, then put through a medium strainer, using a pestle or the bowl of a ladle to push the soup through. Return to the pot, heat through, and adjust the salt and pepper.

4. Serve, topping each bowl with a dollop of whipped crème fraîche and a sprinkling of chives.

VARIATION / SPINACH AND POTATO SOUP WITH SALT PORK

Add to the above recipe 4 ounces bacon when you add the bouquet garni. Simmer 45 minutes. While the soup is simmering, stem and thoroughly wash 1 pound spinach. Bring a medium pot of water to a boil, season generously with salt, and add the spinach. Boil just until it wilts, about 20 to 30 seconds, and transfer to a bowl of ice cold water. Drain, squeeze dry, and chop. Add to the soup at the end of step 2 and simmer an additional 5 minutes. Remove the bacon along with the bouquet garni and proceed with the recipe.

[NOTE] You may use other greens, such as Swiss chard or kale. The blanching time will be longer, especially for kale, which needs about 4 minutes in boiling water. Add chard or kale to the soup about 15 minutes after adding the potatoes.

green garlic soup [makes 6 servings]

This is a farmers' market dish. In an ideal world, by the time you have this book in your hands you'll be able to find green garlic in a supermarket near you, but if not, seek it out at your local farmers' market during its short spring season. It looks like spring onions, as the bulbs have not yet formed cloves, and it has a mild, nutty, sweet garlicky flavor. There will be no green shoots to remove from green garlic.

¾	pound green garlic (greens included)
2	tablespoons extra virgin olive oil
	Cloves from 1 regular head of garlic, peeled
½	pound spring onions, white parts only, roughly chopped
1	small stalk celery, cut in thick slices
	Kosher salt
1½	quarts water
½	pound russet potatoes, peeled and cut in 1-inch chunks
½	cup fresh flat-leaf parsley leaves
	Freshly ground black pepper

[GARNISH]
Garlic Croutons (page 18)
Chopped fresh flat-leaf parsley, chervil, or chives

1. Trim off the ends of the green garlic bulbs, cut in half lengthwise, and wash away any sand or dirt from the inside with cold water. Cut into 2-inch lengths.

2. Heat the olive oil in a large, heavy soup pot over medium heat and add the green garlic, regular garlic, spring onions, celery, and ½ teaspoon salt. Cook gently for about 10 minutes, until the onions have softened but not colored. Add the water, potatoes, and another 1½ teaspoons salt. Bring to a simmer, cover, and simmer over low heat for 30 minutes. Add the parsley and simmer another 3 minutes.

3. Using an immersion blender or a food mill fitted with the fine screen, puree the soup, or working in 1½-cup batches, ladle into a blender. Cover the blender, placing a towel over the cover and pulling it down tightly to prevent splashing. Blend each batch, then put through a medium strainer, using a pestle or the bowl of a ladle to push the soup through. Return to the pot. Reheat, taste, and adjust the salt. Add freshly ground pepper to taste.

4. Place a handful of garlic croutons in each bowl and ladle in the soup. Garnish with chopped fresh parsley, chervil, or chives, and serve.

roasted winter squash soup [makes 4 to 6 servings]

Roasting winter squash gives this warming winter soup a rich caramelized flavor. You can use kabocha, hubbard, or butternut squash. Choose winter squash that feels heavy for its size. If the squash sounds hollow when you thump it, it's ripe and ready to use. To peel heavy, thick-skinned squash, cut into slices, lay the slices on their sides, and cut away the skin with a chef's knife. You can use a vegetable peeler for butternut squash

2¾	pounds butternut, kabocha, or hubbard squash, peeled, seeds and membranes removed, and cut in 1-inch cubes
1	medium carrot, peeled and thickly sliced
1	medium onion or ½ large onion, peeled and cut in large dice
1	head of garlic, broken into cloves
1	tablespoon kosher salt
½	teaspoon freshly ground black pepper
1	heaped teaspoon coriander seeds, cracked
¼	cup extra virgin olive oil
2	cups Chicken Stock (page 66)
2	cups water (or use 4 cups chicken stock in all)
4	fresh sage leaves
½	cup heavy cream
4	fresh sage leaves, cut in chiffonade

1. Set aside ¼ pound of the squash for garnish. Preheat the oven to 400°F. Toss together the remaining squash, carrot, onion, garlic, 1 teaspoon of the salt, the pepper, coriander seeds, and 3 tablespoons of the olive oil and transfer to a lightly oiled baking dish. Roast uncovered for 1 to 1½ hours, stirring every 20 minutes, or until the vegetables are thoroughly softened and lightly caramelized. If any of the onion pieces are blackened, discard them, as they will give the soup a bitter taste. Remove from the heat and transfer to a soup pot.

2. Add the remaining salt, the chicken stock, water, and whole sage leaves and bring to a simmer. Simmer 30 minutes, until the vegetables are falling apart tender. Remove the sage leaves.

3. Put the mixture through a food mill fitted with the small screen and return to the pot. Stir in the cream and heat through. Taste and adjust the seasonings.

4. Cut the squash that you set aside for garnish into very small cubes, about ¼ inch. Heat the remaining tablespoon of olive oil in a small skillet and add the slivered sage leaves. Cook, stirring, until just crisp, about 1 minute, then remove from the oil and drain on a paper towel. Add the diced squash and cook over medium-high heat until lightly browned and tender.

5. Ladle the hot soup into bowls and top each serving with a spoonful of the diced squash and a sprinkling of sage.

roasted tomato soup [makes 6 to 8 generous servings, plus some extra for the freezer]

This tomato soup is comforting, thick, and creamy, though there's no cream in it. The tomatoes are roasted first, then cooked again with a base of onion, celery, leeks, and herbs. The soup is twice blended, first through a food mill and then with an immersion blender. It may sound complicated, but believe me, that final puree with the immersion blender really pulls all the flavors together and makes a superior soup. You're making a large quantity here, so your efforts will get you two batches, one for the freezer and one for tonight's dinner. Don't bother making it if all you can find are hard, pink tomatoes. Juicy heirlooms, such as Cherokees or Marvels, are best, but good Romas will work too. If you're using juicy farmers' market tomatoes, you'll need 5 pounds; if you're using Romas, which are fleshier but not as intensely flavored, use 6.

5	to 6 pounds vine-ripened tomatoes
⅔	cup extra virgin olive oil, plus additional for drizzling
	Kosher salt
	Freshly ground black pepper
6	ounces country bread, preferably whole wheat or non-seeded rye, cut in 1-inch cubes, plus 6 to 8 slices of baguette, toasted, for garnish
1	large onion, coarsely chopped
2	stalks celery, with leaves, coarsely chopped
½	pound leeks (2 small or 1 large), both white and light green parts, sliced across the grain ½ inch thick and washed (page 54)
1	small red bell pepper, roughly chopped
½	dried red chile, preferably Japanese
1	head of garlic (about 3 ounces), broken into cloves and roughly chopped (no need to peel)
	A handful of thyme sprigs
	A handful of basil sprigs
½	small bunch fresh flat-leaf parsley

1. Preheat the oven to 450°F, with the racks adjusted to the center and the top third. If using round tomatoes, cut them in half at the equator. If using Romas, cut them in half lengthwise. Toss in a very large bowl (or in batches in a smaller one) with 6 tablespoons olive oil, 1 teaspoon salt, and ½ teaspoon freshly ground pepper. Place the tomatoes, cut side down, on one or two baking pans with 1-inch sides, however they'll fit, and pour on the juices from the bowl. Place on the middle and upper racks of the oven and roast for 45 minutes, until the skins are blistered and lightly browned and the tomatoes are soft. Remove carefully from the oven and set aside.

2. Toss the bread cubes with 1 tablespoon olive oil and spread on a baking sheet in an even layer. Place in the oven and toast for 10 to 15 minutes, until crisp.

3. Meanwhile, make the vegetable base: Heat 3 tablespoons olive oil over medium heat in a heavy soup pot or Dutch oven and add the onion, celery, leeks, fresh red pepper, dried chile, and ½ teaspoon salt. When the vegetables just begin to sizzle, turn the heat to low and cook, stirring often, for 15 to 20 minutes, until tender and lightly colored. Add the garlic and herbs and cook for another 5 minutes, stirring often.

4. Add the tomatoes, bread cubes, and 1 quart of water to the pot and bring to a simmer. Add 1½ teaspoons salt and ½ teaspoon pepper. Simmer 30 minutes, stirring from time to time so that nothing sticks to the bottom and burns.

5. Remove the soup from the heat and put through a food mill fitted with the fine blade. Return to the pot, and using an immersion blender, puree until smooth and silky. Taste and adjust the seasonings.

6. Heat through and serve, garnished with a toasted slice of baguette and a drizzle of olive oil.

[WASHING HERBS]

Always wash herbs gently so that they don't bruise. This is especially important for basil, which will oxidize and change flavor quickly if it's bruised.

[USING CHOPPED GARLIC]

Garlic oxidizes quickly once you chop it, and the flavor will change, becoming more acrid. This is why it's always best to chop garlic as close as possible to the time you are going to use it.

green tomato soup with bacon [makes 4 servings]

If you grow tomatoes, you might be at a loss to use up the last crop still on the vine in the fall when the weather has cooled. Those tomatoes will never ripen. Since few people want green tomatoes as a gift (though they may if they've tasted this soup), this soup is a perfect destination for them. You can sometimes find green tomatoes at farmers' markets. You can keep green tomatoes in the refrigerator for weeks; they won't be ruined there as would ripe tomatoes. Even if they turn a little pink, they'll still taste like green tomatoes. This soup has a wonderful chewy texture because of the bread. I recommend serving it with an Alsatian Gewürztraminer, a wine that goes well with spicy and acidic foods.

2½	ounces slab bacon, in 1 piece, or 2½ ounces thick-cut bacon (about 3 strips)
1	tablespoon canola oil
½	medium onion, sliced
1	stalk celery, sliced
3	garlic cloves, crushed
1	large leek, white and dark green parts separated, sliced across the grain and washed (page 54)
	Kosher salt
1	teaspoon cumin seeds, toasted and lightly crushed
1	teaspoon dried oregano
½	dried hot red chile, preferably Japanese
2½	pounds green tomatoes, cut in wedges
1	teaspoon sugar
2	cups Chicken Stock (page 66)
1	cup water
1	ounce country bread, preferably whole wheat or non-seeded rye, cut in 1-inch cubes (1 thick slice baguette or ½ slice country bread)
1	tablespoon unsalted butter
	Freshly ground black pepper

[GARNISH]

2	tablespoons crème fraîche (optional)
4	slices bacon, cooked until crisp and crumbled

1. Combine the bacon and the canola oil in a large, heavy soup pot over medium heat and cook, stirring occasionally, until the bacon renders its fat and begins to color, about 5 minutes for slab bacon, 3 minutes for strips. Add the onion, celery, garlic, the dark green part of the leeks, and ½ teaspoon salt and cook, stirring often, until tender but not colored, about 5 minutes. Add the cumin seeds, oregano, and dried chile and stir together for a minute, then add the green tomatoes, the sugar, and another ½ teaspoon salt. Cover and cook gently over medium-low heat until the tomatoes soften and begin to cook down, about 20 minutes.

2. Add the chicken stock, water, 1 teaspoon salt, and the bread and bring to a simmer. Cover and simmer over low heat for 30 minutes. Stir from time to time to prevent anything from sticking to the bottom of the pot.

3. Meanwhile, heat the butter in a medium skillet over medium heat and add the white parts of the leeks and ¼ teaspoon salt. Cook, stirring, until tender, about 5 minutes. Remove from the heat.

4. Remove the bacon and the chile from the soup. Using an immersion blender, or in batches using a regular blender and taking care to cover the top with a towel to prevent splashing, blend the soup, then put through the medium blade of a food mill or strain through a medium strainer, using a pestle or the bowl of a ladle to push the soup through. Return to the pot and stir in the sautéed leeks. Add salt and pepper to taste and heat through. If you wish, you may dice up the bacon and stir it into the soup.

5. Serve, garnishing each bowl with a spoonful of crème fraîche and a sprinkling of crumbled crisp bacon.

sweet pea soup with walnut croutons [makes 6 to 8 servings]

You can only make this intense pea soup during English peas' short spring season. Its broth is all about pulling as much intense flavor out of ingredients as you can, and the soup is all about freshness. It will be worth your while to buy and shell all of those peas. Look for small pods; if they're big and the peas inside are big, they'll be woody and starchy. The walnut finish here adds a nutty, mildly bitter contrast to the sweet soup.

[BROTH]
2	tablespoons extra virgin olive oil
½	medium onion, chopped
2	garlic cloves, halved, green shoots removed
	Green of 1 large leek, sliced across the grain and washed (page 54)
	Kosher salt
¼	teaspoon freshly ground black pepper
1	pound unblemished pea pods
2	quarts water

[SOUP]
2	tablespoons extra virgin olive oil
1	leek, white and light green parts, sliced across the grain and washed (page 54)
½	medium onion, sliced crosswise across the grain
2	garlic cloves, peeled and halved, green shoots removed
½	pound russet potato, peeled and diced
	Kosher salt
1	pound shelled peas (about 3½ cups)
1½	quarts pea pod broth (above)
	Leaves from 1 stalk celery, roughly chopped
1	sprig fresh mint
2	to 3 sprigs fresh flat-leaf parsley
	Freshly ground black pepper

[WALNUT CROUTONS AND GARNISH]
6	ounces walnut bread
1	tablespoon extra virgin olive oil
1	tablespoon walnut oil

1. Make the broth: Heat the olive oil in a large soup pot over medium heat and add the onion, garlic, and leek greens. Add ½ teaspoon salt and the pepper, and cook gently for about 5 minutes, until the vegetables have softened but not colored. Add the pea pods, cover, and continue to cook gently for another 3 minutes, until the pods are just beginning to soften. Add 2 quarts water and a teaspoon salt and bring to a simmer. Cover and simmer over low heat for 30 minutes. Strain and measure out 1½ quarts.

2. Make the soup: Heat the oil in a large, heavy soup pot or Dutch oven over medium heat and add the leek, onion, garlic, potato, and ½ teaspoon salt. Cook gently for 5 minutes, stirring often, until the onion and leek have softened but not colored. Add the peas and stir together for 1 minute, then add the broth and bring to a simmer. Cover and simmer over low heat for 30 minutes. Add the celery leaves, mint sprig, and parsley, and remove from the heat. Let sit, covered, for 1 minute.

3. While the soup is simmering, make the walnut croutons. Preheat the oven to 325°F. Cut the crusts off the bread and tear the bread into roughly 1-inch pieces. They should be irregularly shaped. Place in a large bowl and drizzle in the olive oil. Toss with your hands until the bread is evenly coated. Spread the bread in an even layer on a baking sheet and bake 20 to 25 minutes, until crisp. Remove from the heat and transfer to a stainless steel bowl. Toss with 1 teaspoon of the walnut oil.

4. Using an immersion blender or a food mill fitted with the fine screen, puree the soup, or working in 1½-cup batches, ladle into a blender. Cover the blender, placing a towel over the cover and pulling it down tightly to prevent splashing, and blend each batch. Put the pureed soup through a medium strainer, using a pestle or the bowl of a ladle to push the soup through. Return to the pot. Heat through and add salt and pepper to taste.

5. Place a handful of the croutons in each soup bowl and ladle in the soup. Drizzle on a few drops of walnut oil, and serve.

beet borscht [makes 8 servings]

There are many versions of borscht, and you've probably eaten one of them, especially if you have Russian or Polish relatives. This soup is all about the beets, so get fresh, sweet, heavy ones. Roasting the beets gives them great depth of flavor.

Don't wear any clothing you value when you make this soup unless it's red. And use kitchen gloves when you peel the beets (you'll see why if you don't).

4	tablespoons (½ stick) unsalted butter
1	medium onion, cut in half and sliced across the grain
2	stalks celery, sliced
2	medium carrots, peeled, quartered lengthwise, and sliced
3	fat garlic cloves, cut in half, green shoots removed
1	medium leek, white and light green parts only, sliced across the grain and washed (page 54)
	Kosher salt
2½	pounds Roasted Beets (page 226), skinned and diced
	A bouquet garni made with a handful each parsley and thyme sprigs, ½ teaspoon cracked black pepper, and ½ teaspoon caraway seeds (page 66)
1	quart Chicken Stock (page 66)
1	quart water
1	cup heavy cream
1	to 2 teaspoons freshly squeezed lemon juice (to taste)
	Crème fraîche and chopped fresh dill, for serving

1. Heat the butter in a large, heavy soup pot over medium-low heat and add the onion, celery, carrots, garlic, leek, and ½ teaspoon salt and cook, stirring from time to time, until the vegetables are tender but have not colored, about 15 minutes.

2. Stir in the roasted beets and bouquet garni, add the chicken stock and water, and bring to a simmer. Add another teaspoon of salt, cover, and simmer over low heat for 40 minutes.

3. Remove the bouquet garni from the soup. Using an immersion blender or a food mill fitted with the fine screen, puree the soup, or working in 1½-cup batches, ladle into a blender. Cover the blender, placing a towel over the cover and pulling it down tightly to prevent splashing. Blend each batch. Return to the pot, stir the soup, bring to a simmer, and simmer another 5 minutes, stirring often so the mixture doesn't stick to the bottom of the pan.

4. Meanwhile, heat the cream to a simmer in a small saucepan, and stir into the soup. Add the lemon juice, taste, and adjust the salt.

5. Put the soup through a medium strainer, pushing it through with a pestle or the bowl of a ladle. Return to the pot and heat through. Garnish each serving with a dollop of crème fraîche and a sprinkling of chopped dill.

ribollito [makes 4 servings]

Ribollito means "reboiled" in Italian. It's a classic way to stretch yesterday's soup and bread into another meal by combining stale bread with leftover minestrone. The bread soaks up the liquid and the mixture is blended. It has the consistency of pap, something the Italians can render absolutely delicious. But I like a prettier dish, and this one fits the bill. Less processed than a traditional ribollito, this looks more like a cassoulet, with thick, garlicky slices of toasted bread layered over the leftover soup like a lid. The bread soaks up the liquid from the soup and becomes crusty on top as the mixture bakes into a casserole. This is so good that it's worth making a double batch of minestrone (see the Fresh Shell Bean Minestrone on page 56) just so you can have enough left over to make the ribollito.

4	ounces country bread, cut in ½-inch-thick slices
1	garlic clove, cut in half, green shoot removed
4	cups Fresh Shell Bean Minestrone (page 57)
3	tablespoons extra virgin olive oil

1. Preheat the oven to 350°F. Toast the bread until crisp and nicely browned. Rub both sides with the cut clove of garlic.

2. Place the soup in a 2-quart casserole or gratin dish. Layer the bread over the top in a single attractive layer. Drizzle on the olive oil. Cover tightly with foil and bake 20 minutes. Uncover and spoon some broth from the bottom of the dish over the bread. Return to the oven and bake, uncovered, for 5 to 10 minutes, until nicely browned. Remove from the heat and serve hot or warm.

wild mushroom and farro soup [makes 8 servings]

The inspiration for this great winter soup comes from the mushroom and barley soup that was my favorite canned soup when I was growing up. Farro is a hard winter wheat you can find in gourmet and Italian markets. Barley can be substituted if you can't find farro.

1	ounce dried morels
½	ounce dried porcini
3	tablespoons extra virgin olive oil
½	cup farro
1	medium onion, diced
1	medium carrot, peeled and cut in ¼-inch dice
2	stalks celery heart, cut in ¼-inch dice
	Kosher salt
1	pound fresh wild mushrooms, such as maitake, hedgehog, oyster, shiitake (remove stems from shiitakes), cleaned, trimmed, and coarsely chopped or sliced
4	fat garlic cloves, cut in half, green shoots removed, and sliced
¼	cup dry white wine
1	tablespoon plus 1 teaspoon tomato paste
	Freshly ground black pepper
	A bouquet garni made with a few sprigs each parsley and thyme, a sprig of tarragon and a bay leaf (page 66)
	Parsley Pesto (page 59), for garnish (optional)

1. Place the dried morels and porcini in a 1-quart Pyrex measuring cup or a bowl and pour on 3 cups hot water. Let sit for 30 minutes. Agitate the mushrooms from time to time to release any sand. Lift the reconstituted mushrooms from the soaking water and squeeze over the water. Rinse the mushrooms in 2 to 3 changes of water until there is no more sand in the bowl, swishing them in a bowl and lifting them from the water. Slice the morels crosswise into rings and chop the porcini coarsely. Strain the soaking liquid through a cheesecloth-lined strainer. Combine with enough water to measure 2 quarts and set aside.

2. In a large soup pot, heat 1 tablespoon of the olive oil over medium heat and add the farro. Cook, stirring, until it begins to smell like popcorn. Add another tablespoon of olive oil and the onion, carrot, celery, and ½ teaspoon salt, and cook for another 5 to 7 minutes, stirring often, until the vegetables have begun to soften. Add the fresh and reconstituted dried mushrooms, the garlic, and 1 teaspoon salt. Cook, stirring, until the mushrooms begin to soften and release liquid, about 5 minutes. Turn the heat to medium-low, cover, and cook slowly for 5 minutes. Add the wine and the tomato paste and stir together for a few minutes, until the mixture is very fragrant.

3. Add another 2 teaspoons salt, ¼ teaspoon freshly ground pepper, the bouquet garni, and the combined mushroom broth and water and bring to a boil. Reduce the heat, cover, and simmer 45 minutes, until the farro is tender and the grains have opened up. Taste and add salt and pepper as desired. Remove the bouquet garni.

4. Serve, drizzling a teaspoon or two of parsley pesto over each bowl, if desired.

[NOTE] It's best to use at least two different kinds of mushrooms for a richer flavor. You could also use half white or cremini mushrooms, half wild mushrooms.

spring onion soup with gruyère croutons [makes 8 servings]

This is a springtime take on traditional French onion soup (another example of a great dish gone bad). The light, sweet spring onion soup is light years away from the onion sludge soup with molten Swiss cheese on top that most French onion soup has become. This one preserves the freshness of new spring onions.

[SOUP]

¼	cup extra virgin olive oil
4	fat garlic cloves, peeled, cut in half, green shoots removed, and sliced
3¼	pounds spring onions, white and light green parts only, sliced in thin rings
	A bouquet garni made with a sprig each savory and thyme, a bay leaf, a small handful of celery leaves and parsley, and ¼ scant teaspoon peppercorns (page 66)
	Kosher salt
1	quart Chicken Stock (page 66)
1	quart water
	Freshly ground black pepper

[CROUTONS]

16	to 24 ½-inch-thick slices French bread, preferably a rustic batard
	Extra virgin olive oil
1	fat garlic clove, cut in half, green shoot removed
4	ounces aged Gruyère cheese, grated or sliced very thin

1. Make the soup: Heat the olive oil in a large, heavy soup pot over medium heat and add the garlic cloves, spring onions, bouquet garni, and 1 teaspoon salt. Cook, stirring often, until the onions have softened, about 5 minutes. Do not allow them to color. Add the chicken stock, water, and another teaspoon of salt. Bring to a simmer, cover, and simmer over low heat for 30 minutes. Taste and adjust the salt.

2. Make the croutons: Lightly toast the bread, then rub with a dab of olive oil and the cut side of the garlic clove. Place on a baking sheet and top each crouton with a small amount of grated Gruyère or a thin slice. Light the broiler and place under the broiler just until the cheese melts. Remove from the heat.

3. Ladle the soup into bowls. Grind no more than 1 to 2 twists of the pepper mill into each serving, top with 2 or 3 Gruyère croutons, and serve.

cold cucumber and yogurt soup [makes 6 to 8 servings]

This beautiful green soup is perfect for summer. It's important to use Japanese or European cucumbers because you use the skin, and regular cucumbers are too bitter or the skin is waxed. It's also important to find good-quality, creamy plain whole milk yogurt (Greek is a good bet), and to serve the soup ice cold.

2	pounds Japanese or English cucumbers
	Kosher salt
2	stalks celery, thinly sliced
1	cup fresh flat-leaf parsley leaves (about ½ bunch), rinsed, dried, and roughly chopped
½	cup mint leaves, rinsed, dried, and roughly chopped, plus 1 tablespoon leaves, cut in fine chiffonade (slivers), for garnish
1	quart whole milk yogurt
1½	teaspoons finely chopped lemon zest
1	tablespoon freshly squeezed lemon juice
6	to 8 ice cubes
1	tablespoon chopped chives

1. Peel the cucumbers, peeling deep so you get some of the flesh with the peels, over a bowl. Place the peels in the bowl. Cut the cucumbers in half lengthwise and scrape out the seeds with a demitasse spoon. Discard the seeds. Roughly chop half the cucumbers and place in the bowl with the peels. Cut the remaining cucumbers into pretty ¼-inch dice and toss in a colander with 1½ teaspoons salt. Set the colander with the diced cucumbers over a bowl or plate for 15 minutes.

2. Working in batches if necessary, combine the cucumber peels, the roughly chopped cucumbers, the celery, parsley, mint, and 1 cup of the yogurt in a blender. Puree, stopping and starting the blender if necessary to make sure all of the ingredients are finely pureed. Scrape into a bowl and stir in the remaining yogurt, the lemon zest, lemon juice, and 2 teaspoons salt. Let sit for 10 to 15 minutes. Strain into another bowl through a fine-mesh strainer, pressing the solids against the sides of the strainer to extract all of the juice.

3. Rinse the salted cucumbers in fresh water. Stir into the soup. Taste and adjust the seasoning if necessary. Cover with plastic wrap and chill in the refrigerator for several hours before serving.

4. Place one ice cube in each of 6 to 8 soup bowls. Ladle in the soup. Top with a sprinkling of mint chiffonade and chopped chives and serve.

chicken noodle soup [makes 6 to 8 servings]

This has the same name and comfort level as the Campbell's version (which is actually not bad). But this one is elegant as well as homey, with carrots and leeks, potatoes and shiitakes added to the mix, and a little caraway seed for an unexpected but delightful accent. When you make the intense double broth for this, make a large quantity and freeze what you don't use for the soup. Make the broth a day ahead so it will be easier to skim. Be careful to follow the directions here; if the soup is simmered for too long it becomes a gray mush.

[BROTH AND CHICKEN]

I	tablespoon canola oil
4	ounces pancetta (optional)
I	medium onion, chopped
I	medium carrot, peeled and chopped
1½	stalks celery, chopped
4	ounces white mushrooms, sliced
4	garlic cloves, cut in half, green shoots removed
	Kosher salt
	Green and light green parts of I large leek, sliced across the grain and washed (page 54)
4	ounces green cabbage, shredded (I cup)
I	large chicken, cut up
	A bouquet garni made with a bay leaf, a few sprigs each parsley and thyme, I dried chile pepper, and 6 peppercorns, crushed (page 66)
3	quarts cold water or Chicken Stock (page 66, or use half broth, half water)

[SOUP]

	Kosher salt
	Freshly ground black pepper
I	leek, white part only, sliced across the grain and washed (page 54)
½	pound waxy potatoes, such as White Rose, cut in ½-inch dice
½	cup sliced celery, from the inner stalks (the heart)
I	medium carrot, peeled, cut in ½-inch oblique slices (see below)
½	teaspoon caraway seeds
2	ounces fresh shiitake mushrooms, stemmed, sliced very thin, and seared (see right)
2	ounces (about ½ cup) soup pasta, such as elbow macaroni, small shells, or broken spaghetti
½	cup chopped celery leaves
2	tablespoons chopped fresh parsley or tarragon, or a combination

1. Make the broth a day ahead. Heat the canola oil and pancetta together in a large soup pot over medium heat and cook until the pancetta renders its fat, about 5 minutes. Add the onion, carrot, celery, mushrooms, and garlic, and cook, stirring often, until tender, about 5 minutes. Add 1 teaspoon salt and the leek and cabbage. Continue to cook, stirring often, for another 5 minutes. Add the chicken, the bouquet garni, and the water or stock. Bring to a simmer, reduce the heat to low, cover partially, and simmer 1 hour and 15 minutes. Remove from the heat.

2. Remove the chicken pieces from the broth and place in a bowl. Cover with plastic wrap and refrigerate. Strain the broth through a fine strainer into a bowl, cover, and refrigerate overnight.

3. Lift the fat off the chilled broth. Measure out 2½ quarts. Add salt and pepper to taste and bring to a simmer in a large saucepan or soup pot (freeze the remaining broth in small containers). Meanwhile, remove the chicken from the bones, discard the skin, and dice or shred the meat. You will need 2 cups for the soup.

4. Add the white part of the leek, the potatoes, celery, carrot, and caraway seeds to the soup pot and simmer 15 minutes. Add the seared shiitakes, chicken, pasta, and pepper, and simmer until the pasta is cooked al dente. Add the celery leaves and salt and pepper to taste. (If not serving right away, chill in an ice bath so the vegetables do not continue to cook.) Stir in the fresh herbs and serve.

[HOW TO CUT OBLIQUE SLICES]
Peel the carrot and make one slice on the diagonal. Turn the carrot 120 degrees (one third turn), and cut on the diagonal again. Continue to turn and cut on the diagonal to get oblique cuts.

[SEARING SHIITAKE MUSHROOMS]
Searing shiitakes brings out maximum flavor, and the mushrooms retain a soft, yet firm texture. Heat a pan over medium-high heat. Add 1 teaspoon oil and when very hot, add the mushrooms. Shake the pan once, then let the mushrooms cook without moving them around (resist the urge) until they begin to sweat and soften. After about a minute or two, when they have begun to sear and release moisture, you can move them around in the pan. Cook for about 5 minutes and remove from the heat.

clam, corn, and potato chowder [makes 6 to 8 servings]

This is a rich, savory soup, but I think of it as a summer dish because it's as much about sweet corn, at its best only from late June to early October, as it is about clams. Everything else is available year-round. Do this recipe as I've written it, even the part with the corncobs. The flavor will be marvelous. White corn is generally sweeter than yellow corn, but yellow corn has more flavor and vitamin A.

[CLAMS]

2	tablespoons extra virgin olive oil
I	medium onion, coarsely chopped
8	garlic cloves, crushed
¼	cup chopped celery
¼	cup chopped fennel
I	dried red chile, preferably Japanese
½	teaspoon cracked black peppercorns
4	pounds Manila or littleneck clams, purged (see right)
I	cup dry white wine
2	sprigs each fresh flat-leaf parsley, thyme, and tarragon

[SOUP]

6	to 7 cups Chicken Stock (page 66), as needed
1¼	pounds White Rose, Red Rose, or Yukon Gold potatoes, peeled
4	large ears of sweet corn (4 to 4½ cups kernels)
	Kosher salt to taste (3 teaspoons, or more)
2	cups heavy cream
4	tablespoons (½ stick) unsalted butter
I	medium onion, finely chopped
I	stalk celery, finely diced
½	small fennel bulb, finely diced
	Freshly ground black pepper
½	teaspoon dried thyme

1. Cook the clams: Heat the olive oil in a large, heavy pot over medium heat and add the onion, garlic, celery, fennel, chile, and pepper. Cook, stirring often, until the vegetables are tender, fragrant, and lightly colored, about 10 minutes. Add the clams and stir together. Add the wine, parsley, thyme, and tarragon, raise the heat to high, and bring to a boil. Cover and cook 3 to 4 minutes, or until the clams have started opening up. Stir once during this time so the clams on the bottom don't overcook before the clams on top even open up. As the clams start opening up, use tongs to remove them one by one, and transfer to a bowl. Set aside.

2. Make the soup: Carefully pour the liquid in the pot through a cheesecloth-lined strainer, pressing the juice from the vegetables in the strainer. Measure the liquid and add chicken stock to equal 2 quarts. Rinse the pot briefly to get rid of any residual sand and place back on the stove over medium heat. Add the stock to the pot.

3. Slice half the potatoes and add to the stock. Cut the remaining potatoes into ¼-inch dice, cover with water, and set aside. Cut the corn kernels from the cobs. Set aside half and add half to the stock. Add the corncobs to the stock. Bring to a simmer over medium-high heat. Add 2 teaspoons salt and simmer, partially covered, for 30 minutes.

4. While the soup is simmering, remove the clams from their shells and discard the shells. Rinse the clams several times to remove any lingering sand. Cut them into halves or quarters (depending on the size). Place in a bowl, cover, and refrigerate until ready to serve the soup.

5. Remove the corncobs from the broth. Allow to cool slightly, and holding onto each one with a towel so you don't burn your hand, scrape them with the back of a chef's knife to extract more of the kernels from the cob. This will make a bit of a mess but is worth it for the extra flavor you'll obtain. Add the scrapings to the soup and discard the cobs.

6. Using an immersion blender, blend the soup until smooth. Alternatively, blend the soup in batches in a regular blender, placing a towel over the top of the blender to prevent hot soup from splashing out of the blender, then return to the pot. Bring back to a simmer.

7. In a separate saucepan, bring the cream to a simmer. Stir into the soup. Taste and adjust the seasonings.

8. Heat the butter in a large skillet over medium heat and add the onion, celery, and fennel. Cook 5 minutes, stirring often, until the vegetables are translucent. Do not allow them to color. Add the remaining corn kernels. Cook, stirring,

until tender, about 5 minutes. Add 1 teaspoon salt and ½ teaspoon ground pepper. Drain the diced potatoes and add to the mixture. Cover and continue to simmer for 5 to 6 minutes, until the potatoes are cooked but still firm. Add all of these vegetables to the soup and simmer for another 5 to 8 minutes, until the potatoes are tender. Add the thyme and remove from the heat. Let steep for 15 minutes (the soup can sit for several hours at this point). Taste and adjust the seasonings. Just before serving, stir in the clams, heat through, and serve.

[HOW TO PURGE CLAMS AND MUSSELS]

Even though most clams and mussels we buy have been purged once, it's always a good idea to purge them again. They will undoubtedly have more sand to expel, and even a little bit of sand is very unpleasant if you bite into it. Do this just before you cook them because they will die soon after purging. Brush the clams and mussels thoroughly and rinse several times with cold water. Place in a large bowl and cover with cold water. Add 2 tablespoons of salt and swish the shellfish around. Taste the water: it should taste like the ocean. Add more salt if necessary. Let the shellfish sit undisturbed for 15 minutes (undisturbed is important because you want the clams and mussels to spit out the sand, and if they are disturbed they'll clamp down and not spit). At this point the clams should be moving a little bit in the water. Lift from the water into another bowl. Rinse again in several changes of water.

mussel soup with saffron and kale [makes 6 servings]

I think of this soup as a minestrone with mussels. It's not a rich, creamy mussel soup, but a brothy one, with greens, tomatoes, potatoes, and an aromatic pinch of saffron. Although there's a long list of ingredients here, the soup is not labor intensive.

½ pound Swiss chard or kale, stemmed and washed thoroughly in several changes of water

2 tablespoons extra virgin olive oil

⅔ cup chopped onion
Kosher salt

4 garlic cloves, cut in half, green shoots removed, then sliced

1 pound canned or fresh tomatoes, peeled, seeded, and chopped
Freshly ground black pepper

½ cup dry white wine

1 dried red chile, preferably Japanese

1 bay leaf

1 pound mussels, purged (page 83)

3 cups Chicken Stock (page 66)

3 cups water
Generous pinch of saffron

1 pound Yukon Gold, White Rose, or Red Rose potatoes, peeled and cut in ½-inch dice

½ teaspoon dried oregano

1 tablespoon chopped fresh parsley

[GARNISH]

16 slices baguette, toasted, brushed with olive oil, and rubbed with a cut garlic clove

1 cup Rouille (page 175) or 3 tablespoons Basil Pesto or Parsley Pesto, without the cheese (page 59)

1. Bring a large pot of generously salted water to a boil and add the chard or kale. Blanch chard for 2 minutes, kale for 3, and transfer to a bowl of ice water. Drain and squeeze dry. Chop coarsely and set aside.

2. Heat the olive oil in a large, heavy soup pot over medium heat and add the onion and ½ teaspoon salt. Cook, stirring often, until it softens, 3 to 5 minutes, and add the garlic. Cook for another minute, until the garlic smells fragrant, then add the chard or kale. Cook, stirring often, until the greens have cooked down slightly and smell fragrant, 5 to 10 minutes, stirring occasionally. Add the tomatoes and cook for another 10 minutes, until they cook down slightly. Season to taste with salt and freshly ground pepper. Spoon everything into a bowl and set aside. Place the pot back on the heat.

3. Add the wine, chile pepper, bay leaf, and mussels to the pot. Bring to a boil, cover, and cook 3 minutes. Check the mussels and using tongs, transfer them as they open to a second bowl. Remove the pot from the heat once all the mussels have opened up and have been moved to the bowl. When they are cool enough to handle, remove the meat from the shells, holding them above the bowl to catch the juices, and discard the shells. Rinse briefly. Pour any liquid from the mussels into the pot, then pour all of the liquid in the pot through a cheesecloth-lined strainer into a third bowl. Rinse the pot with fresh water to eliminate any residual sand.

4. Return the broth, chile pepper, bay leaf, and the sautéed onion-tomato mixture to the pot. Add the chicken stock and water and bring to a simmer. Add a fat pinch of saffron, 2 teaspoons salt, the potatoes, and the oregano. Bring to a simmer and cook 20 to 30 minutes, until the potatoes are tender and the broth fragrant. Taste, add pepper, and adjust the salt.

5. Just before serving, coarsely chop the mussels and add them to the soup. Heat through. Stir in the parsley and serve, topping each bowl with a couple of croutons spread with rouille. Alternatively, stir a heaped teaspoon of pesto into each serving.

wild fennel soup [makes 6 to 8 servings]

In California and other warm, semi-arid places, wild fennel grows freely, and it's considered a weed. It's an invasive plant, so you can feel good about taking it when you find it. I get most of mine from a vacant lot a few blocks from the restaurant. If you can get wild fennel, take only the pale tender growth and leave the hard, woody stalks. Wild fennel doesn't bulb; it produces generous feathery fronds that look like dill and have a sweet, anisy flavor. If you can't get your hands on the wild stuff, use all bulb fennel, with the fronds. Remember to wash wild fennel well, in several changes of water. Aphids love it even more than I do.

¼	cup extra virgin olive oil
1	pound wild fennel, washed well in several changes of water and roughly chopped
1¼	pounds bulb fennel, washed and diced (or use 2¼ pounds bulb fennel in all if wild fennel is not available)
1	pound russet potatoes (2 medium), peeled and diced
½	large or 1 medium onion, diced
1	large leek, both white and light green parts, sliced ½ inch thick across the grain and washed (page 54)
1½	stalks celery, sliced
	Cloves from ½ head garlic, peeled
2	ounces mushroom stems (optional)
	Kosher salt
	A bouquet garni made with 1 bay leaf, 3 sprigs each of fresh parsley and thyme, 1 sprig of fresh tarragon, ½ teaspoon fennel seeds, and ¼ teaspoon cracked black pepper (page 66)
2	quarts Chicken Stock (page 66) or water
	Freshly ground black pepper

[GARNISH]

	Chopped fresh fennel fronds (the tender pale green part only)
1½	teaspoons fennel seeds, lightly toasted and cracked (page 33)

1. Heat the olive oil in a large, heavy soup pot or Dutch oven over medium heat and add all of the vegetables and 1 teaspoon salt. Cook gently until the vegetables have softened but not colored and lost some of their volume, 10 to 15 minutes. Add the bouquet garni and the stock or water and bring to a simmer. Add another teaspoon of salt, cover, and simmer over low heat for 45 minutes.

2. Remove the bouquet garni. Using an immersion blender, puree the soup. Or, working in 1½-cup batches, ladle into a blender; cover the blender, place a towel over the cover, and pull it down tightly to prevent splashing. Put the soup through a medium strainer, using a pestle or the bowl of a ladle to push the soup through. Return to the pot. Heat through and add salt and pepper to taste. Serve, garnished with cracked toasted fennel seeds and chopped fennel fronds.

[NOTE]

This recipe includes mushroom stems, which I had on hand when I was developing the recipe. Whenever you're preparing mushrooms for a dish, save the stems to use in soups and stocks. They're a natural source of MSG, a flavor enhancer. They are optional here—you don't have to go out and buy mushrooms just for the stems.

[3]

PASTA AND RISOTTO

The recipes in this chapter range from simple spaghetti and meatballs to giant homemade ravioli. I've included some of my favorite Italian and Italian-American dishes like Pasta Carbonara (page 98) and Linguine and Clams (page 101), sometimes with a twist but true to their original form, and a couple of updates of those American comfort food classics, macaroni and cheese and tuna noodle casserole. Some of the pasta dishes are vehicles for our complex and delicious Bolognese Sauce (page 91), while others can be made quickly with ingredients you should have in your pantry or refrigerator—garlic, olive oil, Parmesan cheese, and dried red chile peppers.

In Italy pasta isn't regarded as a main course, but here people love pasta as the main dish. At Campanile we do both. Our family dinners feature the more substantial dishes in this chapter as main courses and the lighter, simpler ones as starters. You will probably want to make a dinner out of all of them. The ravioli on page 105 is the only dish here that requires you to make fresh pasta, and I urge you to make it at least once. It's one of those dishes you can't slap together: You must pay attention. Once you've made it, everything else here will seem easy.

Pasta and risotto are usually grouped together on restaurant menus, as they are in this chapter. In the restaurant risottos can be first courses or main dishes, but at home risotto is dinner, since it takes at least 30 minutes to make. Once you've learned how to make risotto, a constellation of dishes will open up. Every risotto recipe is done using the same method, with some variations at the beginning and end. Let the market be your guide as to what kind of risotto you're going to make. It's a great vehicle for seasonal foods, from squash to wild mushrooms, cavolo nero to fresh English peas. But don't use more than two or three main ingredients in each risotto. In cooking as in most things, restraint, like brevity, is the soul of elegance.

fresh pasta dough [makes I pound]

This is a simple, straightforward, and definitive pasta recipe. I've seen recipes with more or less egg and more or less semolina. This one is somewhere in the middle and works well.

I	cup all-purpose flour
I	cup semolina
½	teaspoon salt
I	tablespoon olive oil
I	large egg
2	large egg yolks
	Up to 3 tablespoons ice water

I. Mix together the flour, semolina, and salt with your hands in a very large bowl. Make a well in the middle.

2. In a small bowl, beat together the olive oil, egg, and egg yolks. Add the mixture to the well in a steady stream, leaving the last teaspoon in the bowl (if there are any bits of eggshell in the mixture they will be in that last teaspoon). Then, using your fingertips, swirl the flour mixture into the egg mixture. Use your hands to mix together until the mixture is like coarse cornmeal. Add the water a tablespoon at a time, and when the dough can be gathered together into a ball, remove from the bowl and knead briefly, about 5 minutes. The dough will be stiff.

Alternatively, you can mix the dough in a standing mixer fitted with the paddle or in a food processor. If using a standing mixer, add the dry ingredients and mix together. With the machine running at low speed, add the egg mixture (again reserving the last teaspoon) and 1 to 2 tablespoons water. If the dough does not come together and seems dry, add another tablespoon of water and beat on low speed until the dough comes together. Gather it into a ball and knead briefly, about 5 minutes.

If using a food processor, pulse the dry ingredients in the food processor. With the machine running, pour in all but the last teaspoon of the egg yolk mixture and finally the water as needed. When the dough comes together, remove from the food processor and knead briefly, about 5 minutes.

3. Wrap the dough in plastic and let rest for 1 hour.

4. To roll out the dough using a pasta roller, cut the dough into 3 equal pieces. Keep the other pieces covered in plastic while you roll out one piece at a time. Attach the pasta roller securely to a table with a smooth surface. Set the rollers at the widest opening. Flatten the first piece of dough into a thick strip no wider than the machine to enable it to pass through the rollers. If necessary, dust the pasta very lightly with semolina. Run the pasta through the machine. Fold in half crosswise and run through the machine again. Repeat this procedure several more times, until the dough is smooth and elastic. Set the machine to the next smaller opening and run the dough through the rollers twice. Continue rolling and stretching the dough, using a smaller setting each time, until the ribbons reach the thinness you desire. If they become too long and unwieldy to work with, cut them in half and keep the unused half covered with plastic.

5. Shape and cut the pasta as directed in your recipe. Sprinkle with semolina so it doesn't become sticky. Store for up to 3 days in the refrigerator on a flat tray sprinkled with semolina between sheets of parchment paper.

spaghetti with meatballs [makes 4 main course servings or 8 starters]

What can I say that hasn't been said about spaghetti and meatballs? Because our meatballs are so good (no, really) this dish is still one of our best sellers when we make it for a family dinner. The dish is a perfect illustration of the principle "It's not what you do, it's how you do it." Make the meatballs right; make the tomato sauce right; cook the spaghetti right; use the best Parmesan, and you might just expiate the sins of Chef Boyardee.

1	tablespoon extra virgin olive oil
24	meatballs (page 132)
1	recipe Simple Tomato Sauce (page 90)
	Kosher salt
¾	pound spaghetti
⅓	cup freshly grated Parmesan cheese

1. Heat the olive oil in a large, heavy skillet over medium-high heat and add the meatballs, in batches if necessary. Brown on all sides, about 3 minutes per side, and transfer to a medium saucepan. Add the tomato sauce to the saucepan and bring to a simmer. Cover and simmer for 20 minutes.

2. Meanwhile, bring a large pot of water to a boil. Add a generous tablespoon of salt and the spaghetti. Cook al dente, following the timing recommendations on the package but checking to see if the pasta is done a minute or two before the time listed on the package. The pasta should be cooked all the way through but resistant to the bite in the middle. Drain and transfer to a warm pasta bowl. Add the sauce with the meatballs, toss together, and serve, passing the Parmesan at the table.

simple tomato sauce [makes 2 cups]

Tomato sauces don't get much simpler than this one, especially if you use canned tomatoes, which I recommend if you're making the sauce any time other than the peak of tomato season, July through October.

3 tablespoons extra virgin olive oil

2 fat or 4 medium garlic cloves, halved, green shoots removed, and thinly sliced

2 pounds fresh ripe tomatoes, peeled, seeded, and roughly chopped, or one 28-ounce can chopped tomatoes, with juice

½ to 1 teaspoon kosher salt

¼ teaspoon freshly ground black pepper
A small handful of basil leaves, without the stems

TOMATO STORY

Ripeness, above all, determines the quality of a tomato. When I went to UC Davis to study agriculture, one day in late June I picked up a tomato in a field that was just about to be harvested for ketchup or canning. This tomato was an industrial tomato, grown with pesticides and chemical fertilizer. But it had ripened on the vine, and it had a sweet, rich, sun-filled flavor that only a truly vine-ripened tomato can have. This is the taste I look for when I buy tomatoes, and if I can't find it in a fresh one, I turn to canned.

[SEEDING TOMATOES AND RETAINING THE SWEETEST PART]

The gelatinous, juicy seed of a tomato contains some of the fruit's sweetest, most intense flavors. When you seed tomatoes, place a strainer over a bowl. Cut the tomatoes in half at the equator and squeeze over the strainer. Rub the seeds and surrounding pulp against the strainer so the juice goes through. Add the juice to your dish along with the chopped tomatoes.

Heat the olive oil with the sliced garlic in a heavy saucepan over medium-low heat and simmer the garlic gently until transparent, about 3 minutes. Add the tomatoes, ½ teaspoon salt, and the pepper and simmer 45 minutes, stirring often to make sure the sauce does not stick to the pan, until thick. If you have used canned tomatoes, crush the tomatoes with the back of your spoon to get a finer texture. Taste and adjust the seasoning. Stir in the basil and remove from the heat. Allow the basil to infuse for 15 minutes or longer, then remove. This will keep for 5 days in the refrigerator, and freezes well.

VARIATION / SIMPLE ROASTED TOMATO SAUCE

Before you begin, preheat the oven to 450°F. Cut the tomatoes in half, oil a baking dish, and place the tomatoes on it, cut side down. The tomatoes should fit snugly in the baking dish so the edges don't burn. Sprinkle on 1 teaspoon salt and drizzle on ¼ cup olive oil. Place in the oven and roast until lightly caramelized, 30 to 45 minutes. Remove from the heat and put through the medium or fine screen (fine enough to keep out the seeds) of a food mill. Proceed with step 1 above. You will not have to cook the sauce for as long (20 to 30 minutes).

bolognese sauce and three pastas [makes 3 cups]

This is a long recipe, but entirely worth it. There's nothing difficult or unusual about this regal ancestor of American spaghetti sauce. It just takes time. I think its best characteristic is that it's made with shredded beef, not ground beef, which gives it a succulence and toothiness unlike any other type of Bolognese sauce. Any of the tougher, flavorful cuts of beef, like chuck or brisket, will work for this. To enrich the flavor, we roast the tomatoes first, and the resulting caramelization gives this a great depth of flavor. I'm giving you a recipe for a large quantity here, as it freezes well. If you're going to take the trouble to make this, you might as well make a lot and use it for several meals. Thaw it slowly, overnight in the refrigerator. You will need a day to marinate the meat before you make the sauce, and ideally another day to refrigerate the sauce. It's easier to skim off the fat if you chill it, and the flavors intensify overnight.

[MARINADE]

3	pounds beef chuck or brisket, in 1 piece
1	medium onion, coarsely chopped
1	large carrot, peeled and coarsely chopped
2	stalks celery, coarsely chopped
¼	cup coarsely chopped fresh flat-leaf parsley
2	cups red wine
1½	teaspoons cracked black peppercorns

[SAUCE]

5	pounds tomatoes, or four 28-ounce cans plus 1 cup of the liquid from the cans
6	tablespoons extra virgin olive oil
4	fat garlic cloves, halved, green shoots removed, and minced
	Kosher salt
	Freshly ground black pepper
	Canola oil
3	ounces pancetta, diced
2	cups Chicken Stock (page 66, or 1 cup canned chicken broth and 1 cup water)
3	tablespoons extra virgin olive oil
1	large carrot, peeled and cut in ¼-inch dice
2	large stalks celery, cut in ¼-inch dice

1	medium onion, cut in ¼-inch dice
4	fat garlic cloves, halved, green shoots removed, and thinly sliced
	A bouquet garni made with a handful each of parsley and thyme sprigs, and 2 bay leaves (page 66)
1	6-ounce can tomato paste, dissolved in ½ cup water (if using fresh tomatoes only)

1. Cut the meat across the grain into roughly 2-inch pieces. Toss with the coarsely chopped onion, carrot, celery, parsley, 1 cup of the red wine, and 1 teaspoon of the cracked pepper in a large bowl. Cover and refrigerate for 12 to 24 hours, stirring once after a few hours.

2. The next day, preheat the oven to 400°F. If using fresh tomatoes, cut the tomatoes in half at the equator. If using canned whole tomatoes, remove from the liquid in the cans (do not discard the liquid in the cans), but do not cut. Toss either fresh or canned tomatoes in a large bowl with 3 tablespoons olive oil, 4 minced garlic cloves, 1 teaspoon salt, and ¼ teaspoon pepper. Place on baking sheets and pour on the juice from the bowl, but not from the can. Fresh tomatoes should be cut side down. Roast for 45 minutes to an hour, until the tomatoes are soft and beginning to blister (45 minutes for canned tomatoes). Remove from the heat.

3. Remove the meat from the marinade, wipe off the chopped vegetables, pat dry, and season with 1 teaspoon salt. Heat 1 tablespoon canola oil in a large skillet over medium-high heat until the oil is rippling, then put the meat in the pan in one layer. Sear the meat on all sides, working in batches so you don't crowd the pan. Each batch should take about 5 minutes. Transfer to a large Dutch oven or casserole.

4. When all the meat has been seared, reduce the heat to medium and add the pancetta to the pan. Stir for a couple of minutes, then add the vegetables and wine from the marinade and stir, scraping the bottom of the pan to deglaze. Cook for 5 minutes, then add the remaining cup of red wine and bring to a boil. Reduce the mixture to half its volume, which should take 5 to 10 minutes. Scrape into the Dutch oven with the meat and add the chicken stock, the roasted tomatoes with their juice, 1 cup of the liquid from the canned tomatoes if using canned, and 1 teaspoon salt. Return to the heat and bring to a simmer. Reduce the heat to low, cover, and simmer 2 hours, stirring occasionally. The meat should be fork-tender and the broth fragrant.

5. Using tongs, remove the meat from the stew and allow to cool until you can handle it. Shred the meat, using your fingers or 2 forks. Do not shred too finely.

6. If possible, refrigerate the meat in a covered bowl and the stew in its pot overnight. The next day, lift off the fat from the top of the stew and discard. If you do not have the extra day, use a ladle to skim the fat from the top of the liquid in the pot and discard (see page 121). Put the contents of the pot through a food mill fitted with a medium or fine screen (fine enough to keep out the tomato seeds) and return to the pot. Stir the meat back into the sauce and bring to a simmer over medium-low heat.

7. Heat 3 tablespoons olive oil in a large skillet over medium heat and add the finely diced carrot, celery, and onion, along with ½ teaspoon salt and ¼ teaspoon ground black pepper. Cook, stirring often, 5 minutes and add the sliced garlic. Continue to cook for another 5 minutes, or until the mixture is tender and very fragrant. Stir into the sauce. Add the bouquet garni and the dissolved tomato paste. Simmer for 30 minutes to an hour, until thick and aromatic, stirring often to make sure the stew doesn't stick on the bottom. If it becomes too thick, add water, a tablespoon at a time. Remove the bouquet garni. Taste and adjust the seasoning. Use as a sauce or filling for pasta. Freeze what you don't use in 2-cup containers.

pappardelle with bolognese sauce [makes 4 main course servings or 6 to 8 starters]

Most of the pasta dishes in this collection call for dried pasta. But there is nothing quite like these wide fresh pasta ribbons with Bolognese sauce. I think of all the ways to serve Bolognese sauce, this simple dish is one of my favorites.

½   pound (½ batch) Fresh Pasta Dough (page 88)
1½ cups Bolognese Sauce (page 91)
    Kosher salt
¼   cup freshly grated Parmesan cheese

1. Roll the pasta out with a pasta roller into thin sheets. With a sharp knife, cut into 12 x ¾-inch ribbons. Dust with semolina and set aside on a parchment-covered baking sheet.

2. Bring a large pot of water to a boil while you warm the Bolognese sauce in a saucepan. When the water reaches a boil, add a generous tablespoon of salt and the pasta. As soon as it boils to the surface, it should be cooked al dente; it should not take longer than 3 minutes. Test by biting into a piece; it should still be a bit firm in the center. When ready, drain and toss with the Bolognese sauce. Serve, passing the Parmesan for sprinkling.

stuffed shells with bolognese sauce [makes 6 servings]

I love stuffed shells like these, with their soft, rich interior and a lightly caramelized, ever-so-crunchy exterior (I like pot roast for the same reason). The dish is both comforting and elegant because of its presentation. It looks like a delicate casserole.

½	pound large macaroni shells (conchiglieri)
1	tablespoon extra virgin olive oil (plus additional for the baking dish)
1	cup fresh ricotta cheese
2	garlic cloves, green shoots removed, minced
1	tablespoon minced fresh flat-leaf parsley
1	teaspoon fresh thyme leaves
½	cup heavy cream
	Kosher salt
6	ounces fresh mozzarella cheese, cut in very small dice
3	ounces Gruyère cheese, cut in very small dice
1⅔	cups Bolognese Sauce (page 91)
½	cup freshly grated Parmesan cheese

1. Bring a large pot of water to a boil. Add a generous tablespoon of salt and add the shells. Cook 10 to 12 minutes, or until cooked through but still al dente (firm to the teeth). Drain and toss gently with 1 tablespoon olive oil. Set aside on a platter.

2. In a medium bowl, stir together the ricotta, garlic, parsley, thyme, cream, and ½ teaspoon salt. Taste and adjust the seasoning.

3. Toss together the diced mozzarella and Gruyère.

4. Preheat the oven to 400°F. Oil a 2-quart baking dish with 1 teaspoon olive oil. Fill the shells with approximately 1 teaspoon of the ricotta mixture, a heaped teaspoon of the Bolognese sauce, and a generous pinch of the mozzarella/Gruyère mixture. Place the shells in the baking dish as you fill them, packing them in tight.

5. Cover the dish tightly with oiled foil and place in the preheated oven. Bake 30 minutes. Remove the foil and sprinkle on the Parmesan. Return to the oven and bake for another 10 to 15 minutes, until the top is lightly browned and the mixture is bubbling. Allow to sit for a few minutes before serving.

VARIATION
You can also make this dish using wide tubes. Cook them al dente, as above (about 12 minutes), drain, and toss with the olive oil. Then cut the tubes in half. Fill them with the same mixture, and stand them, cut side down, in the baking dish (so they look like corks). Bake as above.

lasagne bolognese [makes 8 generous servings]

This uses the exact same ingredients as the shells on page 95 but in different proportions. It's further proof that Bolognese is a mother sauce with endless possibilities.

1	tablespoon extra virgin olive oil, plus about 1 teaspoon for the baking dish
1	cup fresh ricotta cheese
2	garlic cloves, cut in half, green shoots removed, and minced
1	tablespoon minced fresh flat-leaf parsley
1	teaspoon fresh thyme leaves
½	cup heavy cream
½	teaspoon kosher salt
2¾	cups Bolognese Sauce (page 91)
8	ounces no-boil lasagna noodles
¾	cup freshly grated Parmesan cheese
½	pound fresh mozzarella cheese, cut in very small dice
4	ounces Gruyère cheese, cut in very small dice

1. Preheat the oven to 400°F. Oil a rectangular baking dish with olive oil (approximately 1 teaspoon).

2. In a medium bowl, mix together the ricotta cheese, garlic, parsley, thyme, cream, and salt. Taste and adjust the seasoning.

3. Spread ⅓ cup Bolognese sauce over the bottom of the baking dish and top with a layer of noodles. Top the noodles with the ricotta mixture. Place another layer of noodles over the ricotta mixture and spread 1 cup of Bolognese sauce over the noodles. Sprinkle on ¼ cup Parmesan.

4. Add a third layer of pasta and top this with 1 cup Bolognese sauce. Mix together the mozzarella and Gruyère cheeses and sprinkle over the Bolognese sauce. Add a final layer of pasta and the remaining Bolognese sauce. Sprinkle on the remaining Parmesan and drizzle on the olive oil.

5. Oil a sheet of aluminum foil and cover the baking dish. Bake 30 minutes and remove the foil. Bake another 15 minutes uncovered, or until lightly browned. Remove from the heat and allow to sit for 5 to 10 minutes before serving.

[HOW TO WRAP A BAKING DISH]

If you want to really seal a baking dish, don't just cover it and crimp the foil over the sides. Pull out a large sheet of foil and place your baking dish on top of it. Pull the long edges up over the dish, gather them together in the middle, and crimp them so that there is a fold in the middle of the baking dish. Bring the sides up and around the dish.

lasagne with bolognese sauce, creamed spinach, and poached egg [makes 4 main course servings or 6 starters]

You can make everything from scratch for this dish, or you can view it as a festival-of-leftovers dish. That was how it evolved on our Monday Night Family Dinner menu.

1	recipe Creamed Spinach (page 228)
1	tablespoon extra virgin olive oil, plus more for the baking dish
4	ounces fresh or dry lasagna noodles, preferably the no-boil variety
1	tablespoon white wine vinegar
4	to 6 large eggs (depending on the number of portions)
1¼	cups Bolognese Sauce (page 91), warmed Kosher salt and freshly ground black pepper
½	cup freshly grated Parmesan cheese

1. Make the creamed spinach. Do not drain the cooking water from the spinach. You'll use it to cook the noodles.

2. Preheat the oven to 450°F. Brush a square or rectangular baking dish with olive oil.

3. Bring the water back to a boil and cook the lasagne noodles al dente, following the timing instructions on the package, or if using no-boil lasagna, check after the pasta becomes flexible in the water. Drain and toss with 1 tablespoon olive oil in a bowl.

4. Fill a medium saucepan with water and bring to a simmer. Add the vinegar. Using a spoon or a whisk, swirl the water vigorously in the pot, then one by one, break the eggs into the pot. Cook 4 minutes, then using a slotted spoon, transfer to a bowl of cold water. Be careful not to overcook the eggs. Drain on paper towels.

5. Layer half the noodles over the bottom of the baking dish. Spread the Bolognese sauce over the noodles in an even layer, and top with the remaining noodles. Spread the creamed spinach over the noodles in an even layer.

6. Imagine how you will divide the lasagne into 4 to 6 servings (depending on the shape of your dish), and place a poached egg in the middle of each serving. Season each egg with salt and pepper. Sprinkle the Parmesan over the eggs and spinach, and place in the oven for 10 minutes, or until the cheese has melted. Remove from the heat and serve at once.

pasta carbonara with asparagus [makes 4 main course servings or 6 to 8 starters]

Despite the many recipes you see for this Roman classic that call for it, cream is not an ingredient in pasta carbonara. Far be it from me to disparage cream, but it doesn't belong here. The dish is creamy, yes, but that's because of egg yolks that cook gently as they're heated through with the hot pasta. What makes a carbonara is the intertwining of the pork, the cheese, and the pasta. The asparagus is my own addition, and it works as long as you don't overcook it.

4	ounces pancetta, guanciale, or bacon, cut in thin strips or roughly chopped
12	medium asparagus spears, woody ends snapped off
4	large egg yolks
¼	cup freshly grated Parmesan cheese
¼	cup freshly grated Pecorino Romano cheese Kosher salt (to taste)
½	teaspoon freshly ground black pepper, plus more for serving
2	tablespoons extra virgin olive oil
1	tablespoon finely chopped fresh flat-leaf parsley
¾	pound spaghetti or linguine

1. Begin heating a large pot of water for the pasta.

2. Meanwhile, combine the pancetta (or guanciale or bacon) and ¼ cup water in a wide skillet and cook over medium heat until the water evaporates and the pork is browned and just slightly crisp. Remove from the pan and set on a paper towel-lined plate. Do not discard the fat; leave it in the pan.

3. Add the asparagus to the hot pan, along with 2 tablespoons water. Cover and return to the heat. Cook 4 minutes and check the asparagus. It should be just tender to a fork, not too soft. Transfer the asparagus to the plate with the pancetta. Remove the pan from the heat and allow it to cool until it is warm rather than hot (you do not want it to cook the egg yolks when you put them in the pan. To cool down the pan quickly, put some ice-cold water in a wide bowl and dip the bottom of the pan into the water).

4. Beat the egg yolks in a bowl. Combine the cheeses and stir half into the egg yolks, as well as ¼ to ½ teaspoon salt, pepper, olive oil, and parsley. Making sure the pan is not too hot, pour this mixture into the warm frying pan, scraping out every last bit from the bowl with a rubber spatula.

5. When the water comes to a boil, add a generous tablespoon of salt and the pasta. Cook al dente, following the timing instructions on the package but checking the pasta a minute or two before the indicated cooking time. It should be cooked through but firm to the bite. Lift the pasta out of the water with a strainer and immediately toss with the egg yolk mixture and the pancetta in the warm pan. If the mixture seems too thick, add 2 to 4 tablespoons of the pasta cooking water. Cover and let stand for 1 minute, then toss again and serve at once, topping each serving with a tablespoon of the remaining cheese and 3 spears of asparagus. Serve with lots of freshly ground black pepper and more cheese.

spaghetti with garlic, olive oil, and basil

[makes 4 main course servings or 6 to 8 starters]

The traditional Italian dish this is modeled after is called *aglio e olio*, but I can never pronounce that right so let's just leave it with the English name, with its basil embellishment. It's a quick and easy dish, and if you've got a pot of basil growing near your kitchen it's ethereal. Be very careful not to brown the garlic; that's the only tricky point in the recipe. If it gets darker than a manila file folder, it's gone too far and you must start over.

6	tablespoons extra virgin olive oil
3	fat garlic cloves, cut in half, green shoots removed, and minced
1	dried red chile (preferably Japanese), broken in half, or ¼ teaspoon red chile flakes
	Kosher salt
¾	pound spaghetti
	Freshly ground black pepper
3	tablespoons slivered fresh basil (chiffonade)
¼	cup freshly grated Parmesan cheese, as needed

1. Begin heating a large pot of water for the pasta.

2. Meanwhile, heat the olive oil in a small saucepan or frying pan over medium-low heat with the garlic and chile. Cook until the garlic turns pale blond, about 2 minutes. Remove from the heat. If using a whole chile, remove it and discard.

3. When the pasta water comes to a boil, add a generous tablespoon of salt and the spaghetti. Cook al dente, following the timing directions on the package but checking the pasta a minute or two before the time on the package. Remove ½ cup of the pasta water and add it to the pan with the garlic and oil, along with ½ teaspoon salt and several twists of the pepper mill. Return the pan to the heat and drain the pasta.

4. Return the drained spaghetti to the hot pasta pot and toss immediately with the garlic, water, oil, and basil. Serve, topping each serving with a spoonful of Parmesan. Have the pepper mill available for extra seasoning.

pasta with roasted asparagus and pecorino romano

[makes 4 main course servings or 6 to 8 starters]

This is a quick spring pasta dish, to make when asparagus is at its best. It's delicious if you use homemade pappardelle, but if making your own pasta is a problem, you can find perfectly good dried pappardelle. If you can't, use fettuccine or fusilli. Make sure to turn on your oven fan when you roast the asparagus.

¾	pound dried pappardelle, fettuccine or fusilli, or ½ pound fresh pasta (½ batch, page 88)
¾	pound medium-thick asparagus, tough base ends snapped off
2	tablespoons extra virgin olive oil
½	teaspoon kosher salt
	Leaves from 4 fresh thyme sprigs
2	garlic cloves, halved, green shoots removed, and minced
	Freshly ground pepper
¼	cup freshly grated Pecorino Romano cheese
¼	cup freshly grated Parmesan cheese

[BUYING ASPARAGUS]
When you shop for asparagus, look for stalks with tight, firm heads. The heads are the bud ends of the stalk, and when they open they loose their flavor and texture. They are also the most vulnerable part of the stalk, so look closely to make sure that the tips aren't soft, broken, or spoiled.

1. Preheat the oven to 450°F. Begin heating a large pot of water for the pasta.

2. Place the asparagus on a baking sheet and toss with 1 tablespoon of the olive oil, making sure to rub the oil over each stalk. Spread in a single layer on the baking sheet and sprinkle with the salt and thyme. Place in the oven for 10 minutes, until the asparagus is just beginning to wrinkle. Remove from the heat and, using tongs, immediately transfer the asparagus to a cutting board. Cut in 1-inch lengths and place in a pasta bowl, along with the juices and thyme from the pan.

3. Heat the remaining tablespoon of olive oil over low heat in a small pan and add the garlic. Cook for 1 to 2 minutes, just until fragrant and beginning to color, and transfer to the pasta bowl with the asparagus.

4. When the pasta water comes to a boil, add a generous tablespoon of salt and the pasta. Cook the pasta al dente, until firm to the bite, following the timing instructions on the package but checking the pasta a minute or two before the designated cooking time. Fresh pasta should take no longer than 4 minutes. Remove ½ cup of the pasta cooking water and add to the bowl with the asparagus, and drain the pasta. Toss at once with the asparagus, a generous amount of black pepper, and the pecorino. Serve immediately, passing the Parmesan at the table.

VARIATION
You can add other vegetables to this, such as blanched green beans, as well as fresh herbs like slivered basil or fresh marjoram, but not too many things at once.

linguine and clams [makes 4 main course servings or 6 starters]

Linguine with clams is another traditional Italian-American restaurant dish that was wonderful in its original incarnation but was often abused, eventually becoming a cliché. Make it right and it's a brilliant combination of briny clams, pungent garlic, spicy olive oil, dry white wine, and chewy pasta. This is the "white" version of the dish, meaning it has no tomatoes. A red version follows.

3	tablespoons extra virgin olive oil
3	fat garlic cloves, halved, green shoots removed, and minced
½	cup dry white wine
1	dried chile (preferably Japanese)
36	littleneck or cherrystone clams, or 48 Manila clams, purged (page 83)
	Kosher salt and freshly ground black pepper
¾	pound linguine
2	tablespoons cold unsalted butter, cut into small pieces
¼	cup chopped fresh flat-leaf parsley

1. Begin heating a large pot of water for the pasta.

2. In a wide skillet over high heat, combine 1 tablespoon of olive oil, 1 garlic clove, the white wine, and the chile. Add the clams and bring to a boil. Cover and cook 3 to 5 minutes, shaking the pan from time to time, until the clams begin to open up. Using tongs, remove the open clams from the pan and place in a bowl. Discard any clams that have not opened. Remove the pan from the heat.

3. Allow the clams to cool, then remove the meat from the clam shells, holding them over the pan to catch the juices. Rinse briefly to rid them of any lingering sand, and cut in half or chop coarsely. Rinse out the bowl and strain the liquid in the pan through a cheesecloth-lined strainer into the bowl. Set aside.

4. Heat the remaining olive oil in the pan in which you cooked the clams over medium-high heat and add the remaining garlic. Cook, stirring, until fragrant and just beginning to color, about 30 seconds to a minute. Add the cooking liquid from the clams. Bring to a simmer. Taste and add salt as needed and about ¼ teaspoon pepper. Keep at a low simmer while you cook the linguine.

5. When the pasta water comes to a boil, add a generous tablespoon of salt and the pasta. Cook al dente, following the timing directions on the package but checking the pasta to see if it is cooked through but firm to the bite a minute or two before the end of the cooking time designated on the package.

6. Meanwhile, a little at a time, whisk the butter into the broth. Remove ¼ cup of the pasta cooking water and set aside. Drain the pasta and add to the pan, along with the clams and parsley. Add the cooking water you set aside if the mixture seems dry. Toss together and serve, passing a vial of olive oil and the pepper grinder for extra seasoning.

VARIATION / LINGUINE AND CLAMS WITH RED SAUCE
To the above recipe add 2 large tomatoes, peeled, seeded, and finely chopped, or one 14-ounce can, drained and chopped. Add the tomatoes after sautéing the garlic in step 4 and cook, stirring often, for about 10 minutes before proceeding with the recipe.

spaghetti with mussels and peas [makes 4 servings]

Fresh peas seem to be on the market for about a day in early spring, and when I see them, I buy as many as I can. If the pea pods are fat, round, and heavy, they are probably past their prime. Open up a pod and taste a pea. Even raw it should be sweet, not starchy. This dish is in the same family as the Linguine and Clams on page 101, but it's a bit more complex. There is something about the combined flavors of mussels, marjoram, and peas that makes the dish wonderful.

3	tablespoons extra virgin olive oil
½	small onion or 1 medium shallot, chopped (about ⅓ cup)
2	fat garlic cloves, halved, green shoots removed, and sliced
1	dried red chile (preferably Japanese)
½	cup dry white wine
½	cup chicken stock or water
1½	pounds mussels, purged (page 83)
2	tablespoons unsalted butter
2	teaspoons chopped fresh marjoram
	Kosher salt and freshly ground black pepper
¾	pound spaghetti
1	cup shelled fresh peas
2	tablespoons chopped fresh flat-leaf parsley

1. Begin heating a large pot of water for the pasta.

2. Heat a wide saucepan or lidded frying pan over medium-high heat and add 2 tablespoons of the olive oil. Add the onion or shallot, the garlic, and the chile and cook, stirring, until the onion is just tender, 3 to 5 minutes. Add the wine and stock or water, and bring to a boil. Add the mussels, cover, and cook 3 to 4 minutes, shaking the pan once or twice, or until the mussels begin to open. Remove the open mussels from the pan using tongs and place in a bowl. If a few mussels refuse to open, discard them. Set aside 4 of the prettiest mussels for garnish, then, holding them over the bowl to catch the liquid, remove the meat from the shells of the remaining mussels, and discard the shells. Rinse briefly to remove any lingering sand. Remove the dried red pepper from the pan and discard.

3. Return the mussels to the pan and strain in any liquid you may have caught in the bowl through a fine strainer. Add the butter and the marjoram. Taste the liquid in the pan and season with salt and pepper. Keep warm while you cook the pasta.

4. When the pasta water has reached a rolling boil, add a generous tablespoon of salt and the spaghetti. Cook 5 minutes and add the peas. Continue to cook until the pasta is al dente (usually about 5 more minutes). Drain the spaghetti and return to the hot pot. Add the mussels and their liquid to the spaghetti pot, along with the parsley and a tablespoon of olive oil. Toss together and serve. Pass a vial of olive oil and a pepper grinder for extra seasoning if you wish.

giant ravioli with spinach, ricotta, and egg yolk

[makes 6 main course servings or 12 starters]

This is a labor-intensive dish to make on a Saturday or Sunday afternoon. It's worth the effort. The sauce is created inside these giant ravioli, a perfectly soft-boiled egg yolk that will ooze out when you cut the ravioli, enriching both the filling and pasta. Don't separate the eggs until you are assembling the ravioli, because the yolks will become too fragile if they sit. Lay out the ravioli squares and spoon on the filling, then one by one, separate the eggs and gently lay the yolks on the filling.

12	ounces baby spinach or 1½ pounds fresh bunch spinach, stemmed and washed
1	pound (2 cups) fresh ricotta
2	garlic cloves, halved, green shoots removed, and finely minced
¼	cup finely chopped fresh flat-leaf parsley, or a combination of parsley and other sweet herbs such as basil, chervil, tarragon
¾	cup freshly grated Parmesan cheese, plus additional for sprinkling
	Kosher salt and freshly ground black pepper
	Up to ½ cup heavy cream
1	recipe Fresh Pasta Dough (page 88)
12	large egg yolks
¼	cup extra virgin olive oil

1. Bring a large pot of generously salted water to a boil and add the spinach. Blanch baby spinach for 10 seconds only (bunch spinach for 20 to 30 seconds), and transfer to a bowl of ice water. Cool for a few minutes, then drain and, taking up a handful at a time, squeeze hard to get out the excess water. Chop fine. You should have about 1 cup chopped spinach.

2. In a large bowl, mix the ricotta, garlic, chopped spinach, parsley, Parmesan, and salt and pepper to taste. Fold in enough cream to make the mixture soft and malleable.

3. Roll out the pasta to thin sheets. Cut twelve 4½-inch squares and twelve 5-inch squares. Cover with a damp cloth while you make the ravioli. Working 2 or 4 squares at a time, spoon 2 tablespoons of the filling onto the middle of each 4½-inch square. With the back of your spoon or with your fingers, make a depression in the middle of the mound. Carefully place an egg yolk in the depression, and season with salt and pepper. Carefully cover the egg yolk with another tablespoon of filling and spread it over, without pressing down, so that it joins the bottom mound of filling. Gently pinch the bottom and top layers together.

4. Brush the edges of the pasta square with water. Place a 5-inch square of pasta over the top and gently pinch the edges together. Continue until you have 12 squares.

(continues)

TOP LEFT Working 2 or 4 squares at a time, spoon 2 tablespoons of the filling onto the middle of each 4½-inch square.
MIDDLE With the back of your spoon or with your fingers, make a depression in the middle of the mound.
BOTTOM Carefully place an egg yolk in the depression, and season with salt and pepper.

5. Bring a large pot of water to a simmer and add a generous tablespoon of salt. Add the giant ravioli. Cook for 5 minutes, until the pasta is cooked al dente (break off a corner of one to test it). Be careful not to allow the water to reach a rolling boil or the ravioli may fall apart. Remove with a skimmer and place 1 or 2 on each deep soup plate. Drizzle with olive oil and sprinkle with Parmesan and freshly ground pepper. Serve at once.

[HOW TO KEEP RAVIOLI FROM SOAKING THROUGH]

The main challenge when you make ravioli and have to hold it for a while before cooking it—and who doesn't?—is to keep the moist filling from soaking through the pasta. If that happens the pasta will tear when you're transferring it to the pot for cooking. The way to get around this is to clear a space in your freezer for a half-sheet pan. Line the pan with parchment and sprinkle the parchment generously with semolina. Place the assembled ravioli on the parchment, and immediately place the baking sheet in the freezer. No need to cover if you are just keeping it for a few hours. Transfer directly from the freezer to the simmering water. If it is frozen solid, then you'll need to add a minute or two to the cooking time.

TOP Carefully cover the egg yolk with another tablespoon of filling and spread it over, without pressing down, so that it joins the bottom mound of filling.
MIDDLE Brush the edges of the pasta square with water.
BOTTOM Place a 5-inch square of pasta over the top and gently pinch the edges together.

penne with uncooked puttanesca sauce

[makes 4 servings]

This is a quick and easy, robust pantry pasta. With the exception of the fresh, ripe tomato, you should have the remaining ingredients on hand.

1	to 2 garlic cloves (to taste), cut in half, green shoots removed
	Kosher salt
3	tablespoons plus 1 teaspoon extra virgin olive oil
2	fat anchovy fillets (or 4 thin ones), soaked in cold water for 5 minutes, drained, rinsed and dried on paper towels
1	tablespoon capers, rinsed
3	tablespoons chopped fresh flat-leaf parsley
½	pound fresh ripe tomatoes, cored and peeled
8	imported black olives, pitted and cut into strips
	Freshly ground black pepper (to taste)
12	ounces penne
2	tablespoons slivered fresh flat-leaf parsley leaves
2	to 4 tablespoons freshly grated Parmesan cheese

1. Begin heating a large pot of water for the pasta. In a mortar and pestle, mash the garlic with a generous pinch of salt and 1 teaspoon of the olive oil. Add the anchovy fillets and capers and mash together. Work in the chopped parsley and 2 tablespoons of the olive oil.

2. Cut the tomatoes in half at the equator. Place a strainer over a bowl and squeeze out the tomato seeds and pulp. Rub the pulpy seeds against the strainer to extract as much juice as possible. Discard the seeds. Coarsely chop the tomatoes and mix with the olives, garlic, and anchovy paste, and the strained tomato juice. Add salt and pepper to taste, and 1 more tablespoon of olive oil.

3. When the water comes to a boil, salt generously and cook the pasta al dente, about 8 minutes (see the recommendation on the package and begin testing a minute before the recommended time). Drain the pasta and return to the pot with the sauce. Mix together and warm through in the pot for a minute, then transfer to a platter. Garnish with the slivered parsley and Parmesan, and serve.

macaroni and cheese with mushrooms [makes 8 servings]

I firmly believe that macaroni and cheese is one of the great American dishes. It's been ruined by Kraft and other companies that would have you believe macaroni and cheese consists of overcooked pasta smothered in iridescent "cheese food." A true macaroni and cheese is a creamy casserole with a crisp, cheesy crust. Made properly, it's delicious, even without the wild mushrooms. Though, why not gild the lily? I use penne for the pasta because I like it better than the smaller, smoother macaroni. In early American usage all pasta was macaroni. Remember the Yankee Doodle who stuck a feather in his cap and called it macaroni? He probably meant *penne*, because the word derives from the word for "pen," or "quill," which at that time would have been a feather.

[BÉCHAMEL]

½	ounce dried porcini mushrooms
3	tablespoons unsalted butter
3	tablespoons all-purpose flour
⅓	cup minced onion
1	dried red chile (preferably Japanese), whole
1	small bay leaf
	Kosher salt
2	cups whole milk

[MACARONI]

¾	pound penne
1	tablespoon extra virgin olive oil
½	ounce dried morels
2	tablespoons unsalted butter
½	cup finely chopped onion or shallot
	Kosher salt
2	fat garlic cloves, halved, green shoots removed, and minced
6	ounces fresh wild mushrooms, such as hedgehogs, maitake, or oyster mushrooms, washed and quartered or cut into thick slices
1½	teaspoons chopped fresh thyme leaves
2	tablespoons chopped fresh flat-leaf parsley
	Freshly ground black pepper
3	ounces Gruyère cheese, grated (¾ cup, tightly packed)
1½	ounces Parmesan cheese, grated (⅓ cup, tightly packed)
3	ounces fresh mozzarella cheese, finely chopped (about ¾ cup)
¼	cup fresh or dried bread crumbs

BÉCHAMEL

It's important to cook béchamel long enough to rid it of any raw flour taste. This is one reason you always add cold milk to your roux.

1. Make the béchamel: Place the porcini in a bowl and pour in 1 cup hot water. Let sit for 30 minutes. Drain through a cheesecloth-lined strainer. Squeeze the mushrooms over the strainer to extract the soaking liquid, then rinse well in several changes of water, swishing them around in the water until you no longer see any sand. Squeeze dry, chop coarsely, and set aside. Measure out ¾ cup of the soaking liquid.

2. In a medium saucepan over medium heat, melt the butter and add the flour. Stir together with a wooden spoon until the roux is just barely golden and has a popcorn aroma, 3 to 5 minutes. Add the onion, chile, and bay leaf and continue to cook, stirring, until the onion softens slightly and the raw onion smell is gone. Add ¼ teaspoon salt. The popcorn smell will dissipate and the roux will thicken, then loosen up.

3. Change from the wooden spoon to a whisk and whisk in the milk and the mushroom-soaking liquid all at once. Bring slowly to a simmer, whisking constantly.

4. Turn the heat to low and simmer, stirring very often with a wooden spoon or a heatproof rubber spatula so that nothing sticks to the sides and bottom of the pot. If the flour sticks and scorches, the béchamel will be ruined and you'll have to begin again. It helps to cook the béchamel in a wide pan you can tip to see the bottom to make sure the sauce is not sticking. Simmer for about 15 minutes, until there is no raw flour taste and the sauce is quite thick.

(continues)

5. Remove from the heat and press through a sieve immediately, while hot. You can store the béchamel for a few days in the refrigerator. Place a piece of plastic directly over the surface to prevent a skin from forming. When you reheat it, whisk it vigorously.

6. Make the macaroni: Bring a large pot of water to a boil and add a generous tablespoon of salt and the penne. Cook for a minute less than usual. It should be cooked through but a little more al dente or chewy than you'd like it if you were serving it right away. Drain and toss with a tablespoon of olive oil. Set aside.

7. Preheat the oven to 400°F and butter a 2-quart gratin or baking dish. Place the dried morels in a bowl and pour on 1½ cups hot water. Allow to soak for 20 to 30 minutes. Agitate the mushrooms in the soaking water to release more sand, then lift them from the water and let the water sit for a few minutes. Strain into a bowl through a cheesecloth-lined strainer. Rinse the mushrooms, swishing them around in several changes of water to release more sand. Slice lengthwise and set aside with the reconstituted porcini.

8. Heat 1 tablespoon unsalted butter in a wide, heavy saucepan and add the onion and ½ teaspoon salt. Cook gently until tender, about 5 minutes, and add the garlic.

Cook for another minute, until the garlic is fragrant, and stir in the reconstituted morels and porcini. Cook, stirring for a minute or two, until the liquid cooks out. Add the fresh mushrooms and ¼ teaspoon salt, and cook, stirring, until the mushrooms are tender and have cooked down somewhat, about 5 minutes. Add the strained soaking liquid from the dried mushrooms and stir together. Bring to a boil and cook until the liquid has reduced by about three quarters, to a thick gravy coating the mushrooms and the bottom of the pan. Rub the thyme between the palms of your hands to release its aroma and stir into the mushrooms along with 1 tablespoon of the parsley; add salt and pepper to taste. Stir in the béchamel and remove from the heat.

9. In a large bowl, toss together the cooked penne, the béchamel and mushrooms, the Gruyère, all but 2 tablespoons of the Parmesan, and the mozzarella. Spoon into the buttered baking dish. Combine the bread crumbs, the remaining Parmesan, and the remaining tablespoon of parsley and sprinkle over the top in an even layer. Dot with the remaining butter.

10. Cover the macaroni with foil and place in the oven. Bake 40 minutes, or until bubbling. Uncover, turn the heat down to 375°F, and bake another 10 to 15 minutes, until the top has browned. Remove from the heat and, once the macaroni has stopped bubbling, serve.

campanile tuna noodle casserole [makes 6 servings]

My mother could only make ten dishes, and this was one of them. With all due respect, I think this is even better than hers. I love using the Southern Italian ring-shaped pasta called calamarata, which are like rounds of squid (calamari) and make a harmonious foil for this rich tuna and noodle casserole. The classic choice is elbow macaroni, and that will do just fine if you can't find calamarata. Whichever noodles you do use, undercook them slightly as they will soften up more when you bake the casserole.

My guests are amused and often surprised when they see this on the menu. If they've brought their children, they're delighted, as this is something that children love to eat, even without the traditional potato chip topping.

[BÉCHAMEL]

3	tablespoons unsalted butter
3	tablespoons all-purpose flour
¼	cup minced onion or shallot
1	small dried red chile (preferably Japanese), whole
1	small bay leaf
	Kosher salt
2½	cups whole milk

[CASSEROLE]

½	pound calamarata or elbow macaroni
2	tablespoons olive oil from the tuna
¾	pound tuna confit (page 197) or two 6-ounce cans imported tuna packed in olive oil
4	ounces Gruyère cheese, grated (1 cup tightly packed)
3	tablespoons minced fresh flat-leaf parsley
1½	cups (2 ounces) fresh bread crumbs
1½	ounces Parmesan cheese, freshly grated (⅓ cup tightly packed)

1. Make the béchamel: In a medium saucepan over medium heat, melt the butter and add the flour. Stir together with a wooden spoon until the roux is just barely golden and has a popcorn aroma, about 5 minutes. Add the onion or shallot, chile, and bay leaf and continue to cook, stirring, until the onion softens slightly and the raw onion smell is gone. Add ½ teaspoon salt. The popcorn smell will dissipate and the roux will thicken, and then, after 2 to 3 minutes, it will loosen up.

2. Change from the wooden spoon to a whisk and whisk in the milk all at once. Bring slowly to a simmer, whisking. Whisk continuously until the sauce thickens. Use a heatproof rubber spatula to scrape the sauce from the bottom and edges of the pot so it doesn't stick and burn. It helps to cook the béchamel in a wide pan you can tip to see the bottom to make sure the sauce is not sticking. Reduce the heat and simmer gently, scraping the sides and bottom of the pot from time to time, for about 15 minutes, until there is no trace of a floury taste.

3. Remove from the heat and strain immediately, while hot, through a medium strainer into a bowl. Taste and adjust the seasoning (you will probably want to add up to ¼ teaspoon salt); it should be well seasoned and medium thick. You can store the béchamel for a few days in the refrigerator. Place a piece of plastic wrap directly over the surface to prevent a thick skin from forming. When you reheat, whisk vigorously.

(continues)

4. Assemble the casserole: Preheat the oven to 375°F. Butter a 2-quart baking dish. Bring a large pot of water to a boil and add a generous tablespoon of salt. Add the pasta and cook for a minute less than usual. It should be cooked through but a little more al dente or chewy than you'd like it if you were serving it right away, about 10 minutes for calamarata. Remove a ladleful of the cooking water and set aside in a bowl. Drain the pasta and toss with a tablespoon of the olive oil from the tuna in a large bowl.

5. Crumble the tuna into the bowl with the pasta and toss together. Gently fold in the béchamel, the grated Gruyère, and 2 tablespoons of the parsley. If the sauce seems to coat the pasta too thickly, thin out with a small amount of pasta cooking water (2 tablespoons or a little more). Spoon into the baking dish. Mix together the bread crumbs, Parmesan, remaining tablespoon of parsley, and the remaining tablespoon of olive oil from the tuna. Sprinkle over the top in an even layer.

6. Cover the casserole with foil and bake in the preheated oven for 30 minutes. Remove the foil and continue to bake for another 15 minutes, until the top has browned and the casserole is bubbling and hot all the way through. Remove from the heat, let stand until no longer bubbling, and serve.

wild mushroom risotto [makes 4 to 6 servings]

I like to use an assortment of mushrooms for this. At the restaurant we often get bluefoots, which have a nice meaty texture and lots of pronounced flavor; hedgehogs, which are more delicate; and black trumpets, another delicate mushroom with an earthy flavor. I also use dried morels, which contribute the intense flavor of dried mushrooms to the broth as well as a nice chewy texture. Use other dried mushrooms, such as porcini or shiitakes, if you can't find dried morels.

½ ounce dried morels or porcini
6 cups Chicken Stock (page 66)
1 to 2 tablespoons canola oil, as needed
½ pound assorted wild mushrooms, washed, trimmed, and thickly sliced
Kosher salt
1 tablespoon extra virgin olive oil (plus additional if desired for drizzling)
1½ cups arborio or Carnaroli rice
¼ cup minced shallot (1 fat shallot)
1 fat garlic clove, green shoot removed, minced
½ cup dry white wine
Freshly ground black pepper
A few drops of freshly squeezed lemon juice (optional)
2 tablespoons unsalted butter
⅓ cup freshly grated Parmesan cheese
2 tablespoons chopped fresh flat-leaf parsley

1. Place the dried mushrooms in a bowl or a large Pyrex measuring cup and pour on 2 cups boiling water. Let sit for 20 minutes. Strain through a cheesecloth-lined strainer. Squeeze the mushrooms over the strainer, then rinse in several changes of cold water, swishing the mushrooms around in the water to rid them of lingering sand. Cut in half or quarters and set aside.

2. Combine the mushroom water and the chicken stock in a saucepan and bring to a simmer.

3. Heat 1 tablespoon canola oil in a large, heavy saucepan over high heat and when hot, add the sturdiest of the fresh wild mushrooms, along with ¼ teaspoon salt. Cook for 1 to 2 minutes, until they begin to soften, and add the remaining, more delicate mushrooms, and more oil if needed. Add another ¼ teaspoon salt, and cook the mushrooms, stirring often, until softened and fragrant. Add the reconstituted

dried mushrooms and stir together. Reduce the heat to medium and continue to cook for 3 to 4 more minutes, until the mushrooms are tender, juicy, and fragrant. Remove from the heat and transfer to a bowl.

4. Add the olive oil to the saucepan and stir in the rice. Place over medium heat and stir constantly over the heat until the rice begins to smell toasty, like popcorn, and the kernels are opaque. Add the shallot, garlic, cooked mushrooms, and 1 teaspoon salt, and cook gently, stirring for a few minutes, until the shallot softens.

5. Add the wine all at once and stir until it has been absorbed by the rice.

6. Begin adding the simmering stock, a couple of tablespoons at a time. It should just cover the rice and should immediately begin to bubble, though not too hard. If it is boiling hard, turn down the heat a bit. Stir until just about absorbed, and add another few tablespoons. Stir often (almost constantly) and continue to add stock whenever you see that there is not much left in the saucepan. Gradually the mixture will become creamy as starch from the rice dissolves into the broth.

7. After about 25 minutes, the rice should be cooked al dente, the grains just a bit chewy in the center, and the broth creamy. Taste and adjust the seasoning with salt, pepper, and a few drops of lemon juice, if desired. Continue to add stock and cook if necessary. It should not take more than 30 minutes. Be careful not to let the rice stick to the bottom of the pan. The final risotto should be creamy and the rice kernels should not stick together.

8. Remove from the heat, add another ladleful of stock, and stir in the butter, Parmesan, and parsley. Serve immediately in wide soup bowls or on plates. Drizzle some great olive oil over and around the risotto on the plate.

saffron risotto with cavolo nero [makes 4 to 6 servings]

Cavolo nero (Italian for "black cabbage" and the name often used even at American markets) is my favorite kale or cabbage. The flavor melts into this risotto, but structurally it stands up to a surprising amount of cooking. If you can't find black kale you can substitute regular green kale for this dish.

Kosher salt
5   ounces cavolo nero (black kale), washed and stemmed
7   cups Chicken Stock (page 66)
1½   cups arborio or Carnaroli rice
2   tablespoons extra virgin olive oil, plus more for drizzling
Generous pinch of saffron
½   cup finely chopped onion
2   fat garlic cloves, green shoots removed, thinly sliced
½   cup dry white wine
2   tablespoons unsalted butter
⅓   cup freshly grated Parmesan cheese

1. Bring a large pot of water to a boil and add a generous tablespoon of salt and the kale. Blanch for 2 minutes and transfer to a bowl of ice water. Drain, squeeze out the water, and roughly chop. Set aside.

2. Bring the stock to a simmer in a medium saucepan.

3. In a heavy, large saucepan over medium heat, combine the rice and the olive oil. Stir constantly over the heat until the rice begins to smell toasty, like popcorn, and the kernels are opaque. Crush the saffron threads between your fingers and stir into the rice, along with 1½ teaspoons salt (less if your stock is salted). Add the onion and garlic and continue to stir for 1 to 2 minutes.

4. Add the wine all at once and stir until it has been absorbed by the rice. Stir in the kale.

5. Begin ladling in the simmering stock, a couple of tablespoons at a time. It should just cover the rice and should immediately begin to bubble, though not too hard. If it is boiling hard, turn down the heat a bit. Stir until just about absorbed, and add another few tablespoons. Stir often (almost constantly) and continue to add stock whenever you see that there is not much left in the saucepan. Gradually the mixture will become creamy as starch from the rice dissolves into the broth.

6. After about 25 minutes, the rice should be cooked al dente, the grains just a bit chewy in the center, and the broth creamy. Taste and adjust the seasoning. Continue to add stock and cook if necessary. It should not take more than 30 minutes. Be careful not to let the rice stick to the bottom of the pan. The final risotto should be creamy and the rice kernels should not stick together.

7. Remove from the heat, add another ladleful of stock, and stir in the butter and Parmesan. Serve immediately in wide soup bowls or on plates. Drizzle some great olive oil over and around the risotto on the plate.

[CUTTING UP THE KALE]
The kale is not finely chopped, but roughly cut. Once the greens are cooked and shocked in ice water, drain and squeeze out the water. The squeezed kale will form a ball in your hand. Set the ball of kale on your cutting board and cut into ½-inch-wide strips. Turn the ball a quarter turn and cut across the strips at ½-inch intervals. Now your kale is coarsely chopped.

VARIATION
For a delicious variation, add 2 ounces sliced uncooked bacon to the rice at the beginning of step 3.

risotto with caramelized squash [makes 4 substantial main dish servings or 6 to 8 starters]

We make this risotto in fall and winter, when the winter squash is at its best, fat and heavy for its size. We cook the squash first until it's lightly caramelized, then set it aside and stir it into the risotto at the last minute. If you add it too soon, it will turn to mush.

3	tablespoons unsalted butter
1	pound peeled, seeded winter squash, such as butternut, kabocha or acorn, cut in ½-inch dice (about 3 cups)
	Kosher salt
4	garlic cloves, halved, green shoots removed, 1 minced, 3 sliced
2	teaspoons slivered fresh sage leaves
7	cups mild chicken stock, or 3½ cups stronger chicken stock and 3½ cups water
2	tablespoons extra virgin olive oil
1½	cups arborio or Carnaroli rice
½	cup finely chopped shallot or onion
½	cup dry white wine
	Freshly ground black pepper
½	cup freshly grated Parmesan
1	tablespoon chopped flat-leaf parsley
1	tablespoon pumpkin seed oil (optional)

1. Caramelize the squash: Heat 2 tablespoons of the butter in a medium saucepan or skillet over medium heat and add the squash. Cook slowly, turning the pieces as they color. When the cubes are just about done, evenly golden on all sides and tender (after about 20 minutes), add 1 teaspoon kosher salt, the minced garlic clove, and the slivered sage, and stir together for a minute. Remove from the heat and set aside.

2. Make the risotto: Heat the stock or stock and water in a saucepan to simmering. Heat the olive oil in a wide, heavy saucepan over medium heat and add the rice and 1½ teaspoons (less if your stock is salted) salt. Stir constantly over the heat until the rice begins to smell toasty, like popcorn, and the kernels are opaque. Add the shallot or onion and sliced garlic and continue to stir for 1 to 2 minutes.

3. Add the wine all at once and stir until it has been absorbed by the rice. Reduce the heat to medium-low.

4. Begin ladling in the simmering stock, a few tablespoons at a time. It should just cover the rice and should immediately begin to bubble, though not too hard. If it is boiling hard, turn down the heat a bit. Stir until just about absorbed, and add another few tablespoons. Stir often (almost constantly) and continue to add stock whenever you see that there is not much left in the saucepan. Gradually the mixture will become creamy as starch from the rice dissolves into the broth.

5. After about 25 minutes, the rice should be cooked al dente, the grains just a bit chewy in the center, and the broth creamy. Taste and adjust seasoning. Continue to add stock and cook if necessary, then stir in the squash. Be careful not to let the rice stick to the bottom of the pan. The final risotto should be creamy and the rice kernels should not stick together.

6. Remove from the heat, add another ladleful of stock, and stir in the remaining tablespoon of butter, freshly ground pepper to taste, the Parmesan and the parsley. Serve immediately in wide soup bowls or on plates. To make it extra special, drizzle some pumpkin seed oil over and around the risotto.

[4]
MEAT AND MEAT STEWS

Meat is an important part of what we do at Campanile. We use prime, corn-fed, dry aged beef, which has environmental issues attached to it; but this kind of beef is and should be an expensive luxury item, not something you eat every day. This is why most of our Monday Night Family Dinner menus and recipes in this chapter call for inexpensive cuts, and use rubs and flavorings to pull out the natural flavors of the meats. There are a few wonderful steak recipes here, and our signature prime roast. But you'll find many more braises and stews. I love the flavor and complexity of these dishes: You put your effort in long before the dish is cooked; once it's in the oven or gently bubbling on the stove, most of your work is done. These are informal dishes that hold well and are perfect for entertaining or family dinners.

In addition to the beef, lamb, and pork dishes in this chapter, you'll find several veal recipes. It may not be politically correct to serve veal, but as long as there is a dairy industry in this country, there will be veal. Dairy cows have to have calves to produce milk, and most male calves are destined to be veal. They should not be treated cruelly, and many producers do treat their veal calves well. Veal lends itself to a range of cooking styles: You'll find delicious classic recipes here for thinly pounded veal scaloppine cooked in minutes, and, at the other end of the spectrum, marinated and slowly roasted vitello tonnato, where everything except the slicing and serving is done the day before.

There was a time in America when a meal meant meat. We still eat too much meat, but that is an individual choice. These recipes reflect that center-of-the-plate mentality. Whether you eat meat every day, rarely, or somewhere in between, you'll find a range of dishes here with big flavors for hearty appetites.

beef bourguignon [makes 6 servings]

There are many different recipes for this classic beef stew, but they all include beef, aromatics, and red wine. I intensify the flavor in the marinade by first cooking the aromatics that go into it. The recipe requires little in the way of skill, but it does require time and attention.

¾	pound mushrooms, stems removed but retained for cooking, caps halved or quartered if large, left whole if small
¼	cup extra virgin olive oil
4	ounces lean pancetta, diced
1	large yellow onion, finely chopped
1	large carrot, chopped
1	stalk celery, chopped
3	fat garlic cloves, halved, green shoots removed, and sliced
	Kosher salt
	A bouquet garni made with a few sprigs each thyme and parsley, 1 or 2 bay leaves, ½ small dried chile with the seeds removed (preferably Japanese, optional), and about ½ teaspoon cracked black peppercorns (page 66)
3½	cups good red burgundy or California, Washington, or Oregon Pinot Noir
3	pounds beef chuck, cut in 2-inch pieces
	Freshly ground black pepper
2	tablespoons canola oil
3	tablespoons all-purpose flour
2	cups water
2	tablespoons unsalted butter
	Rice, potatoes, or noodles, for serving

Whenever a recipe calls for mushroom caps, use the stems along with onions, carrots, and celery in the broth. Mushrooms are a natural source of MSG, and the stems will add a lot of flavor to the mix.

1. Rough-chop the mushroom stems and set aside; refrigerate the caps. Heat the olive oil over medium heat in a large, heavy frying pan or a wide saucepan and add the pancetta, onion, carrot, and celery. Cook, stirring, until tender, about 5 minutes, and add the garlic, the mushroom stems, and ½ teaspoon salt. Cook, stirring often, for about 10 minutes, until very fragrant. Add the bouquet garni and 3 cups of the wine and scrape the bottom and sides of the pan with a wooden spoon to deglaze, Bring to a simmer and simmer 3 minutes. Remove from the heat and allow to cool.

2. Toss the meat in a large bowl with the cooled wine and vegetable mixture. Cover the bowl with plastic wrap, or transfer the meat and marinade to a zipper bag and refrigerate overnight, preferably for about 24 hours.

3. Remove the pieces of meat from the marinade. Brush the vegetables adhering to the meat back into the marinade. Pat the meat dry. Sprinkle the meat all over with salt and pepper. Heat 2 tablespoons canola oil over medium-high heat in a wide, heavy skillet and brown the meat, in batches, on all sides. Pour off the fat from the pan between batches. Transfer to a casserole or Dutch oven. When all the meat has been browned, add the remaining ½ cup red wine to the pan and stir and scrape with a wooden spoon to deglaze. Pour into the casserole with the meat.

4. Place the casserole over medium heat and sift in the flour. Cook, stirring constantly, for about 3 to 5 minutes, until all the meat is well coated, the wine is almost completely absorbed, and you can smell the flour beginning to brown. Add the marinade with all of the vegetables and the bouquet garni, along with 2 cups water, and turn the heat to high. Using a wooden spoon, stir the bottom and sides of the pan to bring up any browned bits of flour or meat that may have stuck. Bring to a simmer, reduce the heat to very low, cover, and simmer, stirring occasionally, for 2½ to 3 hours, until the meat is fork-tender. Taste and add salt and pepper as desired.

5. Toward the end of the 2½ hours, sear the mushrooms. Heat the butter over medium-high heat in a large skillet and add the thickly sliced mushrooms and about ¼ teaspoon salt. Cook, stirring often, until they soften and begin to sweat, 5 to 8 minutes. Stir into the beef stew, along with any juices from the pan. Cover and simmer another 30 minutes. Taste, adjust the seasonings, and serve with potatoes, rice, or noodles.

[NOTE] If you can make this stew a day ahead, it will be all the better. Make through step 4. Using a slotted spoon, remove the meat and vegetables from the liquid and place in a bowl. Pour the liquid into another bowl. Cover and refrigerate overnight. The next day, lift off the fat that has accumulated on top of the liquid and discard. Combine the meat and gravy in a pot, reheat gently, and adjust the seasonings. Proceed with step 5.

campanile hamburgers with cheddar cheese [makes 4 servings]

Like all of the standard dishes in this book, our hamburgers are great because we pay attention to the ingredients that go into them. We don't use the leanest, most expensive beef in the market because hamburgers require fat; if they're too lean they'll be dry. We use chuck, which has the best flavor, with a fat content between 20 to 23%, and we grind it ourselves. We put Dijon mustard on the bottom bun and top the hamburger with crumbled Grafton white cheddar cheese (never pre-sliced yellow cheddar), seared or grilled onion, thinly sliced tomato, butter lettuce, and Russian dressing (which I prefer to ketchup—I reserve that for the fries—but you can use both).

You will probably buy your hamburger meat already ground, which is fine. Just make sure that it has the right fat content, and don't handle it too much. The hamburger should be formed by gently patting it, not by squeezing or pressing. Hamburgers should be crumbly, not solid. They are delicate and a little tricky to flip, but the resulting texture is worth the extra care. The size and thickness of the patty should be determined by the size of your hamburger bun; it should be slightly bigger, as it will shrink during cooking. So if the bun you are using is big, your patty will be fairly thin and will probably only require about 1½ to 2 minutes cooking on each side. Make sure the bun you use is a soft one; if the crust is hard, everything will squeeze out onto your lap when you bite into it.

1½	pounds chuck (20 to 23% fat)
1½	teaspoons kosher salt
½	teaspoon freshly ground black pepper
4	hamburger buns, sliced in half
1	to 2 tablespoons Dijon mustard
2	to 3 teaspoons canola oil
4	ounces white cheddar cheese, crumbled (½ cup)
1	medium or ½ large onion, sliced in rings (about 6 ounces)
3	tablespoons Russian Dressing (page 22)
1	large or 2 medium tomatoes, sliced about ¼ inch thick (thin slices are important)
4	leaves bibb lettuce

1. If grinding the meat yourself, season with ½ teaspoon of the salt and ¼ teaspoon of the pepper and keep the meat and the grinder very cold until ready to grind. Grind the meat. If using ground chuck, gently and quickly mix in ½ teaspoon of the salt and ¼ teaspoon of the pepper with your fingertips. Measure out four 6-ounce portions. Using the buns as your guide, gently form into a patty that is a little larger than your buns. Set on a plate or a platter and keep in the refrigerator while you heat a cast iron pan over medium-high heat.

2. Grill or toast the buns very lightly. Spread 1 to 1½ teaspoons Dijon mustard over the bottom of each bun and arrange on plates or on a platter. Season the hamburger patties on both sides with the remaining salt and pepper. Add the canola oil to the pan and two of the hamburger patties (you will probably have to cook them in batches). Cook ½ inch thick patties for 1½ to 2 minutes on each side for rare, 2½ minutes for medium-rare. To test for doneness, press gently in the middle. They should give a little. Use a spatula to turn them and flip gently, as they will be crumbly. Once you turn them over, arrange the cheese on top and cover with a lid or a bowl so that the cheese will melt quickly. Remove from the pan and place on top of the bun.

3. Add the sliced onions to the pan and sear for about 2 minutes, just until slightly soft and colored. Remove from the heat.

4. Place about 1½ teaspoons Russian dressing on top of the cheese, and a layer of onion on top of that. Add a tomato slice and a lettuce leaf. Top with a little more Russian dressing (or ketchup if desired), then the top bun. Cut in half, and serve.

beef goulash [makes 6 servings]

Paprika is the most important ingredient in this Austro-Hungarian classic. It should be sweet Hungarian paprika, not smoked Spanish paprika. Keep it in the freezer in a well-sealed container and it will stay fresh for several months. If it's been sitting out for more than 6 months, discard it and get a new batch. Begin this stew a couple of days ahead so you can marinate the meat and easily degrease the finished sauce.

3	pounds skirt steak or beef chuck or round, cut in 1½-inch pieces
2	tablespoons canola oil
3	tablespoons sweet Hungarian paprika
	Kosher salt and freshly ground black pepper
6	fat garlic cloves, halved, green shoots removed, and sliced
1	large or 2 medium onions, chopped
3	ounces thick-cut bacon, cut in ¼-inch-wide strips
¾	teaspoon caraway seeds
2	teaspoons tomato paste
1½	cups chopped, peeled, and seeded tomatoes (fresh or canned)
½	pound sweet red peppers (1 large or 2 medium), roasted (page 175), peeled, seeded, and sliced (retain any juices)
1½	cups (one 12-ounce bottle) lager beer

1. This is best if you begin 2 days before you wish to serve it. Marinate the meat. Place it in a large bowl and toss with the canola oil, paprika, 1 teaspoon salt, ½ teaspoon freshly ground pepper, 4 of the garlic cloves, and half the onion. Knead the mixture well so that the seasonings penetrate the meat. Cover and refrigerate overnight.

2. The next day, scrape the onions and garlic off the meat and set aside with the remaining onions and garlic. Heat a large, heavy casserole or Dutch oven over medium-high heat and add the bacon. Cook until the bacon renders its fat, then remove it from the pan with a slotted spoon. Set aside in a bowl.

3. Add the meat to the pan in batches and brown on all sides. Remove with a slotted spoon and set aside in a bowl with the bacon (there will be a lot of juice in the pan; pour off the liquid from the pan between batches but retain with the meat.).

4. Add the remaining onions to the pan with ½ teaspoon salt and ½ teaspoon pepper. Turn the heat to medium and cook, stirring, until the onions soften, about 5 minutes. Add the remaining garlic, caraway, and tomato paste and cook, stirring, until the tomato paste caramelizes slightly (it will turn a rusty color). Add the tomatoes and cook, stirring, for about 5 minutes, until they have cooked down slightly. Add the roasted peppers and their juice and stir together for a few more minutes, then return the meat and bacon to the pan with any juices that have accumulated in the bowl. Add the beer, 1 teaspoon salt, and water if necessary. The meat should be almost submerged. Bring to a simmer, cover, and simmer over low heat for 3 hours, until the meat is fork-tender. From time to time, skim the fat from the top of the simmering stew. Taste and adjust the seasonings.

5. Using a slotted spoon, remove the meat and vegetables from the liquid and place in a bowl. Pour the liquid into another bowl. Cover and refrigerate overnight if serving the following day (if serving the same day, allow to rest for 1 hour and degrease, following the directions below). The next day, lift off the fat that has accumulated on top of the liquid and discard. Combine the meat and gravy in a pot, reheat gently, correct the seasonings, and serve, with noodles, Spaetzle (page 211), rice, or Parsleyed Potatoes (page 206).

[HOW TO DEGREASE A WARM BROTH]
Allow the broth to rest for 15 minutes, or up to 1 hour if possible, so that the fat rises to the surface. Dip the bottom of a ladle into the center of the pot and rotate it around in a small circle to push the grease to the edges of the pot. Without tipping the bowl of the ladle into the liquid, push the ladle bowl straight down and push it toward the edge of the pot, then slowly press down until the top of the ladle bowl is just barely level to the top of the grease, so that the grease slips into the ladle. Continue, beginning in the center of the pot and pushing out to the sides, until you no longer see a greasy layer on the surface of the broth or gravy.

flemish beef and beer stew [makes 4 to 6 servings]

Most of us can imagine what French, German, and Italian cooking is, but the word *Belgian* doesn't conjure up an image. If it did, this would be the dish. It's a layered beef stew, sweet with caramelized onions and dark beer, with a bit of a vinegary edge. If you want to make this a day ahead, refrigerate before proceeding with step 5. The next day, scrape the fat from the top, then reheat and proceed with step 5.

2	pounds boneless chuck or round steak
	Kosher salt and freshly ground black pepper
2	tablespoons all-purpose flour
2	tablespoons canola oil
4	ounces bacon, diced
2	tablespoons unsalted butter
2	large or 3 medium onions, cut in half, then thinly sliced crosswise
1	tablespoon dark brown sugar
1	tablespoon cider vinegar
2¼	cups dark beer
	A bouquet garni made with a bay leaf, a tarragon sprig, a few parsley sprigs and a few thyme sprigs (page 66)
6	ounces country bread, cut in ½-inch-thick slices
2	tablespoons Dijon mustard
	Steamed or boiled potatoes, mashed potatoes (page 202), or rice, for serving

1. Cut the meat with the grain into ½-inch-thick slices. Season with about 1 teaspoon salt and ½ teaspoon pepper, and lightly dredge in the flour.

2. Heat 2 tablespoons canola oil in a wide, heavy skillet over high heat and brown the meat for about 2½ minutes on each side, in batches so you don't crowd the pan. Set aside on a plate.

3. Allow the skillet to cool slightly and add the bacon. Cook over medium heat until it begins to soften all the way through and render its fat, about 3 minutes, then add the butter. When the butter begins to foam, add the onions and 1 teaspoon salt. Cook, stirring and scraping the bottom of the pan to deglaze, and turn the heat to medium-low. Cook the onions gently until light brown, stirring often, about 20 minutes. Add the sugar and vinegar and cook for a few minutes. Add the beer and bring to a boil, stirring and scraping the bottom of the pan. Add ½ teaspoon salt and ¼ teaspoon pepper, and remove from the heat.

4. Preheat the oven to 350°F (or you can cook this over a low heat on top of the stove). Layer one third of the onions on the bottom of a 3-quart casserole. Layer half the meat over the onions. Layer another third of the onions over the meat, and the remaining meat over the onions. Top with the remaining onions. Insert the bouquet garni into the onions and pour on the liquid from the pan. Cover the pot and place in the oven or over low heat and simmer gently for 2½ hours, or until the meat is fork-tender.

5. Spread the slices of bread with mustard on both sides. Lay the slices over the top of the casserole in a single layer, and press them down slightly so they absorb some moisture. Return to the oven for 20 minutes. Remove from the heat and serve with steamed or boiled potatoes, mashed potatoes, or rice, and accompany with beer.

short rib pot au feu [makes 8 servings]

This is a French classic. We call it "Pot of Food" in the kitchen at Campanile because it makes enough for a crowd. Although this isn't labor-intensive, it is time-consuming and requires a watchful eye because the meat must be brought to a simmer very slowly and then cooked slowly, skimming often, for a long time.

[MEAT]

3	pounds beef short ribs, off the bone
3	pounds veal short ribs, cut into single-bone portions
3	quarts water
1	quart Chicken Stock (page 66) (or use 4 quarts water in all)
4	teaspoons kosher salt
	A bouquet garni made with a bay leaf, 5 parsley sprigs, 1 teaspoon peppercorns, 2 thyme sprigs, and ¼ teaspoon fennel seeds (page 66)
	Greens from 4 leeks, cut in half lengthwise and cleaned
1	head of garlic, cut in half horizontally
2	medium onions, each peeled, halved, and each half studded with a clove
3	medium carrots, peeled and quartered

[VEGETABLES]

1	small cabbage, cut in 8 wedges
1	bulb fennel, cut in eighths or thick slices
4	parsnips or small turnips (or both), peeled and quartered
12	medium boiling potatoes, scrubbed and cut in half
4	carrots, peeled and quartered
12	boiling onions, peeled
	The white part of 4 leeks, cut in half lengthwise (save the greens for the meat stock)

[CONDIMENTS]

Coarse sea salt or fleur de sel
Cornichons (can serve a selection)
French Dijon mustard or a selection of coarse and smooth mustards

1. The day before you wish to serve this dish, cook the meat: Arrange the meat in a large stockpot or Dutch oven. Add the water and chicken stock. Place over medium-high heat and bring to a bare simmer, being careful not to allow the liquid to boil; this will take some time. Skim off any impurities and foam that rise to the top, wait 10 minutes, then skim again. Turn the heat to low, and continue to cook and skim, keeping the mixture at a bare simmer for 30 minutes. Strain over a bowl and rinse the pot. Line a strainer with a linen napkin and strain the liquid again, then return to the pot with the meat. Bring back to a simmer. Add the salt, bouquet garni, leek greens, garlic bulb, onions, and 3 medium carrots. Skim again, cover, and continue to simmer gently, skimming often, for 3 hours, until the meat is moist and fork-tender. Remove from the heat and allow to cool for 30 minutes.

2. Using tongs or a perforated spoon, remove the meats from the stock and transfer to a bowl. Strain the stock into another bowl through a strainer lined with a double thickness of cheesecloth, pour over the meat, and refrigerate overnight.

3. Remove the stock and meat from the refrigerator and lift off the fat. Remove the meat from the gelatinous stock and transfer the stock to a large pot. Reheat until it has become liquid again, and strain again through a napkin-lined strainer. Return to the pot, without the meat, bring to a simmer, taste, and adjust the seasonings.

4. Cook the vegetables: Bring a medium-size pot of generously salted water to a boil and add the cabbage. Blanch for 5 minutes and transfer to a bowl of ice water. Add the fennel to the boiling water and blanch for 2 minutes. Now add all of the vegetables (including the blanched ones) to the simmering stock. Cover and boil gently until tender, 20 to 25 minutes. Using tongs or a skimmer, transfer the vegetables to one or two platters. Keep warm.

5. Add the meat to the simmering broth and heat through. Remove from the broth and arrange on a platter. Spoon some broth over the meat and the vegetables, and sprinkle with coarse salt, preferably fleur de sel. Serve the meat and vegetables hot, with the condiments and additional broth.

[NOTE] You can serve the broth as a first course. Keep the meat and vegetables warm and serve as directed.

beer-braised brisket with caramelized root vegetables

[makes 8 to 10 servings]

Brisket is one of our most popular fall/winter Monday Night Family Dinners. There are times when you need a brisket recipe, and this one will serve that purpose. Marinate the meat overnight for the best flavor and make sure to buy your brisket with all of the fat on. Don't trim it before you cook it; trim it afterward. The fat bastes the meat as it cooks, so your brisket won't be dry. For these caramelized vegetables you can substitute other root vegetables, like turnips for the parsnips, if you wish. Root vegetables are by nature high in sugar, so they caramelize well (as opposed to, say, spinach). If butter is a problem, substitute extra virgin olive oil when you finish them in the pan before serving.

[BRISKET]

1	5- to 6-pound brisket
	Kosher salt
2	teaspoons cracked black peppercorns
1	medium onion, sliced
1	large carrot, halved lengthwise and sliced
1½	cups (one 12-ounce bottle) dark beer
3	garlic cloves, crushed
	Handful of thyme sprigs
2	tablespoons canola oil
3	cups Chicken Stock (page 66, or commercial)

[CARAMELIZED VEGETABLES]

1	pint boiling onions
2	tablespoons canola oil
¾	pound carrots, peeled and halved lengthwise if small, quartered if large
¾	pound parsnips, peeled, halved lengthwise if small, quartered if large, and cored, or ¾ pound turnips, peeled and quartered
1	celery root, peeled and cut in 1-inch chunks
	Kosher salt and freshly ground black pepper
2	tablespoons unsalted butter

1. The day before you wish to serve this, marinate the meat: Sprinkle both sides with kosher salt and cracked pepper, using about 1 teaspoon of each per side, and place in a roasting pan. Top with the onion and carrot and pour in the beer. Turn the meat over, add the garlic and thyme sprigs, and cover the pan tightly. Refrigerate overnight.

2. The next day, remove the meat from the marinade, brush off the vegetables back into the marinade, and pat the meat dry with paper towels. Preheat the oven to 350°F. In a skillet large enough to hold the meat, heat 2 tablespoons canola oil over high heat and sear the meat, fat side down first, on both sides, about 5 minutes per side. Place fat side up in the roasting pan and dispose of the fat from the skillet. Add the vegetables and marinade to the skillet and bring to a boil, stirring to deglaze the bottom of the pan. Boil for 5 minutes and add the chicken stock. Bring to a simmer and add 1 teaspoon salt. Pour over the brisket. Spoon the vegetables on top of the meat and cover the pan tightly with foil. Place in the oven and roast for 4 hours, or until the meat pulls apart easily with a fork. Remove from the oven and allow to cool for 30 minutes.

3. Remove the meat from the roasting pan and place on a cutting board. Cover with foil to keep warm. Strain the braising liquid through a medium strainer or a colander into a bowl. Cool for 1 hour if possible and skim off the fat (page 121). Turn the oven up to 400°F.

4. Make the vegetables: Bring a medium pot of generously salted water to a boil. Meanwhile, fill a bowl with ice and water. Blanch the boiling onions for 3 minutes. Transfer to the ice water, allow to cool slightly, then drain and peel.

5. Heat the oil in a large skillet over medium-high heat. Add the vegetables and sear until lightly browned on the surface, about 8 minutes. Transfer to the roasting pan, season with salt and pepper, and add 1 cup of the strained roasting liquid. Cover and return to the oven. Braise for 20 to 30 minutes, until tender. Remove from the liquid with a slotted spoon.

6. When ready to serve, trim the fat from the meat, slice, and place on a platter. Warm the braising liquid. Heat the butter in the skillet in which you seared the vegetables over medium-high heat and add back the vegetables. Cook until lightly caramelized. Serve the meat with the vegetables and broth.

prime rib with yorkshire pudding [makes 6 servings]

I'll admit, this beef is not the healthiest thing in the world either to eat or to raise. But once in a while it's irresistible. We use prime beef that has been dry aged for 28 days. Make sure to let the meat come to room temperature before you roast it.

1	2-rib standing roast, bone in, cut from the bottom end, at room temperature
	Kosher salt
1	tablespoon canola oil
2	tablespoons cracked black peppercorns
	Yorkshire Pudding (page 216)
	Horseradish Cream or Anchoïade (recipes follow), for serving

1. Preheat the oven to 350°F. Season the meat with a light dusting of kosher salt. Rub with the canola oil, then cover with a thin crust of cracked black peppercorns and place in a roasting pan.

2. Place in the oven and roast 15 minutes for each pound of meat. If you have 6 pounds, check after 1½ hours. Insert a meat thermometer into the middle of the rib roast. It should read 120°F to 125°F for rare. Remove from the oven and allow to stand for 15 minutes or longer before slicing.

3. Meanwhile, pour off the fat and use for Yorkshire pudding.

4. Serve with horseradish cream or anchoïade and Yorkshire pudding.

[HORSERADISH CREAM makes about ¾ cup]

Use the thick bottom part of the horseradish, which is more pungent and less woody than the thin end. Use a good sharp grater, and be careful of your eyes when grating the radishes.

1	cup finely grated horseradish
2	tablespoons champagne vinegar
½	cup crème fraîche
¼	cup heavy cream
½	teaspoon kosher salt
	Pinch of freshly ground black pepper

Combine all the ingredients. Refrigerate in a covered container until shortly before using. Taste and adjust the vinegar to the desired sharpness. Stir again before serving. Serve with roast beef, steak, or other cold leftover meat.

[ANCHOÏADE makes 1⅓ cups]

Anchoïade falls into the mayonnaise family of French sauces, and specifically into the loud, opinionated Mediterranean garlic mayonnaise branch. It's one of my favorite variations.

2	fat garlic cloves, peeled, halved, green shoots removed
4	anchovy fillets, soaked in water for 15 minutes (see Note)
¼	teaspoon kosher salt
2	teaspoons capers, rinsed
6	kalamata olives, pitted
1	large egg yolk
2	teaspoons white wine or champagne vinegar
½	cup canola oil
½	cup extra virgin olive oil

[NOTE] If you're using salt-packed anchovies, which are packed whole, rinse them and take the fillets off the bone. Soak for 30 minutes in cold water, then rinse and pat dry.

1. Place the garlic, anchovy fillets, salt, capers, and 3 olives in a mortar and pestle and mash to a smooth paste. Add the egg yolk and vinegar and work in. Slowly begin to drizzle in the canola oil, stirring constantly with the pestle. When you've added about a third of the canola oil and the mixture has begun to emulsify, scrape the mixture into a medium bowl. Switch to a whisk. Wet a dish towel and wrap it around the base of the bowl so the bowl doesn't move around and walk away while you whisk.

2. Continue to add the remaining canola oil while whisking constantly. When all the canola oil has been added, drizzle in the olive oil, whisking all the while. Once the mixture has emulsified you can add the oil a little more quickly. When all the oil has been added, taste and adjust the seasoning. Cut the remaining olives into slivers and fold in. Cover and refrigerate until ready to use.

steak bordelaise [makes 4 servings]

We've made this sauce every night at Campanile for twenty years; we like to call it our A-1 sauce. It's important to use a heavy skillet, such as a well-seasoned cast-iron pan, so the pan will be hot enough to cook the steak properly without scorching it. It's also important to choose steaks that are at least one inch thick. That said, you do not have to use the most expensive steaks (porterhouse, sirloin, New York); as long as they're thick enough, flatiron and hanger steaks will work for this. You also needn't use an expensive Bordeaux for the sauce, despite the name. A California Merlot will be just fine.

1	tablespoon canola oil
	Kosher salt and cracked black peppercorns
2	16-ounce steaks, at least 1 inch thick, at or just below room temperature
3	tablespoons unsalted butter
3	tablespoons minced shallots
¼	cup red wine, such as Merlot
½	cup Port wine
½	cup beef stock
2	tablespoons minced fresh flat-leaf parsley

1. Heat the canola oil over high heat in a heavy skillet until just below smoking. Meanwhile, generously salt and pepper the steaks on both sides and press the seasoning into the meat.

2. Add the steaks to the pan and cook for 4 to 5 minutes per side, depending on how rare you like them. Remove to a warm platter and pour off the fat from the pan.

3. Turn the heat down and add 1 tablespoon of the butter, the minced shallots, and a generous pinch of cracked pepper to the pan. Cook the shallots until tender, about 3 minutes, then add the red wine and port, stirring the bottom and sides of the pan with a wooden spoon to deglaze. Reduce the liquid by about two-thirds, until the bubbles breaking in the pan are tiny. Add the beef stock, bring to a boil, and reduce by half, about 5 minutes. Stir in the minced parsley. Strain and return to the pan, but keep the pan off the heat. Swirl in the remaining 2 tablespoons of butter, a teaspoon at a time.

4. Slice the steak and serve with the sauce.

steak with anchovy butter [makes 4 to 6 main course servings]

Anchovy is an important ingredient in all steak sauces because it goes so well with beef. Even if you don't think you like anchovies, you're eating them every time you use Worcestershire, A-1 Sauce, or any of the many commercial prepared steak sauces. For this recipe you can grill the steaks or cook them in a very hot pan (the instructions here are for pan-cooking). You can use an economical steak like a flatiron or hanger steak, or a more expensive New York, porterhouse, or sirloin. No matter which type you cook, if you like steak you'll like it even more with anchovy butter.

[ANCHOVY BUTTER]
- 1 fat garlic clove, cut in half, green shoot removed
- 3 anchovy fillets, soaked in water for 15 minutes (30 minutes if salt-packed), rinsed and patted dry
- ⅛ teaspoon kosher salt
- 1 teaspoon extra virgin olive oil
- 2 tablespoons coarsely chopped fresh flat-leaf parsley
- ½ cup (1 stick) unsalted butter, at room temperature
  A few grinds of the pepper mill

[STEAK]
- 2 pounds steak (individual steaks or larger steaks), at or just below room temperature
  Kosher salt and freshly ground black pepper
- 1 tablespoon canola oil

I always cut my garlic cloves in half if I'm going to mash them. I do it to look for the green shoot, which must be removed, but also because it's easier to mash them if they have a flat side. Otherwise they'll bounce around when you hit them with a pestle.

I use a rough chop of parsley for this, rather than finely chopped parsley, because there will be more flavor to extract as I grind the leaves in my mortar and pestle.

1. Combine the garlic, anchovy fillets, salt, and olive oil in a mortar and pestle and mash to a smooth paste. Add the parsley and grind with the pestle until well blended with the garlic and anchovies. Work in the butter and add a few grinds of the pepper mill. Set aside. Taste and adjust the salt (add up to another ⅛ teaspoon).

2. Heat a heavy skillet over high heat. Pat the steaks dry and season generously on both sides with salt and pepper. With your fingertips, press the seasonings into the steaks.

3. When the pan is hot, add the canola oil. Heat to just

below smoking and add the steaks, in batches if necessary to avoid crowding the pan. Cook for 3 minutes on each side for rare 1-inch-thick steaks, 4 to 5 minutes for thicker steaks.

4. Remove the steaks from the pan and immediately dollop 4 to 6 heaped tablespoons of the butter over the top. Let the meat rest for a couple of minutes, then slice and serve at once.

VARIATION / STEAK WITH STILTON (OR ROQUEFORT)
Cook the steaks as instructed above. Substitute 2 ounces Stilton or Roquefort and 4 tablespoons softened butter, creamed together, for the anchovy butter. Place 4 to 6 dollops over the cooked steaks and proceed as instructed above.

VARIATION / STEAK WITH BÉARNAISE
Béarnaise is a variation on hollandaise, and it's almost as easy to make. What makes it sing are the fresh herbs, particularly the chervil and tarragon, and the splash of vinegar. It's a classic sauce with meats, especially steak, and it's delicious on a hamburger. You can make other variations by substituting different herbs, such as dill or marjoram. Use about half the amount this recipe makes with the steak. Refrigerate the remaining sauce and use up within 2 days.

- 2 tablespoons minced shallot
- 2 tablespoons white wine vinegar
- ½ cup dry white wine
- 1½ teaspoons finely chopped chervil
- 1½ teaspoons finely chopped tarragon
- 1½ teaspoons finely chopped fresh flat-leaf parsley
- 1 tablespoon finely chopped chives
- 1 large or extra-large egg yolk
- 1 cup (2 sticks) unsalted butter, melted and hot (but not scalding)
- ½ teaspoon freshly squeezed lemon juice
  Very small pinch of cayenne
- ¼ teaspoon kosher salt

(continues)

1. Combine the shallot, vinegar, wine, and herbs in a small saucepan and bring to a boil over medium heat. Boil until the mixture is reduced to ¼ cup.

2. Bring 1 cup of water to a boil in the bottom of a double boiler, which you can fashion out of a saucepan and a bowl that sits on the top. The bottom of the bowl should not touch the water.

3. Transfer the wine mixture to the bowl and add the egg yolk. Whisk together over the simmering water. Keep the heat at medium-low and whisk continually. From time to time, test the temperature of the mixture with the back of your middle finger, at the knuckle, where it is most sensitive to heat. When the mixture is hot and thick, remove from the heat.

4. Moisten a towel, make a ring with it on your work surface, and set the bowl on the ring. This will keep it from spinning and walking away from you as you whisk. Gradually whisk in the butter, a small ladleful at a time. The mixture should emulsify and become glossy. When all the butter has been added, whisk in the lemon juice, cayenne, and salt. Allow it to sit for 5 minutes so the salt dissolves. Taste and adjust seasoning.

[NOTE] If the sauce begins to curdle around the edges while you're making it, immediately remove the bowl from the heat and add ½ teaspoon of cold water to drop the temperature. Whisk vigorously.

santa maria barbecue [makes 6 to 8 servings]

Santa Maria is in the Central Coast region of California, a grassy area with wet winters, dry summers, and lots of oak trees. The Spanish made this cattle country when they colonized California. The tradition of the barbecue evolved during the nineteenth century, when vaqueros from the huge cattle ranches would gather at round-up time to help each other with branding. The host would prepare Spanish-style barbecues that included beef grilled over hot oak fires, accompanied with salsa, stewed pinquito beans, and bread for dipping in the meat juices. The steak that was favored was a triangular cut from the bottom sirloin called the tri-tip. It's a flavorful cut, leaner than top sirloin and less expensive. My Santa Maria barbecue uses a spicy dry rub, and the traditional tri-tip is my beef of choice. Yours will be truly authentic if you grill it over a hot oak fire, but any barbecue will do. A two-pound tri-tip will do for a family of four to six. This one serves a bigger crowd. This is a great dish for the Fourth of July. Serve it with the Grilled Corn with Herb Butter on page 232.

3	fat garlic cloves, cut in half, green shoots removed
1	tablespoon olive oil
	Kosher salt
2	tablespoons cumin seeds
1	tablespoon plus 1 teaspoon whole or cracked peppercorns
1	dried ancho chile, seeded, deveined, and broken up
2	teaspoons paprika
½	teaspoon cayenne
1	3-pound tri-tip steak

When working with chiles and rubs, wear rubber gloves. If you don't wear rubber gloves, make sure you don't handle your contact lenses for at least 12 hours. I learned this the hard way.

1. Make the paste and marinate the meat 12 to 24 hours before cooking: To make the paste, first place the garlic in a mortar and pestle with 1 teaspoon of the olive oil and a pinch of salt, and mash to a paste. Set aside. Then, in a small pan over medium-high heat, toast the cumin seeds and peppercorns until fragrant, watching the pan closely and shaking it so the spices don't burn. Add the ancho chile, paprika, and cayenne to the pan and continue to heat until the spices are fragrant and their heat volatile. Together they should emit a toasty popcorn aroma and just begin to smoke.

2. Transfer the toasted spices immediately from the pan to a bowl. Allow to cool, then grind in a spice mill. Stir into the garlic puree. Add 2 teaspoons olive oil and 2 to 4 teaspoons water as necessary to make a dense but spreadable paste.

3. Sprinkle each side of the tri-tip with 1 teaspoon salt, and rub it into the meat. Rub the paste into both sides of the tri-tip, massaging it well into the meat. Wrap tightly with plastic and refrigerate for 12 to 24 hours.

4. Make a very hot fire in a barbecue. Remove the beef from the refrigerator and using your fingertips or a pastry scraper, scrape off any excess paste. Season the meat again with salt. Sear the beef on the hottest part of the grill, about 4 minutes per side. Move it to the side, where the heat is cooler and not so direct. Cook for another 10 to 20 minutes, depending on the thickness of the steaks, turning the meat halfway through. Insert a meat thermometer at the thickest part of the tri-tip and remove the steaks when the temperature reaches 125°F for rare or 135°F for medium-rare. Allow the steak to sit for at least 15 minutes before serving. Serve with Fresh Tomato Salsa (page 144) if desired and Campanile Beans (page 218).

campanile beef, pork, and chicken meatballs

[makes 6 cups of meatball mixture, yielding about 70 small meatballs]

These are moist, light, and delicate. Use them for the world's best Spaghetti with Meatballs (page 89). The recipe makes a lot of meatballs, which takes some time, but they freeze well, and if you have them on hand you can have terrific spaghetti and meatballs in no time. If you don't have a meat-grinding attachment for your mixer, have your butcher grind the pork, beef, and chicken breast. You shouldn't try to do this with a food processor because the mixture will be pasty.

¾	pound pork butt or shoulder, cut in 1-inch cubes or ground
¾	pound chicken breast, cut in 1-inch cubes or ground
¾	pound beef chuck, cut in 1-inch cubes or ground
1	tablespoon extra virgin olive oil
1	medium or ½ large onion (about 6 ounces), finely chopped
2	garlic cloves, halved, green shoots removed, and minced
4	ounces white or cremini mushrooms, cleaned and chopped
1½	teaspoons kosher salt
1	teaspoon cracked fennel seeds
¾	cup cold dry white wine
4	ounces bread, crusts removed, cut in 1-inch cubes
3	tablespoons minced fresh flat-leaf parsley
½	teaspoon freshly ground black pepper

1. [IF THE MEAT HAS ALREADY BEEN GROUND]

Combine the meats in a large bowl. Heat the olive oil in a large, heavy skillet over medium heat and add the onion. Cook gently until tender, 5 to 8 minutes, and add the garlic. Stir until fragrant, about 1 minute, and add the mushrooms, ½ teaspoon salt, and the cracked fennel seeds. Cook until tender, about 7 minutes. Add ¼ cup of the white wine, bring to a simmer, add the bread, and stir together. Remove from the heat and stir together so that the bread absorbs the moisture in the pan. Transfer to a food processor fitted with the steel blade and pulse to a coarse puree. Stir in the parsley and toss the mixture with the meat. Add the remaining 1 teaspoon salt and ½ teaspoon pepper, and combine well. Chill for at least 30 minutes in the refrigerator.

[IF YOU ARE GRINDING THE MEAT YOURSELF]

Combine the meats in a large bowl. Heat the olive oil in a large, heavy skillet over medium heat and add the onion. Cook gently until tender, 5 to 8 minutes, and add the garlic.

Stir until fragrant, about 1 minute, and add the mushrooms, ½ teaspoon salt, and the cracked fennel seeds. Cook until tender, about 7 minutes. Add ¼ cup of the white wine, bring to a simmer, add the bread, and stir together. Remove from the heat and stir together so the bread absorbs the moisture in the pan. Stir in the parsley and toss the mixture with the meat. Add the remaining 1 teaspoon salt and ½ teaspoon pepper and combine well. Put the mixture in the refrigerator and chill for 2 to 4 hours or overnight, or place in the freezer for 1 hour, until very cold. Grind the mixture through the meat-grinding attachment of your standing mixer.

2. Place the ground meat mixture in a standing mixer fitted with the paddle attachment. Add the remaining ½ cup very cold white wine and beat at medium speed for about 1 minute. Turn the speed to low and beat for another 2 to 3 minutes, until well mixed and it holds together when you pinch off a clump. Scrape into a container, cover, and refrigerate until very cold.

3. To check the seasoning, sauté a small spoonful in a small amount of olive oil and taste. Adjust the seasonings if necessary. To form meatballs, fill a small container with water and dip 2 spoons into the water. Line a sheet pan with parchment. Scoop up a spoonful of the meat mixture and scoop the meatball off the first spoon with the help of the other spoon. Scrape off onto the parchment paper. Shape all the meatballs, dipping the spoons into the water each time to keep the meat from sticking to them. Freeze the meatballs you won't be using, right on the parchment-covered baking sheet, and when frozen transfer to freezer bags. Thaw overnight in the refrigerator.

4. To cook, lightly flour the meatballs and brown on both sides over medium heat in a small amount of canola oil, about 4 minutes per side, until firm to the touch. If using in tomato sauce, simmer the browned meatballs in the tomato sauce for 20 minutes.

bacon-wrapped meat loaf [makes 10 to 12 servings]

This one is not my mother's meat loaf, although meat loaf is one dish my mother could make and I have a good memory of hers. Our bacon-wrapped meat loaf is much more moist and flavorful than Mom's, with three kinds of meat instead of one; but it isn't much harder to make it. The meat should be coarsely ground, and you should use meat that has around 20 percent fat. Otherwise your meat loaf will be dry and flavorless. Meat loaf is the closest thing Americans have to pâté. We certainly don't associate it with fine dining, but it can be very good, and when we offer it at the restaurant, it flies off the menu.

8   to 10 thin-cut slices bacon, as needed
1   cup fresh bread crumbs
½   cup whole milk
1   tablespoon canola oil
1   cup finely diced onion
½   cup finely diced celery
2   fat garlic cloves, halved, green shoots removed, and minced
1   tablespoon plus ½ teaspoon kosher salt
2   large eggs, beaten
3   tablespoons chopped fresh flat-leaf parsley
1   pound ground beef
1   pound ground pork
1   pound ground veal
1   teaspoon freshly ground black pepper
2   tablespoons ketchup
8   to 10 large sage leaves

1. Preheat the oven to 350°F. Slice 2 bacon slices into ¼-inch-wide strips and set aside. Line a 9 x 5-inch loaf pan with the remaining slices, alternating the fat and thin ends.

2. In a small bowl, soak the bread crumbs in the milk for a few minutes, then drain and squeeze out the excess milk.

3. Heat the canola oil in a medium skillet over medium heat and add the slivered bacon, the onion, celery, and garlic with ½ teaspoon salt. Cook, stirring often, until the vegetables are tender, about 5 minutes. Remove from the heat and transfer to a plate.

4. In a medium or large bowl, beat together the eggs and soaked bread crumbs. Add the onion mixture and the parsley and combine well. In another large bowl, or in the bowl of a standing mixer fitted with the paddle, combine the meats, the remaining tablespoon of salt, and the pepper, and knead together with your hands or mix at low speed for 2 minutes to combine.

5. A handful or a large spoonful at a time, add half the meat to the egg mixture and combine well. Now stir the combined egg and meat mixture into the remaining meat mixture in the large bowl and combine well. Take up handfuls and slap between your hands to expel air, then fill the loaf pan. It should fill right to the top. Using a spoon, make a depression—a shallow trough—down the center of the loaf, and fill the trough with the ketchup. Garnish with sage leaves, pressing them into the top.

6. Place the filled loaf pan on a baking sheet and place in the oven on the middle rack. Bake for 1½ hours, or until a meat thermometer registers at least 140°F when stuck into the middle. Remove from the oven and allow to rest for at least 30 minutes. There will be quite a lot of liquid in the pan, some of which will be reabsorbed by the meat loaf as it cools and settles.

7. Tip the remaining liquid from the pan into a bowl, then strain the liquid and skim off the fat (or, if not serving right away, refrigerate until the fat congeals on the top, then lift it off). Slice the meat loaf and serve the juice on the side, to spoon over each serving. You can also serve it with more ketchup.

[NOTE] This is also excellent cold. If you wish, you can make this more like a pâté by placing another loaf pan on top of the cooked meat loaf and weighting the pan, then refrigerating for several hours.

seven-hour leg of lamb [makes 8 servings]

This will not turn out medium-rare. When you cook leg of lamb at a very low temperature for a very long time, it becomes so tender you can eat it with a spoon. The ingredients that accompany the lamb during its long roast dissolve into a ready-made sauce. The shiitakes and sun-dried tomatoes act as seasoning and contribute great depth of flavor, quite different from fresh mushrooms and tomatoes.

1	4½- to 5-pound leg of lamb, trimmed of fat
9	garlic cloves, halved, green shoots removed, and sliced
6	anchovy fillets, cut in ½-inch pieces
	Kosher salt and freshly ground black pepper
2	tablespoons canola oil
1	pound onions, sliced
½	cup dry white wine
1½	cups Chicken Stock, (page 66, or commercial)
2	fresh rosemary sprigs
1	pound whole cherry tomatoes or chopped tomatoes
½	ounce dried shiitake mushrooms, broken into pieces
½	ounce sun-dried tomatoes
1	teaspoon anchovy paste

1. Preheat the oven to 250°F. Make several slits in the leg of lamb and place a slice of garlic and a piece of anchovy into each slit. Salt and pepper the lamb generously.

2. Heat the canola oil over high heat in a large, heavy, ovenproof casserole large enough to accommodate the lamb. Brown the lamb on both sides and remove to a sheet pan. Lay the onions over the bottom of the pot. Add the wine and bring to a simmer. Let simmer for a few minutes, then return the lamb to the pot. Add the chicken stock, rosemary, tomatoes, any remaining garlic, dried mushrooms and dried tomatoes, and the anchovy paste, and bring back to a simmer. Simmer 10 minutes. Add 1 teaspoon salt, cover, and place in the oven. Braise for 7 to 8 hours, basting every 45 minutes or so. When the lamb is done, you should be able to pull it from the bone with a spoon (but don't do it).

3. Remove the lamb from the broth and place on a platter. Cover with foil to keep warm. Strain the broth through a colander. Degrease (page 121) and strain through a fine-mesh strainer into a saucepan. Bring to a boil and reduce by half. Correct the seasoning and serve as gravy with the lamb. Serve with Campanile Beans, preferably flageolets or white beans (page 218; I suggest you omit the bacon).

braised lamb shanks [makes 6 servings]

Braised lamb shanks look dramatic. They're big, about the size of a turkey leg, and they're braised until they have a deep, glossy sheen. Use a deep baking dish or casserole, and cook them slowly like a stew, either in the oven or over a low burner. If you can start a couple of days ahead, you will be able to refrigerate the braising liquid overnight and easily lift off the fat before reheating.

[LAMB AND MARINADE]

6	lamb shanks, about 1 pound each
	Kosher salt and freshly ground black pepper
5	large garlic cloves, halved, green shoots removed, and coarsely chopped
3	anchovy fillets, coarsely chopped
8	whole allspice berries, crushed
8	whole juniper berries, crushed
¼	cup chopped fresh flat-leaf parsley
1	tablespoon chopped fresh thyme
1	tablespoon chopped fresh rosemary
¼	cup extra virgin olive oil

[BRAISING INGREDIENTS]

2	tablespoons canola oil
1	medium onion, coarsely chopped
2	medium carrots, peeled and coarsely chopped
2	stalks celery, coarsely chopped
10	large garlic cloves, halved, green shoots removed
	Kosher salt
3	or 4 whole allspice berries
2	rosemary sprigs
2	thyme sprigs
1	bay leaf
4	cups Chicken Stock (page 66), or 2 cups commercial broth and 2 cups water (more as needed)

1. Marinate the lamb shanks at least a day before you wish to serve them. Place the lamb shanks in a large bowl or on a baking sheet. Season with 1 teaspoon salt and about ½ teaspoon freshly ground pepper. Combine the garlic, anchovies, and ¼ teaspoon salt in a mortar and pestle and mash to a paste. Add the allspice, juniper berries, parsley leaves, thyme, rosemary, and 1 tablespoon of the olive oil, and mix together. Rub the shanks with the remaining olive oil, then with the spice, herb, and garlic mixture, making sure that the lamb shanks are well coated. Wrap each shank in plastic and place in a resealable plastic bag. Refrigerate for 24 hours.

2. Preheat the oven to 350°F. Heat 1 tablespoon of the oil in a large sauté pan over medium-high heat and, working in batches, brown the lamb shanks on all sides, about 5 to 10 minutes for each batch. Take care not to crowd the pan or to burn the glaze while browning. Remove from the pan and transfer the shanks to a roasting pan, a Dutch oven, or a wide, straight-sided lidded ovenproof skillet. Pour off most of the fat from the pan and allow the pan to cool slightly.

3. Heat the remaining tablespoon of oil in the same sauté pan over medium heat and gently cook the onion, carrots, celery, and garlic with ½ teaspoon salt until tender, 5 to 10 minutes. Add the allspice, rosemary, thyme, and bay leaf; stir together, add 2 cups of the hot stock to the sauté pan, and bring to a boil. Scrape the glazed meat juice off the bottom of the pan with a wooden spoon and pour into the pot or roasting pan with the lamb shanks, scraping the bottom of the pan clean. Add enough of the remaining stock to cover the lamb shanks halfway. Cover, place in the oven, and braise for 3 hours, until the meat is very tender. Check the stock from time to time and replenish as needed.

4. Remove the pan from the heat and let the shanks cool for 30 minutes in the liquid to firm up (they'll fall apart if you try to remove them too soon). Then remove to a large platter.

5. Strain the braising liquid into a bowl through a colander. If serving the following day, cover the lamb shanks and the braising liquid and refrigerate overnight. The next day, lift the fat from the top of the congealed broth and discard. Reheat the broth. If serving right away, allow the liquid to stand for at least 15 minutes. Using a ladle, skim the fat off the top and discard (see page 121). Return the lamb shanks to the pan and strain the skimmed braising liquid over the shanks.

6. Before serving, heat the shanks and liquid, uncovered, in a 400°F oven, about 15 to 25 minutes, until they are mahogany brown. While reheating, baste the shanks a couple of times with the broth, using a large spoon. Serve with barley, farro, rice, potatoes, or noodles.

lamb daube [makes 6 to 8 servings]

This is a classic Provençal stew heady with orange zest, wine, and Provençal herbs. The lamb has a more assertive flavor than beef, which is more traditional. Marinate the meat 2 days ahead and make the Daube a day ahead. Like all of us, it gets better with age.

4   pounds lamb shoulder or stew meat, cut into 2-inch pieces
     Kosher salt and freshly ground black pepper

[MARINADE]
1   medium carrot, peeled and diced
1   stalk celery, diced
1   medium onion, diced
4   juniper berries, crushed
2   whole cloves, crushed
     A bouquet garni made with a bay leaf, a few sprigs each thyme and parsley, and a tarragon sprig (page 66)
1   leek green, sliced and rinsed (about ½ cup)
1   teaspoon kosher salt
½   teaspoon cracked black peppercorns
1   1-inch-wide strip of fresh orange zest, finely minced
1   bottle tannic red wine, such as a Côtes du Rhone

[STEW]
¼   cup extra virgin olive oil
     Kosher salt and freshly ground black pepper
4   ounces salt pork or pancetta, cut in small dice
6   fat garlic cloves, crushed, plus 1 fat clove, halved, green shoot removed, minced
2   tablespoons tomato paste
1   cup Chicken Stock (page 66, or commercial) or water
1   strip of dried orange peel, in 1 piece, washed if waxy
½   large or 1 medium onion, diced
½   pound carrots, peeled and cut in oblique slices (page 81)
2   medium leeks, white and light green part only, sliced and cleaned (page 54)
     Noodles, rice, or potatoes, for serving

1. Two days before you wish to cook this, place the meat in a bowl, season with the salt and pepper, and add the marinade ingredients. Gently massage the meat with the wine and toss together. Cover and refrigerate for 12 to 48 hours. Stir the mixture 2 or 3 times.

2. Remove the pieces of meat from the marinade, scrape off the vegetables and spices, blot thoroughly dry with paper towels, and set aside. Drain the marinade into a colander set over a bowl. Heat 2 tablespoons olive oil in a large, heavy casserole over high heat, season the lamb with salt and pepper, and brown in batches, adding more oil as necessary. Transfer the meat to a bowl. Pour off most of the fat from the pan between batches and discard.

3. Turn the heat to medium and add the salt pork or pancetta. When the pork begins to render its fat, add the vegetables from the marinade and stir to deglaze the bottom of the pan. Add the garlic and cook until the vegetables soften, about 5 minutes. Add the tomato paste and 1 tablespoon water, and continue to cook, stirring, until the tomato paste coats the vegetables and begins to caramelize, about 2 minutes. Stir in the wine and the juices that have accumulated on the plate or in the bowl with the meat and the chicken stock or water, and bring to a boil, scraping the bottom of the pot with a wooden spoon to lift off the meat glaze. Return the meat to the pot, along with the bouquet garni, 1 teaspoon salt, and the piece of dried orange peel. Bring to a gentle simmer, skimming off any foam. Cover the pot and simmer over very low heat for 2 hours, or until the meat is very tender.

4. Remove the meat from the pot. Strain the liquid through a medium strainer, remove the bouquet garni, and push on the vegetables so that a portion goes through the strainer to thicken the liquid. If serving the next day, refrigerate the meat and the broth separately overnight, then lift the fat off the top of the broth the following day. If serving the same day, allow to rest for 15 to 30 minutes, then skim off the fat with a ladle (page 121).

5. Return the meat and liquid to the pot and bring back to a simmer, uncovered.

6. Meanwhile, heat the remaining 2 tablespoons olive oil in a wide, heavy skillet over medium heat and add the onion, carrots, leeks, and ½ teaspoon salt. Cook, stirring often, until tender, about 10 minutes, and add to the stew. Simmer very slowly for another 30 minutes. Taste and season with salt and pepper. The meat should be fork-tender. Adjust the seasonings and serve with pasta, rice, or potatoes.

lamb and prune tagine (moroccan-style shoulder of lamb)

[makes 6 to 8 servings]

This is a Moroccan lamb stew. The prunes, sweet aromatic spices, sugar (which is really a spice in this dish), and the soft, melting texture of the lamb evoke the essential flavors of North Africa. As this and many other North African tagines prove, not all stews require alcohol; but the prunes do add a mellow, winey richness. Think ahead for this one, and let the meat sit in the refrigerator with the spice rub for a day before you make the stew, and make the stew a day before you serve it. Serve the tagine with couscous.

[SPICE RUB]
1	teaspoon ground ginger
1	teaspoon ground cinnamon
2	tablespoons sugar
1	teaspoon kosher salt
½	teaspoon freshly ground black pepper
	Generous pinch of saffron
1	tablespoon extra virgin olive oil
1	tablespoon water

[TAGINE]
1	tablespoon canola oil
3	pounds boneless shoulder of lamb, cut in 3-inch pieces
2	tablespoons unsalted butter
1	medium onion, chopped
1	3-inch cinnamon stick
¼	teaspoon ground ginger
	Kosher salt
1	cup Chicken Stock (page 66, or commercial)
1	cup water
½	pound pitted prunes
1	teaspoon sugar
2	tablespoons toasted sesame seeds
	Couscous (page 215), for serving

1. Make the spice rub: Mix together the ginger, cinnamon, sugar, salt, pepper, and saffron. Add the olive oil and water and mix until you have a paste. Toss with the meat and knead to rub the paste in. Seal in a small bowl or resealable plastic bag and refrigerate overnight or for up to 2 days.

2. Make the tagine: Heat the oil in a large, heavy casserole or Dutch oven over medium-high heat and brown the meat lightly on all sides. Remove to a platter, bowl, or baking sheet. Pour off the fat from the pan.

3. Add the butter, onion, cinnamon stick, ginger, and ½ teaspoon salt to the casserole and lower the heat to medium. Cook, stirring often, until the onion is tender, 5 to 10 minutes. Return the meat to the casserole. Stir together to combine well, then add the chicken stock and water (there should be enough liquid to barely cover the meat). Bring to a simmer, add 1 teaspoon salt, cover, reduce the heat, and simmer over low heat, stirring often, for 1½ hours. At this point, if possible, remove from the heat, take out the meat, strain the broth through a colander, and refrigerate the meat and broth separately overnight.

4. Lift off the congealed fat from the top of the broth and discard. Combine the meat and broth in the casserole. Place on the stove over medium-low heat and bring back to a simmer. Add the prunes and sugar, and simmer for another 30 minutes, or until the meat falls apart when you poke it with a fork. Taste and adjust the salt. Transfer to a serving dish or a deep platter. Sprinkle the sesame seeds over the top. Serve with couscous

[NOTE] If you do not make this a day ahead, you will need to degrease the stew before serving, and you may need to reduce the liquid in the pot. Remove the meat and the prunes from the casserole and transfer to a bowl. Strain the broth through a colander into a bowl and degrease (see page 121), then return to the pot. Bring to a boil over high heat and boil until it coats the back of a spoon. Taste and adjust the seasonings. Stir the meat and prunes back into the broth and heat through.

breaded veal scaloppine with smoked mozzarella, parmesan, and tomato sauce [makes 4 servings]

Also known as veal Parmesan and veal Milanese, this is an updated version of an Italo-American, red-checked tablecloth, candle-in-the-Chianti-bottle standard. Have the sauce made and the pounded veal cutlets breaded ahead, and all you need to do is quickly reheat the sauce, sauté the veal, and give the assembled dish a few minutes in a hot oven.

4	veal cutlets, about 3 ounces each, pounded ⅛ inch thick (see below)
	Kosher salt and freshly ground black pepper
½	cup all-purpose flour
2	large eggs
1	tablespoon heavy cream
1	cup fresh bread crumbs
1½	cups Simple Tomato Sauce (page 90)
	Olive oil, for the pan
2	tablespoons canola oil (more as needed)
4	ounces smoked or fresh mozzarella cheese, thinly sliced (about ⅛ inch thick)
¼	cup freshly grated Parmesan cheese

[HOW TO MAKE SCALOPPINE]

When veal cutlets (or chicken breasts) are pounded very thin, they're called scaloppine. Place 2 sheets of plastic wrap on your cutting board, overlapping slightly (to make 1 wide sheet), and brush lightly with olive oil. Place wet paper towels underneath your cutting board to steady it, and make sure you are not using the kind of cutting board that has little feet, because those jump around when you pound. Place a veal cutlet in the middle and brush lightly with oil. Place 2 more overlapping sheets of plastic over the cutlet. Working from the center to the outside, pound the meat with the flat side of a meat tenderizer until very flat, about ⅛ inch thick. Make sure you come down flat with the meat tenderizer; if you hit the meat with the edge, you will chop it in two.

1. Season the pounded cutlets with salt and pepper. Place the flour in a wide dish. Beat together the eggs and cream in a wide bowl. Place the bread crumbs in a wide dish.

2. One by one, dredge the seasoned cutlets in the flour. Give them a shake to remove any excess flour, then dip in the egg mixture, and finally in the bread crumbs. Coat evenly and set aside on a baking sheet. Set aside for 10 to 15 minutes, or for up to 24 hours in the refrigerator.

3. Preheat the oven to 450°F. Warm the tomato sauce in a small saucepan. Lightly oil a gratin dish or an ovenproof platter with olive oil. Spoon 1 cup of the sauce over the bottom of the platter. Heat a wide skillet over medium-high heat. Add the canola oil and when it is hot, brown the scaloppine on both sides, cooking in batches so you don't crowd the pan, about 30 seconds per side. Transfer to the baking dish or platter, overlapping the pieces slightly. Place a slice of mozzarella on top of each cutlet. Spoon the remaining tomato sauce over the mozzarella and sprinkle a tablespoon of Parmesan on each cutlet. Place in the hot oven for 5 to 10 minutes, just until the cheese melts. Remove from the oven and serve.

VARIATION

The breaded veal cutlets are also delicious plain, without the sauce and cheese. Then the origin of the dish moves a few hundred miles north to Vienna, and the dish becomes Wiener schnitzel. Serve with lemon wedges.

veal piccata [makes 4 servings]

From about 1947 to 1977 no restaurant could avoid having this on its menu. It's an essential "continental" dish, and like all classic dishes, when done right it's absolutely delicious. As the public lost interest in this dish—because many chefs were doing it badly—it disappeared. But it needn't stay in the museum of mushy food; it deserves a revival.

1	large lemon
4	4-ounce (or eight 2-ounce) veal cutlets, pounded to less than ¼ inch thick (see page 138)
	Kosher salt and freshly ground black pepper
⅓	cup all-purpose flour
2	tablespoons canola oil
¼	cup dry white wine
2	tablespoons unsalted butter, softened
1	tablespoon capers, rinsed (soaked 30 minutes if salt-packed, rinsed, and drained)
1	tablespoon chopped fresh flat-leaf parsley

1. Cut away the skin and white pith from the lemon. To do this, cut the ends off, and standing the lemon upright on your cutting board, cut down the sides, removing the peel and the pith. Hold the lemon over a small bowl and cut out the lemon segments with a paring knife, leaving the membranes behind. When all the segments have been removed, squeeze the membranes over the bowl to extract any remaining juice. Cut the segments into small chunks and return to the bowl with the juice. Pick out the seeds and throw them away. Set aside.

2. Season the pounded cutlets generously with salt and pepper. Dredge in the flour (you will not use all of the flour; discard what you don't use).

3. Heat a wide skillet over high heat and add the canola oil. Sauté the cutlets until brown on both sides, being careful not to crowd the pan (you may have only enough room to cook one at a time). This should only take about 30 seconds to a minute per side. Transfer to a platter and keep warm in the oven.

4. When all of the scaloppine have been cooked, add the wine and lemon juice with the lemon chunks to the pan and scrape the bottom of the pan with a wooden spoon to lift off the meat glaze. Simmer for about 1 minute, then whisk in the softened butter and the capers, and stir until the lemon softens and the sauce is velvety. Pour over the veal scaloppine. Sprinkle with parsley and serve.

vitello tonnato [makes 6 servings]

Vitello tonnato is as classically Italian as macaroni and cheese is American. Every café in Italy seems to have it in the summer, and why not? It's a perfect summer dish, cold and light, but substantial. If you have the time to make your own tuna confit, your sauce will be truly outstanding. But don't let that be an obstacle to making this; you can find perfectly good canned tuna in olive oil, and it's sometimes less expensive than albacore in water. The best imported canned tuna in olive oil comes from Spain, and I wouldn't hesitate to use a Spanish import for this classic Italian dish.

[VEAL]

3	pounds veal top sirloin, trimmed
4	garlic cloves, halved, green shoots removed, cut into slivers
3	anchovy fillets cut into small pieces
¾	teaspoon kosher salt
½	teaspoon freshly ground black pepper
1	teaspoon dried oregano
1	tablespoon fresh thyme leaves
1	tablespoon extra virgin olive oil
½	medium onion, sliced (optional)

[TONNATO SAUCE AND GARNISH]

6	ounces Tuna Confit (page 197) or good-quality tuna packed in olive oil, drained
1	recipe Anchoïade (page 131)
4	large hard-boiled eggs, cut in wedges
3	caper berries, soaked and rinsed, or 2 teaspoons capers, rinsed
1	tablespoon chopped fresh flat-leaf parsley

1. Using the tip of a paring knife, make slits in the veal sirloin and stuff with slivers of garlic and pieces of anchovy. To do this, insert the tip of the knife, twist it slightly to open the slit, and push the garlic and anchovy pieces down the side of the knife tip. Season the meat with the salt and pepper, and fold in the ends to make the sirloin more compact. Truss with kitchen string. Place the sirloin on a piece of plastic wrap and sprinkle with the oregano and fresh thyme, after rubbing the herbs between your hands to extract flavor. Wrap the roast tightly in plastic and refrigerate for 3 hours or longer (up to 24 hours).

2. Roast the veal. Preheat the oven to 425°F. Remove the plastic from the meat, rub the meat with the olive oil, and place it on a baking sheet (I like to place ½ sliced onion underneath the roast to prevent it from sticking and to add flavor). Place in the oven and set the timer for 15 minutes. After 15 minutes, turn the heat down to 350°F and roast for 1 hour to 1 hour and 15 minutes, until a meat thermometer registers 145°F to 150°F when inserted in the middle. Remove from the oven and allow to cool, then wrap the roast in foil or plastic and chill for several hours or overnight.

3. Place the tuna in a large mortar and pestle or bowl and break it up with a fork. Then mash to a paste, using a pestle. Add enough of the anchoïade to make a smooth paste. Once the two are well amalgamated, add the remaining anchoïade. Taste and adjust the seasonings.

4. To serve, spread one third of the sauce down the middle of a platter. Cut the veal in thin slices and arrange on top of the sauce. Spread the remaining sauce over the top and garnish with the hard-boiled egg wedges. Chop the capers or caper berries and toss with the parsley. Sprinkle this mixture over the meat and serve.

barbecued ribs [makes 6 servings]

There's nothing fancy about this dish, but it's one of the most popular family dinners we make. You can make it with beef ribs or with baby back pork ribs. Beef ribs are chewier and fattier, but also richer tasting. They take longer to cook. But whether you use beef or baby back ribs, barbecued ribs always take time.

[SPICY SOY GINGER MARINADE]

1	medium red onion, chopped
1	cup extra virgin olive oil
2	dried chiles (preferably Japanese), broken up
1½	teaspoons cracked black peppercorns
1	bunch scallions, white and light green parts, sliced
4	fat garlic cloves, halved, green shoots removed, thinly sliced
3	ounces fresh ginger, peeled and finely minced (not grated)
⅔	cup soy sauce
½	cup freshly squeezed lime juice

[MEAT]

2	sides beef ribs (7 ribs each), cut into single ribs and trimmed of excess fat, or 3 racks baby back pork ribs, membranes removed
	Kosher salt and freshly ground black pepper
1	recipe Smoked Tomato Barbecue Sauce (page 143)

1. Make the marinade: Combine the onion, olive oil, chile, and pepper in a frying pan or a small saucepan and heat together over medium heat until the onion is softened, 5 to 8 minutes. Remove from the heat and stir in the remaining ingredients.

2. Bring a large pot of water to a boil and blanch the beef ribs for 10 minutes, baby back ribs for 5 minutes. Using tongs, transfer to a large pan and season with salt and pepper. Brush generously with the marinade, pour any excess marinade over the ribs, and cover the dish. Refrigerate for at least 4 hours and up to a day. From time to time, brush the ribs again with the marinade.

3. When you're ready to cook the meat, preheat the oven to 325°F. Brush the ribs again, and add 1 cup water to the pan. Cover tightly and place in the oven. Roast beef ribs for 2½ hours or until tender, baby back ribs for 2 hours or until tender.

4. When the ribs are tender, uncover and, using tongs or 2 spatulas, carefully transfer the ribs to a baking sheet. Brush again with the marinade. Raise the oven temperature to 400°F and return to the oven. Bake for another 20 minutes, basting halfway through, or until dark brown and glazed.

5. Meanwhile, warm the smoked tomato barbecue sauce in a saucepan. When the ribs are done, remove to a serving platter, cut pork ribs into 3-rib sections, ladle the sauce over them, and serve.

[NOTE] You can make these ahead and warm them in a low oven. In this case, pour the barbecue sauce over and warm them in the sauce.

VARIATION

You can also finish the ribs on a medium-hot grill instead of in a hot oven. Prepare a medium-hot grill, and place the ribs along the sides of the grill, not in direct contact with the coals. Grill, uncovered, until glazed, about 10 minutes. Take care not to allow them to burn.

smoked tomato barbecue sauce [makes about 2 cups]

This smoky tomato sauce goes well with grilled and roasted meat, poultry, and fish, and the barbecue sauce variation is a real winner. I use a cedar plank for smoking foods. You can also use oak, which has a slightly milder flavor. But don't use pine; it burns too fast and your food will smell like turpentine. And don't buy those expensive store-bought planks. You can get the wood at any lumber yard. Buy a 6-foot by 6-inch-wide by 1-inch-thick board and have them cut 10-inch lengths. Make sure the wood has not been treated with anything. You'll only be using the planks once, since you burn the wood (that's where the flavor comes from). It would be a health hazard to use them again, particularly if you use them for meat or fish, even if you scrub the wood afterward. Soak the plank for at least 24 hours in water. Pat the wood dry and it's ready to use. You will also need a perforated baking dish insert to set on the plank, easily obtained at restaurant supply stores.

2	pounds tomatoes, cut in half
¼	cup extra virgin olive oil
1	medium or ½ large onion, chopped (about 1 cup)
1	teaspoon coarsely chopped fresh thyme leaves
	Kosher salt
	Freshly ground black pepper
2	to 4 garlic cloves (to taste), halved, green shoots removed, coarsely chopped
1	teaspoon minced fresh ginger
1	tablespoon blackstrap molasses
2	tablespoons cider vinegar
1	tablespoon soy sauce
⅛	to ¼ teaspoon cayenne (to taste)

1. Prepare a hot charcoal or wood-fire grill. Place the plank on the grill and heat while you prepare the tomatoes.

2. In a large bowl, toss together the tomatoes, 2 tablespoons of the olive oil, half the onion, the thyme, 1 teaspoon kosher salt, and a few twists of the pepper mill. Place the tomatoes, cut side up, in the perforated baking pan. Strain the juice remaining in the bowl into a small bowl and set aside. Scatter the onion over the tops of the tomatoes.

3. When the bottom of the plank is smoking, place the pan with the tomatoes on top of it. Close the grill lid or cover the pan with a stainless steel bowl (see Note). Smoke 30 to 40 minutes, until the tomatoes are soft and have a nice smoky aroma. Remove from the grill.

4. In a medium saucepan over medium heat, heat the remaining 2 tablespoons olive oil and add the remaining onion. Cook, stirring often, until tender, about 5 minutes, then add the garlic. Cook, stirring often, until fragrant, about 1 minute, and add the tomatoes, the tomato liquid you set aside, and another ¾ teaspoon salt. Simmer, stirring often, for 15 to 20 minutes, or until thick and fragrant. Allow to cool slightly, then put through the fine blade of a food mill. Taste and adjust the seasonings.

5. Combine the ginger and molasses in the saucepan you cooked the tomatoes in and heat over medium-low heat until it bubbles. Simmer 2 minutes and add the vinegar, soy sauce, and cayenne. Simmer 5 minutes, stirring often, and whisk in the smoked tomato sauce. Bring to a simmer and simmer 10 minutes, stirring often. The sauce will cook down to about 1½ cups. Serve with barbecued meat, poultry, fish, or sausage.

[NOTE] Putting a stainless steel bowl over the tomatoes yields a more intense smoky flavor.

BIG BOWLS AND SMALL CONTAINERS
Always use the largest convenient container for work in the kitchen and the smallest convenient container for storage.

spicy pulled pork [makes 12 servings]

This is great party food. I once made it for the fortieth birthday party of a prominent food critic, and one of the guests complained that it was too good—nobody at the party would talk about anything else. The meat benefits from being rubbed and allowed to sit for 2 days before cooking, and then cooking a day ahead, so do think ahead. The good news is that it's incredibly easy, almost impossible to mess up, because it's difficult to overcook this meat.

[SPICE RUB]

I	tablespoon coriander seeds
I	tablespoon cumin seeds
2	teaspoons cracked black peppercorns
I	tablespoon mild or hot ground chili powder
½	teaspoon cayenne
I	tablespoon sweet paprika
I	tablespoon kosher salt
2	tablespoons canola oil

[PORK]

4½	to 5 pounds pork butt or pork shoulder, trimmed of excess fat and cut into large chunks
¼	cup canola oil
I	medium onion, chopped
	Kosher salt
8	garlic cloves, peeled
1½	cups water

1. Two to three days before you wish to serve, make the spice rub and marinate the pork. Heat a frying pan over medium heat and add the coriander seeds and cumin seeds. Toast, shaking the pan often, until the spices smell fragrant and a bit like popcorn. Add the pepper, chili powder, cayenne, and paprika, stir together briefly, and remove from the heat. Transfer to a small bowl and allow to cool for 5 minutes. Grind the spices in a spice mill to a coarse powder. Add the salt and mix together well.

2. Place the meat in a bowl and toss with 2 tablespoons canola oil and the spice mix. Knead the meat well to work in the spices. Transfer to one or two ziplock plastic bags, or a smaller bowl covered with plastic wrap, and refrigerate for I to 2 days.

3. Cook the pork. Preheat the oven to 350°F. Heat a large, heavy saucepan or Dutch oven over high heat and add I tablespoon of oil. Working in batches and adding oil as necessary, brown the meat lightly on all sides and remove to a bowl. Turn down the heat to medium and add the remaining oil, the onion, and ½ teaspoon salt, and cook, stirring to deglaze the bottom of the pot, until the onion is tender, about 5 minutes. Add the garlic, the pork, the juices that have accumulated in the bowl, and 1½ cups water. Bring to a simmer, cover, and place in the oven.

4. Cook for 2 hours in the oven, stirring from time to time, or until the meat is very tender and can be pulled apart with a fork with no effort. Remove from the heat and allow to cool slightly, or chill overnight and lift off some of the fat if you wish, then reheat. Using forks, shred the meat. Taste and adjust the seasonings. Serve with warm corn tortillas, Pickled Red Onions (page 235), and Fresh Tomato Salsa (below).

[FRESH TOMATO SALSA]

¼	cup finely diced red onion
2	teaspoons white wine vinegar
I	pound fresh ripe tomatoes, seeded and cut in ¼-inch dice
½	teaspoon kosher salt
⅛	teaspoon freshly ground black pepper
I	jalapeño or serrano chile, minced
1½	teaspoons freshly squeezed lime juice
I	tablespoon extra virgin olive oil
2	to 4 tablespoons roughly chopped cilantro (to taste)

Place the diced onion in a bowl and cover with cold water. Add ½ teaspoon of vinegar and allow to sit for 15 minutes. Drain, rinse with cold water, dry on paper towels, and toss with the tomatoes. Add the salt, pepper, chile, lime juice, remaining 1½ teaspoons vinegar, and the olive oil. Allow to sit for 30 minutes for the best flavor. Just before serving, stir in the cilantro.

smothered pork chops [makes 4 servings]

We use thick-cut pork chops (at least 1 inch thick) for this, and we brine them so they're very tender and juicy. The dish is a southern one, but we've added Mediterranean accents (garlic and tomato). We only use a touch of flour in the gravy and cook it until there is no hint of a floury taste. If you find your gravy thickens too much, thin it with water.

2	1½ inch-thick pork chops (about 1 pound each), brined 6 to 8 hours (page 150)
	Kosher salt and freshly ground black pepper
1	tablespoon canola oil
1	ounce thick-cut bacon, cut in ¼ x 1-inch strips
1	tablespoon unsalted butter
1½	teaspoons all-purpose flour
1	medium onion, cut in half, then sliced crosswise
1	fat garlic clove, halved, green shoot removed, and sliced
1	teaspoon tomato paste
1	large tomato, peeled, seeded, and chopped, with juice
2	or 3 small savory or fresh flat-leaf parsley sprigs
1	cup whole milk
¼	cup Chicken Stock (page 66, or commercial)
2	teaspoons chopped fresh flat-leaf parsley

Steaks and chops always have a prettier side, called the "show side" in the restaurant trade. That's the side you cook first. With chops, the bone usually curves up on the show side.

1. Preheat the oven to 375°F. Season the pork chops generously with salt and pepper. Heat the canola oil over medium-high heat in a large, heavy ovenproof skillet and when it is hot, add the pork chops, pretty side down. Sear for 2½ minutes and turn over. Cook on the other side for 2½ minutes and transfer from the pan to a plate. Set aside.

2. Pour the fat off from the pan and lower the heat to medium. Add the bacon and cook, stirring, until it renders its fat. Add the butter and flour and stir together. Cook, stirring, until the mixture begins to smell nutty, a minute or two, and add the onion and ½ teaspoon salt. Cook, stirring often, until the onion is tender, about 5 minutes, then add the garlic and the tomato paste. Stir together for about a minute, until the tomato paste turns a rusty color and smells sweet, and add the tomato and its juice and the savory or parsley sprigs. Cook, stirring often, until the tomato has cooked down and the mixture is fragrant, 5 to 10 minutes.

3. Whisk the milk and the chicken stock into the cooked-down tomato mixture, and bring to a simmer, stirring. Return the pork chops to the pan, show side up, cover with a lid or with foil, and place in the hot oven. Braise for 20 to 25 minutes, until a meat thermometer registers 140°F or higher when inserted in the thickest part of the chop.

4. Transfer the pork chops to a serving platter. Return the gravy to the top of the stove and place over medium heat. Whisk together to amalgamate. If it's runny, cook down slightly, taste, and adjust the seasonings. Remove the savory or parsley sprigs and ladle the gravy over the pork chops. Sprinkle with parsley and serve. A half a pork chop will be plenty for each diner.

[NOTE] You can also slice the pork chops and serve them on the platter, smothered in gravy.

sausages braised in beer with sauerkraut [makes 4 servings]

This is a classic German dish, so make sure to serve it with potatoes. The sauerkraut is the most important element. You need to cook it gently and long enough for it to come together, but not too long. If it is overcooked it will turn to mush.

[SAUERKRAUT]

1	quart sauerkraut, drained
1	medium onion, cut in half, then sliced crosswise
1	tart apple, peeled, quartered, cored, and sliced thinly crosswise
2	cups dry white wine
6	lightly crushed juniper berries, 2 whole cloves, and ½ teaspoon fennel seeds, tied in a piece of cheesecloth

[SAUSAGES]

1	tablespoon canola oil
½	cup roughly chopped onion
½	teaspoon kosher salt
2	whole cloves
7	juniper berries, lightly crushed
½	teaspoon fennel seeds
½	cup dark beer
½	cup Chicken Stock (page 66, or commercial)
1½	pounds pork links or other sausage of your choice (8 large sausages or 16 links)
	Whole-grain mustard and steamed or roasted potatoes, for serving

1. Combine all the sauerkraut ingredients in a medium saucepan. Place over medium heat and bring to a simmer. Cover, reduce the heat, and simmer gently for 1 hour, until the apple is very soft and the liquid in the pan has evaporated.

2. In another saucepan, heat the oil over medium heat and add the onion and salt. Cook gently until tender, about 5 minutes, and add the cloves, juniper berries, and fennel seeds. Cook, stirring, for a few minutes more. Add the beer and chicken stock and bring to a simmer.

3. Pierce the sausages in several places with the tip of a knife and add to the simmering beer mixture. Bring back to a simmer, cover, reduce the heat, and simmer gently until the sausages are thoroughly cooked (small links will take 10 to 15 minutes, larger sausages will take about 30).

4. Distribute the sauerkraut among 4 wide soup bowls. Top with a serving of sausages and drizzle on juice from the pan. Serve with whole-grain mustard and steamed or roasted potatoes on the side.

[5]
POULTRY AND RABBIT

Chicken is the most versatile of all meats. I sometimes refer to it as a "default" dish, because inevitably a customer who can't decide on a meat or fish dish will order chicken. For the home cook a good roast chicken is also often just that, the trusted simple entree you can always turn to. The easiest dishes are often the best; if you can master roast chicken you'll always be able to put a good meal on the table.

The key to great chicken is brine, the first recipe in this chapter. When we get our chickens in, we clean them and brine them right away. If you brine your chicken for the proper length of time—no more than 24 hours for a whole chicken, no more than 8 hours for cut-up chicken pieces, 1 hour for boneless, skinless breasts—you will have succulent, flavorful results. An added benefit is that brining retards the growth of bacteria. Once the chicken has been brined, take it out, pat it dry, place it on a plate, seal it with plastic, and refrigerate until you're ready to cook.

When you shop for chicken, stay away from bargains and don't put much store by the term "free range" (a chicken won't range if it doesn't have to). Instead, look for chicken raised without antibiotics and without hormones by a reputable local producer, and air chilled, not water chilled, when it's processed. The label might not be much help, so ask the butcher or the counterperson, send an e-mail, use your browser. It's amazing what you can find out simply by asking politely. The important thing to know is that if chicken is inexpensive, there's a reason and you will taste it. The more processed a chicken is, the less flavor it will have.

Rabbit and chicken are sold together in the grocery store, and grouped together here, because they're both lean, mild-tasting white meats. I hope you'll never say "It tastes like chicken" again about any food after you've cooked your way through this chapter. Rabbit tastes like rabbit, and chicken tastes like chicken.

brine [makes enough for 1 brined 4-pound chicken, two 2-pound pork loins, or 12 pork chops]

This is the brine we use at the restaurant for our chicken, turkey, and pork. The results are tender and moist. At Thanksgiving we use space at our butcher's to brine about fifty turkeys, because we're open on that day. It's very important to use kosher salt here, or the brine will be too salty. For a turkey, double the recipe and brine the bird in a large pot or a giant ziplock plastic bag. Using this method of making a very concentrated brine, then adding ice water, cuts way down on the heating and chilling times.

8	cups water
⅓	cup kosher salt
¼	cup sugar
1	bay leaf
4	whole cloves
7	juniper berries, gently crushed
1	dried chile (preferably Japanese)
1	teaspoon dried thyme
4	allspice berries, gently crushed
1	teaspoon cracked black peppercorns

BRINING TIMES

Whole chicken or pork loin:	24 hours
Chicken pieces:	8 hours
Boneless, skinless breasts:	1 hour
Pork chops:	6 to 8 hours
Whole turkey:	3 days

1. Place 1 cup of the water in a saucepan and chill the rest with ice.

2. Add the salt, sugar, bay leaf, cloves, juniper berries, chile, dried thyme, allspice berries, and black pepper to the water in the saucepan and bring to a simmer. Simmer until the salt and sugar have dissolved, and remove from the heat.

3. Measure out 7 cups of ice water and add to the hot mixture. Place a whole or cut-up chicken, two 2-pound pork loins, or 12 pork chops in a 1-gallon freezer bag, add the brine, and refrigerate. When the meat has been brined for the appropriate amount of time (see left), remove from the brine and refrigerate, covered, until ready to use.

roast brined chicken [makes 4 servings]

Everyone will marvel at the moistness and rich flavor of this chicken, a result of the brine. Make this recipe, and you might begin to brine your chicken whenever you buy one. It just takes a day of planning. The stuffing is for flavor only (it won't hurt you if you eat it, but you probably won't like it). Allowing the chicken to air-dry for 15 minutes before roasting gives it an evenly colored, crisp, mahogany skin. Use a meat thermometer so you won't overcook it.

1	brined chicken (page150), about 3½ to 4 pounds
1	fat garlic clove, halved, green shoot removed, minced
½	large onion or 1 medium onion, chopped
1	tablespoon chopped fresh flat-leaf parsley stems
5	sage leaves, rubbed between your fingers and chopped
½	small lemon, chopped (skin, pith and all)
½	teaspoon kosher salt
¼	teaspoon freshly ground black pepper

[HOW TO TRUSS A CHICKEN]

Trussing makes the chicken compact, and allows it to cook more evenly and retain more of its moisture. This is one of many ways to truss a chicken or a turkey:

Take a long piece of kitchen twine and pass the middle of it underneath and around the ends of the drumsticks. Cross the ends of the string to make an "X" as if you were playing cat's cradle. Pull the ends of the string down toward the tail, then back along the body, pulling the strings tightly over the joint that connects the thigh and drumstick. Continue to pull the string along the body toward the bird's back, catching the wing underneath the string. Pull one end of the string securely underneath the backbone at the neck opening and tie the two ends of the string with a secure knot.

1. Preheat the oven to 450°F. Lightly oil a rack and place in your roasting pan. Pull the excess fat from the cavity of the chicken and set it aside. Rinse the chicken inside and out and pat it dry with paper towels.

2. Mix together the remaining ingredients. Mince the chicken fat you set aside and mix it in. Spoon this mixture into the chicken cavity.

3. Truss the chicken and place on the rack, breast side down. Let rest for 15 to 20 minutes to dry out the skin.

4. Place in the oven and roast for 15 minutes. Turn the heat down to 375°F and flip the chicken over. Roast for another 45 minutes to an hour, until a meat thermometer registers 160°F when inserted into the thickest portion of the thigh. Remove from the heat, let rest for 10 minutes, and remove string before carving.

ANOTHER TYPE OF ROASTING RACK

Instead of using a rack, you can set the chicken on a sliced onion, which will elevate the bird and also infuse it with its flavor as the chicken roasts. Slice an onion, toss it with ¼ teaspoon salt and ¼ teaspoon freshly ground pepper, and place in the middle of a lightly oiled baking dish. Place the chicken on top and proceed with the recipe. Discard the onion when the chicken is done.

roast chicken with herb butter stuffed under the skin

[makes 4 to 6 servings]

This is a particularly rich variation of the previous recipe, oozing with herb butter pushed under the skin (though some of it is lost with the drippings). The chicken is roasted for the entire time with the breast side up so that the butter doesn't run out. Do not succumb to the fear of fat: This is an incredibly succulent and flavorful roast chicken.

1	fat garlic clove, cut in half, green shoot removed
	Kosher salt
4	teaspoons roughly chopped chervil
1	tablespoon roughly chopped tarragon
1	teaspoon roughly chopped thyme leaves
2	tablespoons roughly chopped fresh flat-leaf parsley
½	cup (1 stick) unsalted butter
1	3½- to 4-pound chicken
	Freshly ground black pepper
1	medium onion, sliced (optional)

1. Preheat the oven to 450°F.

2. In a mortar and pestle, mash the garlic with ½ teaspoon salt until smooth. Add the chervil, tarragon, thyme, and parsley and mash together to a paste. Add the butter and mash together until the mixture is smooth and uniform.

3. Loosen the skin from the surface of the chicken, taking care not to tear it. You can do this by sticking your first and second fingers between the skin and the meat, starting from the breast near the neck and moving them carefully over the surface of the bird. You can also do it with a teaspoon, rounded side out.

4. Season the chicken, inside the cavity and outside, with salt and pepper. Spread the butter under the skin, concentrating on the breast and down into the legs. Truss the chicken and pat the surface dry with a paper towel.

5. If using the onion (the sliced onion acts as a rack and will infuse the chicken with more flavor), toss with ¼ teaspoon salt and ¼ teaspoon freshly ground pepper, and place in the middle of a lightly oiled baking dish. Place the chicken on top, breast side up. If not using the onion, set the chicken on a lightly oiled rack, breast side up. Place in the oven and set the timer for 15 minutes. After 15 minutes turn the heat down to 350°F and continue to bake for 1 hour, until a thermometer registers 160°F when stuck into the thickest part of the thigh. Remove from the heat and let stand for 10 minutes, and remove string before serving. Discard the onion.

(continues)

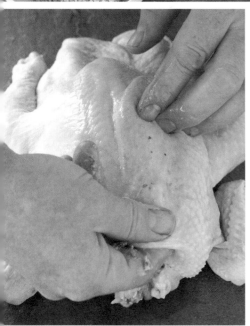

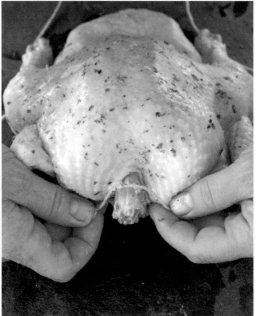

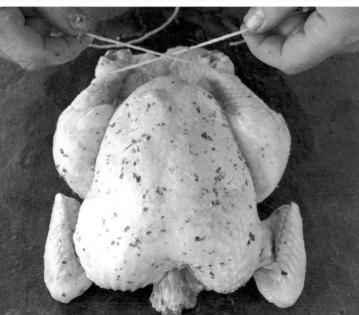

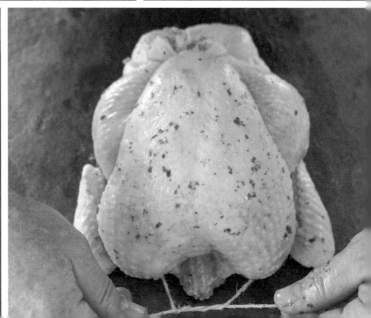

chicken à la king [makes 8 servings]

When I was growing up I thought the name of this dish was "Chicken Allen King," and I thought it had to be good, because Allen King was one of my favorite comedians. Nobody admits it, but everybody loves Chicken à la King, the creamy chicken dish that has graced too many steam tables. When my nouvelle cuisine chef colleagues from the '70s find out that I'm putting a recipe for it into this book, they'll turn up their noses and snort with derision; then they'll make it. This is a great dish to make if you have leftover chicken. You'll need about 4 cups diced meat.

1	ounce dried porcini
¼	cup (½ stick) unsalted butter
2	shallots, minced
2	garlic cloves, minced
½	pound regular or wild mushrooms, sliced
3	tablespoons all-purpose flour
2	cups Chicken Stock (page 66, or commercial)
1	cup whole milk
	Kosher salt and freshly ground black pepper
2	whole chicken breasts, poached in simmering water until cooked through and cut in ½-inch dice (about 4 cups), or 4 cups chopped cooked chicken
2	large egg yolks
⅓	cup cream
1	cup thawed frozen or cooked fresh peas
1	tablespoon dry or amontillado sherry
1	tablespoon minced fresh tarragon
1	tablespoon minced fresh flat-leaf parsley

1. Place the porcini in a bowl and cover with hot water. Let sit for 20 minutes. Remove the reconstituted mushrooms from the water and squeeze over the bowl. Strain the soaking water through a cheesecloth-lined strainer, measure out ½ cup, and add to the chicken stock. Rinse the reconstituted mushrooms and set aside.

2. Heat the butter in a large saucepan over medium heat and add the shallot. Cook, stirring, until tender, about 3 minutes. Add the fresh mushrooms and garlic and cook, stirring, until the mushrooms have softened, about 5 minutes. Add 1 teaspoon salt and the reconstituted dried mushrooms and cook, stirring, for a minute or two. Add the flour, mix together until well blended, and stir for about a minute. Whisk in the chicken stock and milk. Bring to a boil, stirring constantly, then reduce the heat to low and simmer, stirring, until smooth and thick, with no lingering raw flour taste, 10 to 15 minutes. Add freshly ground pepper and adjust salt.

3. Stir the chicken and peas into the sauce.

4. Shortly before serving, beat the egg yolks in a bowl with the cream. Stir ½ cup of the hot sauce into the mixture, then scrape back into the saucepan and bring to a bare simmer, stirring and taking care not to boil (or the egg yolks will curdle). Stir in ¼ teaspoon freshly ground pepper, the sherry, tarragon, and parsley. Taste and adjust seasonings, and serve over rice, puff pastry shells, or toast.

[PREPPING ROAST CHICKEN]

TOP LEFT Loosen the skin by sticking your first and second fingers between the skin and the meat, starting from the breast near the neck and moving carefully over the surface.

TOP RIGHT Carefully spread the herb butter under the skin.

MIDDLE LEFT Spread the herb butter on the breast and down into the legs.

MIDDLE Cut a length of kitchen string at least 48 inches. Loop the string over the neck and draw the strings underneath the wings...

MIDDLE RIGHT...and along the crease between the thighs and the breasts, to the ends of the drumsticks

BOTTOM LEFT Cross the ends of the string to make an "X" and loop them around the ends of the drumsticks, ending underneath the drumsticks.

BOTTOM RIGHT Pull the drumsticks together and bring the strings back along the body, pulling tightly over the joint that connects the thigh and drumstick. Continue to pull the strings toward the bird's back, catching the wings underneath and ending up at the neck. Tie the ends of the strings together.

unabashed, unashamed southern fried chicken [makes 4 servings]

Fried chicken is one of those dishes that should evoke time, place, and often a personality. The first time I put it on the menu for Monday Night Family Dinner, I wasn't prepared for the overwhelming response. I must have done seventy orders in a row. There was so much popping and splattering going on in the kitchen that by the end of the evening I looked like I'd been hit with a load of buckshot. My recipe is inspired by Calvin Trillin's description of the dish in his book *Third Helpings*. He points out the three essential elements for success: a buttermilk marinade, a cast-iron skillet, and pork lard for frying the chicken. To that I add another element—using a brined chicken. Then the resulting fried chicken will be incredibly moist.

1	medium chicken, 3½ to 4 pounds, cut in 8 to 10 pieces and brined (page 150) for 8 hours
½	large onion, sliced
3	fat garlic cloves, unpeeled, crushed
1	cup buttermilk
2	teaspoons kosher salt (3 if the chicken is not brined)
1	teaspoon ground black pepper
1	tablespoon tightly packed, roughly chopped celery leaves
1	tablespoon tightly packed, roughly chopped fresh flat-leaf parsley
10	ounces lard
2	cups all-purpose flour
1	teaspoon paprika
½	teaspoon cayenne

1. Drain the brined chicken and pat dry with paper towels.

2. Place the chicken in a large bowl and add the onion, garlic, buttermilk, 1 teaspoon salt (2 if the chicken has not been brined), ½ teaspoon pepper, the celery leaves, and the parsley. Toss together, making sure the chicken pieces are thoroughly coated with buttermilk. Transfer to a ziplock plastic bag or cover the bowl tightly. Refrigerate overnight.

3. Heat two-thirds of the lard over medium-high heat in a large cast-iron skillet. While it is heating, mix together the flour, 1 teaspoon salt, ½ teaspoon pepper, the paprika, and the cayenne in a large brown paper bag (do this by shaking the bag). You will not use all of the flour—in fact you'll only use about half of it—but it helps to coat the chicken pieces thoroughly if you have a generous amount.

4. Drain the chicken and remove any bits of onion that may be sticking to it. Place the pieces in the bag, fold the bag over, and shake the bag to coat the chicken.

5. Insert a deep-fry thermometer into the fat. When the temperature reaches 375°F, carefully add the chicken pieces, using tongs. The pan can be filled with the pieces, but they shouldn't be touching each other. Cook, turning the pieces every 3 or 4 minutes, until the pieces are a dark, rich brown, 20 to 25 minutes. Once the pieces are lightly browned all over, turn down the heat to medium so the surface doesn't burn before the inside of the chicken is properly cooked (160°F in the thickest part; use the thermometer).

6. Remove the chicken from the pan and drain on newspapers or brown paper bags. Add the remaining lard to the pan and cook the remaining chicken pieces. If not serving right away, place the chicken pieces on a rack set on a half-sheet pan. Keep warm in a low oven. If serving cold, refrigerate, uncovered, until ready to serve.

crispy flattened chicken [makes 4 servings]

This is a signature Campanile dish, whose recipe has evolved since we first published it in *The Food of Campanile* (1997). It's essential that you cook the chicken in a heavy iron skillet. If you use a nonstick skillet the skin won't crisp properly, and if you use one that isn't heavy enough it will burn before the chicken has cooked through. We use another cast-iron skillet to weight the chicken, but this isn't necessary for the home cook, who is not likely to have two cast-iron skillets of the same size. You can weight the chicken by placing a wide pan that fits down into the skillet on top, then a couple of heavy cans of something on top of that. Just make sure that what you put on top of the chicken is flat so the weight is evenly distributed. If your pan isn't big enough to fit all four chicken breasts without crowding, cook two at a time and keep the first two warm by covering with foil while you cook the second two. Select boneless chicken breasts with the skin on and the first wing bone intact; the more skin the better. Also, for super-moist chicken, brine the breasts ahead of time (see page 150).

4	whole boned chicken breasts with the skin on and the first wing bone in, brined if possible (page 150)
3	garlic cloves, halved, green shoots removed, thinly sliced
6	sage leaves
	Kosher salt and freshly ground black pepper
¼	cup extra virgin olive oil

1. Lift up the skin on the cut side of the chicken breasts and insert the garlic slices. Distribute them evenly under the skin, taking care not to break the skin or lift it entirely off. Rub the sage leaves between your hands to release their aroma and insert under the skin with the garlic. Pull the skin back over the breast. If the chicken has not been brined, salt and pepper liberally on both sides. Wrap tightly in plastic and refrigerate for several hours, or overnight if the chicken has not been brined.

2. Heat a large, heavy cast-iron skillet over high heat until hot. Add the olive oil and heat to just below smoking. Place the chicken breasts skin side down in the pan (unless you have a very large pan, do this in 2 batches). Season the other side of the breasts. Turn the heat down to medium-low and place another heavy pan on top of the breasts so they are pressed flat into the pan. If your second pan is not heavy, weight the pan with cans. Make sure the weight is evenly distributed over both breasts. They must cook evenly and at the same time, because once you turn them over you can no longer weight them. Cook until very brown and crisp, 12 to 15 minutes. Turn the breasts over and cook for another 5 minutes, or until cooked through. Remove from the heat, let rest for 5 minutes, then serve.

guinea hen fricassée with red wine, bacon, and mushrooms

[makes 4 servings]

This rich, savory stew is a variation on the classic chicken fricassée or coq au vin. The classic dish is made with a large stewing hen or rooster, whose tough meat requires long cooking. Guinea hen makes a nice substitute. The meat is rich and earthy, gamier and drier than chicken, but it doesn't require as much cooking as a rooster or a stewing hen. If you can't get guinea hen, use chicken legs and thighs, and scale back the cooking time. Serve this dish with egg noodles, steamed or roasted potatoes, or rice.

¼	cup water
4	ounces thick-cut bacon, cut in ¼ x 1-inch strips
1	2½- to 3½-pound guinea hen, cut in 8 pieces, or 8 pieces chicken thighs and legs
	Kosher salt and freshly ground black pepper
¼	cup all-purpose flour
1	tablespoon canola oil
1	medium or ½ large onion, chopped
1	medium carrot, peeled and chopped
1	stalk celery, chopped
4	fat garlic cloves, halved, green shoots removed, minced
2	cups red wine, such as a Côtes du Rhone or Syrah
1	cup Chicken Stock (page 66, or commercial)
	A bouquet garni made with a bay leaf and 3 sprigs each parsley and thyme (page 66)
2	tablespoons extra virgin olive oil
¾	pound cultivated mushrooms or wild mushrooms, thickly sliced (see Note)
2	tablespoons unsalted butter
1	tablespoon chopped fresh flat-leaf parsley

If using shiitakes or other mushrooms with tough stems, remove the stems and sauté them with the vegetables in step 4.

1. Combine the water and bacon in a wide, heavy skillet over medium heat and bring to a simmer. Cook until the liquid boils off and the bacon is lightly browned, about 8 minutes. Remove the bacon to a plate and set aside.

2. Meanwhile, season the guinea hen (or chicken) generously with salt and pepper, and lightly dredge in the flour. (You can put the flour in a brown paper bag with the poultry pieces and shake it if you prefer.)

3. Add the canola oil to the pan in which you cooked the bacon and heat over medium heat. Add the guinea hen

pieces, in batches if necessary so you don't crowd the pan, and brown on both sides, about 10 minutes per side (5 minutes per side if using chicken). Transfer to a platter or baking sheet and pour off some of the fat from the pan.

4. Add the onion, carrot, and celery to the pan, along with any mushroom stems you may have removed, and cook until lightly colored, 5 to 10 minutes, stirring often and scraping the bottom of the pan to begin the deglazing process. Add ½ teaspoon salt and half the garlic and stir together for a minute, then add the red wine. Stir and scrape the pan to deglaze, and bring to a simmer. Return the guinea hen pieces to the pan. Add the chicken stock and the bouquet garni. Bring to a simmer, cover, and simmer 15 minutes. Turn the guinea hen pieces over, cover, and simmer another 15 minutes, or until the meat is tender.

5. While the guinea hen is cooking, in another pan, heat the olive oil over medium-high heat and add the mushrooms. Cook, stirring, until they begin to release water and color, 3 to 5 minutes, and add the remaining garlic, ½ teaspoon salt, and a few grinds of the pepper mill. Stir in the bacon. Continue to cook, stirring often, until the mushrooms are tender and fragrant. Remove from the heat and set aside.

6. Remove the guinea hen from the pan and transfer to a platter. Strain the broth into the pan with the mushrooms. Bring to a boil and reduce by about half. Remove from the heat and a little bit at a time, add the butter, swirling it in as you add it. Taste and adjust the seasonings. Spoon the sauce with the mushrooms and bacon over the guinea hen. Sprinkle with chopped fresh flat-leaf parsley and serve.

[NOTE] You can make this ahead. When the sauce has reduced, turn off the heat and don't add the butter. Place the guinea hen in the pan and cover. When ready to serve, heat through and transfer the guinea hen to a platter. Bring the sauce to a simmer, remove from the heat, swirl in the butter, and proceed with the recipe.

chicken pot pie [makes 4 generous servings]

What Kraft did to macaroni and cheese, Swanson did to the chicken pot pie: they mass-marketed a mediocre version of a classic that then became the benchmark for the dish. But whenever we serve chicken pot pie for a family dinner we can't make enough of it. It's a comforting dish, whether you dress it up or down. This version includes asparagus and sage along with the more traditional carrots and peas; it isn't exactly fancy, but it's far from plain. You can make the filling up to a day ahead and assemble it shortly before baking.

2½	cups Chicken Stock (page 66, or commercial)
	Kosher salt
2	cups thinly sliced carrots
1⅓	cups cooked fresh peas or thawed frozen peas
8	stalks asparagus, tough base snapped off, steamed 5 minutes, and cut in 1-inch pieces
1	cup tiny pearl onions
¾	pound cooked chicken breast, cut in 1-inch pieces or shredded
	Freshly ground black pepper
2	tablespoons unsalted butter
2	tablespoons all-purpose flour
4	fresh sage leaves, cut in chiffonade
¼	cup crème fraîche
1	8-ounce (approximately) sheet frozen puff pastry, thawed
1	large egg
1	teaspoon water

1. Season the chicken stock with salt. Bring to a boil in a small saucepan. Add the carrots, reduce the heat to medium, and boil gently for 4 minutes. Remove the carrots with a slotted spoon and transfer to a bowl with the peas and asparagus. Set aside.

2. Bring a medium saucepan of salted water to a boil while you make a small incision with a paring knife around the root end of each pearl onion. Drop into the boiling water and cook for 10 minutes, until just tender. Remove from the water and transfer to a bowl of ice-cold water, then drain. Peel the onions and add to the bowl with the carrots, peas, and asparagus. Add the chicken and stir together. Season the chicken and vegetables with salt and pepper.

3. Make the sauce. In a medium, heavy saucepan, melt the butter over medium-low heat and add the flour. Stir together with a wooden spoon and cook until the roux is just beginning to color, about 3 minutes. Remove from the heat and whisk in the chicken stock all at once. Return to medium

heat and bring to a simmer, whisking constantly. Reduce the heat to low and simmer for 15 minutes, stirring often to make sure the sauce doesn't stick to the sides and bottom of the pan and scorch. Season to taste with salt and pepper, and remove from the heat. Stir in the sage and set aside to steep for 5 minutes. Whisk in the crème fraîche.

4. Butter four 1½-cup ramekins. Scrape the sauce into the bowl with the chicken and vegetables and mix together thoroughly. Distribute among the 4 ramekins. Cover the ramekins with plastic wrap and place in the refrigerator while you roll out the puff pastry.

5. Roll out the puff pastry into a thin square or rectangle large enough to cut into 4 equal pieces that can be draped over the ramekins.

6. Whisk the egg and water together and brush the outside rim of each ramekin. Set the pastry on top with the dough draping over the sides. Press around the sides of the ramekins to seal and pinch an attractive lip around the edges. Pierce the top with the tip of a paring knife and set in the freezer for 20 minutes.

7. Meanwhile, preheat the oven to 425°F. Place the ramekins on a sheet tray. Brush the tops with the egg wash and place in the oven. Bake until golden brown and bubbling, about 20 minutes. Serve hot, in the ramekins.

VARIATIONS

You can also make one large pot pie in a 2-quart baking dish or soufflé dish. You'll get 6 smaller servings out of it if you make it this way. Butter the dish, spoon in the filling, roll out the puff pastry to cover the dish, and proceed as above, but bake for 30 minutes, or until golden brown and puffed.

Substitute ½ batch Savory Flaky Dough (page 53) for the puff pastry.

braised duck and green olives [makes 4 servings]

Ideally, you should begin this dish a day ahead. If you chill the broth overnight, the fat will congeal on top and it will be easy to discard. If you do serve it on the day you make it, you'll need at least an hour for the broth and fat to separate; then you can spoon it off, though you won't get as much of it. The final flavoring for the sauce is a French preparation called a gastrique, made by caramelizing sugar and adding to it a generous amount of white wine vinegar, cooking this down, and adding it to the broth. This is a classic sauce for duck; the acid and the caramel flavor make a great contrast to the rich duck.

If you have a Chinese market nearby, buy your ducks there. Ask for the bones, neck, feet, and wing tips to use in the broth.

I	duck (about 5 pounds), cut up by the butcher into 8 pieces
	Kosher salt and freshly ground black pepper
I	tablespoon canola oil
I	medium carrot, cut in small dice
I	small stalk celery, cut in small dice
I	medium or ½ large onion, finely chopped
6	ounces imported green olives (not martini olives), preferably large cracked Sicilian green olives, with pits
I	cup dry white wine
I½	cups Chicken Stock (page 66, or commercial)
	A small handful each fresh flat-leaf parsley and thyme sprigs
¼	cup sugar
I	tablespoon water
½	cup white wine vinegar

DUCK FAT
Use duck fat for sautéing potatoes and potato pancakes, for sautéed chicken, and for making duck confit. A teaspoon added to other oils will contribute rich flavor to whatever you're cooking.

1. A day ahead: Preheat the oven to 350°F. Season the duck generously with salt and pepper on both sides. Heat the canola oil in a large, heavy skillet over medium-high heat and add the duck pieces, in batches if necessary to avoid crowding the pan. Brown thoroughly on both sides, about 8 minutes per side. Remove the duck from the pan, using tongs, and transfer to a casserole or Dutch oven, skin side up. Pour off most of the fat into a jar or bowl before you add the second batch of duck pieces.

2. Pour off all but a tablespoon of the fat in the pan and add the duck bones, feet, etc. if you have them and sauté until browned, stirring often. Using tongs, remove to the casserole with the duck. Pour off all but a tablespoon of the fat in the pan again, and add the carrot, celery, onion, and olives. Cook until the vegetables soften, about 5 minutes, and add the white wine. Deglaze the pan, scraping the bottom with a wooden spoon, and cook the wine down by about two-thirds. Add the chicken stock and parsley and thyme sprigs, and stir together. Pour over the duck in the casserole. Bring to a simmer, cover, and place in the oven for I hour, or until the duck is fork-tender.

3. Place a colander over a bowl. Remove the casserole from the oven. Using tongs, transfer the duck and the olives to a plate or bowl. Cover and refrigerate if serving the next day. Strain the stock through the colander into a separate bowl. Don't use a fine strainer, because the fat will not separate out as easily. Transfer to a jar or a smaller bowl to store. Cover and refrigerate overnight. If you are serving the same day, let the broth sit for at least 1 hour, and ladle off the fat (see page 121).

4. Shortly before serving, lift (or skim) off the fat from the broth (which will be congealed if it has been refrigerated) and discard or store in the freezer or refrigerator if you have a use for duck fat, as we do at the restaurant (page 162).

5. To make the gastrique, combine the sugar and 1 table-spoon water in a small saucepan and place over medium heat. Cover and heat until all the sugar has dissolved and the mixture is bubbling, about 3 minutes. Uncover and raise the heat slightly. Let the caramel cook until a golden brown, swirling the pan from time to time so that it cooks evenly. Remove from the heat and wait for the bubbles to subside, then slowly add the vinegar, being careful that the mixture does not splash (it will bubble up), and stir together vigorously. Boil for about 2 minutes, until the mixture has cooked down a bit, and add the duck stock. Stir together well. Season with salt to taste (½ teaspoon or more).

6. Return the duck and olives to the casserole or sauté pan and strain in the sauce through a fine strainer. Spoon some of it over the top of the duck pieces. Heat the mixture through for 15 to 30 minutes over medium-low heat, basting every 5 minutes, until the duck pieces are hot and glazed with the sauce. Taste the sauce and adjust the seasonings. It may need a little salt.

7. Serve with noodles, rice, or boiled or mashed potatoes.

rabbit cacciatore [makes 8 servings]

Rabbit is a meat that has been dealt a bad hand in this country. It's all because of the movie *Bambi*. I can't tell you how many guests tell us that they "don't eat Thumper." If only they knew what they were missing. Rabbit is a lean, flavorful meat, one of those foods that the phrase "It tastes like chicken" was made for—except rabbit has more flavor. Rabbit Cacciatore is a brothy, aromatic one-pot dish. *Cacciatore* (in French it would be *chasseur*) means "hunter's style," which means the dish will contain mushrooms because it's assumed that if a hunter were going to cook a rabbit he had just caught, he would find some wild mushrooms to season the dish and would make something like this. This recipe sounds difficult, but it's not, though it takes some time. Try to have the rabbits cut up by your butcher.

[MARINADE AND BROTH]

2	rabbits, about 2½ pounds each, cut in 8 pieces (page 166; if you have the butcher cut up the rabbit, have him wrap the backbones and necks for you to use for the broth) Kosher salt and freshly ground black pepper
2	tablespoons roughly chopped mixed fresh thyme and rosemary leaves
1½	tablespoons chopped fresh flat-leaf parsley
½	cup whole milk
½	large onion, diced
½	medium carrot, diced
½	stalk celery, diced
⅓	cup chopped washed leek leaves (the light green part)
2	tablespoons canola oil
1	cup dry white wine
2	garlic cloves, peeled and crushed
1½	cups Chicken Stock (page 66 or commercial) plus 1½ cups water

[FINISHED DISH]

	Kosher salt and freshly ground black pepper
1	tablespoon all-purpose flour
3	tablespoons extra virgin olive oil
1	medium onion, cut in large dice
½	pound wild mushrooms, preferably chanterelles, washed and pulled apart by hand into thick pieces
1	pound tomatoes, peeled, seeded (page 90), and cut in chunks
6	garlic cloves, halved, green shoots removed, sliced The strained rabbit broth
1	teaspoon canola oil
1	tablespoon minced fresh flat-leaf parsley Spaetzle (page 211) or wide noodles for serving

1. The day before you wish to serve, marinate the rabbit. Toss the rabbit pieces in a bowl with 1 teaspoon salt, ½ teaspoon pepper, the thyme and rosemary, and the chopped parsley. Cover, or seal in a ziplock plastic bag, and refrigerate several hours or overnight. Place the organs in a small container and cover with milk. Cover and refrigerate.

2. Meanwhile, make the broth. Cut the tailbone, rib cage, and neck into smaller pieces. Combine with the diced onion, carrot, celery, and leek leaves in a medium saucepan. Add the canola oil and place over medium-low heat to brown gently. Stir from time to time, and when the meat and vegetables are lightly browned, after about 10 minutes, add the white wine and scrape the bottom of the pan to deglaze. Add the garlic cloves, bring to a boil, reduce the heat to medium, and boil until the wine has reduced to a syrupy consistency. Add the stock or broth and the water and bring to a simmer. Simmer partially covered over low

(continues)

heat for 1 hour. Strain through a fine strainer set over a bowl, pressing the ingredients against the strainer to extract all of the savory juice. Cover and refrigerate overnight. When you are ready to cook, lift off any fat that has formed on the top. Bring back to a simmer, taste, and adjust the seasoning.

3. Preheat the oven to 375°F. Season the rabbit with salt and pepper. Lightly dust with flour. Heat 2 tablespoons extra virgin olive oil in a wide, lidded skillet or casserole over medium-high heat and brown the rabbit pieces, in batches, until light brown on all sides, about 5 to 8 minutes. Transfer the rabbit pieces to a plate. Once the pieces are browned, add the smaller boneless flaps of rabbit meat and brown on both sides, then remove to the plate. Heat the remaining tablespoon of olive oil in the pan, reduce the heat to medium, and add the onion and mushrooms. Cook, stirring, until the onion is translucent and the mushrooms are slightly softened, 2 to 3 minutes. Add ¾ teaspoon salt, and stir in the tomatoes and garlic. Return the rabbit to the pan, placing the pieces on top of the mushroom mixture. Add the broth and bring to a simmer. Cover and place in the oven. Braise for 1 hour, until the rabbit is very tender, almost falling off the bone.

4. Remove the rabbit pieces from the broth and arrange on a serving dish or deep platter. Remove the flat boneless pieces and cut into slivers. Return them to the broth. Bring to a simmer and reduce by about one-fourth.

5. Meanwhile, cook the liver, kidneys, and heart. Heat the canola oil in a small frying pan over medium-high heat. Remove the organs from the milk, pat dry, and add to the pan. Cook, stirring, until browned on all sides and cooked through, 3 to 5 minutes.

6. Pour the sauce over the rabbit. Cut the liver, heart, and kidneys into quarters and scatter over the top. Garnish with parsley if desired, and serve with Spaetzle (page 211) or wide noodles.

rabbit in mustard sauce with cream and tarragon [makes 8 servings]

This is a classic French rabbit preparation, and you will understand why when you taste it. It's a rich, savory dish with a sauce you'll want to sop up with noodles, rice, or potatoes.

[MARINADE]

2	rabbits, each cut in 8 serving pieces (page 167)
	Kosher salt and freshly ground black pepper
2	cups dry white wine
1	large onion, coarsely chopped
1	medium carrot, peeled and coarsely chopped
1	stalk celery, coarsely chopped
3	garlic cloves, crushed
1	tablespoon mustard seeds

[RABBIT]

2	tablespoons canola oil (more as needed)
	Kosher salt and freshly ground black pepper
½	large or 1 medium onion, cut in small dice
1	medium carrot, peeled and cut in small dice
1	outer stalk or 2 inner stalks celery, cut in small dice
2	tablespoons all-purpose flour

[THE STRAINED MARINADE]

2	cups Chicken Stock (page 66 or commercial)
3	fat garlic cloves, halved, green shoots removed, coarsely chopped
2	teaspoons fresh thyme leaves
1	bay leaf
3½	tablespoons Dijon mustard
½	cup heavy cream
1	tablespoon chopped fresh tarragon

1. The day before you wish to cook this, season the rabbits with salt and pepper and place in a bowl. Add the marinade ingredients—the wine, onion, carrot, celery, garlic, and mustard seeds—and toss together. Cover and refrigerate for 12 to 24 hours, shifting the pieces around from time to time. You can also place the ingredients in a heavy ziplock plastic bag.

2. Preheat the oven to 375°F. Remove the rabbit pieces from the marinade and wipe off all the mustard seeds and vegetables. Pat dry and salt and pepper generously. Strain the marinade and set aside.

3. Heat the canola oil over medium-high heat in an ovenproof casserole or Dutch oven and brown the rabbit on both sides, in batches so you won't crowd the pan. Transfer to a baking sheet as the pieces are done (each batch should take about 8 minutes). Add more oil as needed. Set aside.

4. Turn the heat down to medium and add the onion, carrot, and celery to the pot. Add ½ teaspoon salt and cook gently, stirring often, until they soften, 5 to 8 minutes. Add the flour and cook, stirring, for about 3 minutes, until you no longer see any flour and the mixture has just begun to brown. Add the marinade to the pan and stir and scrape the bottom and sides of the pan to deglaze. Add the chicken stock, garlic, thyme, bay leaf, ½ teaspoon salt, and a few grinds of the pepper mill, and bring to a simmer.

5. Meanwhile, set aside 1½ teaspoons of the mustard and brush the tops of the rabbit pieces with the remaining 3 tablespoons. When all the pieces have been coated and the mixture in the pot is simmering, place the rabbit in the pot, mustard side up. Pour in any juice that has accumulated in the sheet pan. Cover and place in the oven for 1½ hours, basting every 30 minutes, or until the meat is fork-tender and falling from the bone.

6. Using tongs, remove the rabbit from the pot and place in an attractive serving dish. Keep warm in a low oven. Strain the broth, making sure to press out all of the liquid, and return to the pot. Add the cream, combine well, and bring to a simmer. Whisk in the 1½ teaspoons Dijon mustard you set aside and a pinch of freshly ground pepper. Taste and adjust the seasoning.

7. Stir the tarragon into the hot sauce and let steep, on or off the heat, for another minute. Pour over the rabbit and serve, with noodles, rice, or potatoes.

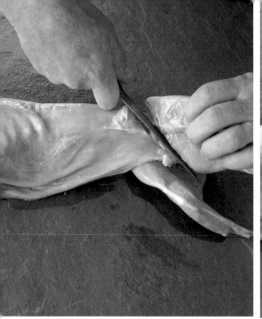 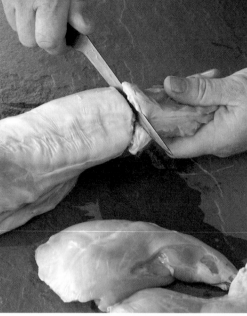 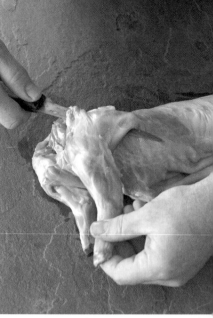

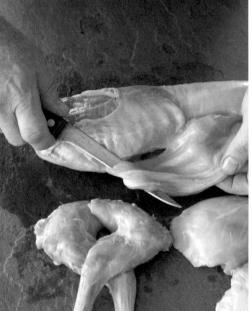  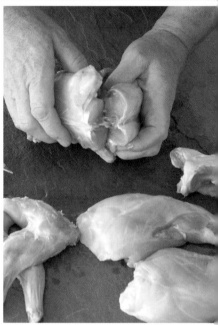

[JOINTING A RABBIT]

Rabbits have the hardest bones of any animal. Chefs are always nicking their knives on them when they cut them up, and farmers will tell you that if you run over one, the bones will puncture your tires. So have both a sharp cleaver and boning knife for this task. First, cut off the hind legs, cutting into the joint from the thigh and twisting off. Next, split the rabbit down the middle at the breastbone, remove the heart, kidneys, and liver, and set aside. Cut off the front legs, including the shoulder. Find the second to last rib, cut through the rabbit, and break the tailbone. Cut off the flaps that go out from the sides, then cut the torso in two across the spine. Cut away the backbone. You should end up with eight pieces plus the tailbone and rib cage with the neck.

TOP LEFT First cut off the hind legs, cutting below the pelvis into the hip joint and twisting off.
TOP MIDDLE Cut through the spine just above the pelvis to remove the tail bone and pelvis, and snap off.
TOP RIGHT Cut off the front legs, including the shoulder.
MIDDLE LEFT Cut off the belly flaps just below the ribs.
MIDDLE AND MIDDLE RIGHT Cut the section of the torso below the ribs (the saddle) away from the rib cage and snap off.
BOTTOM LEFT Cut the saddle in half across the spine and snap in two.
BOTTOM RIGHT You should end up with eight edible pieces plus the tailbone and rib cage for stock.

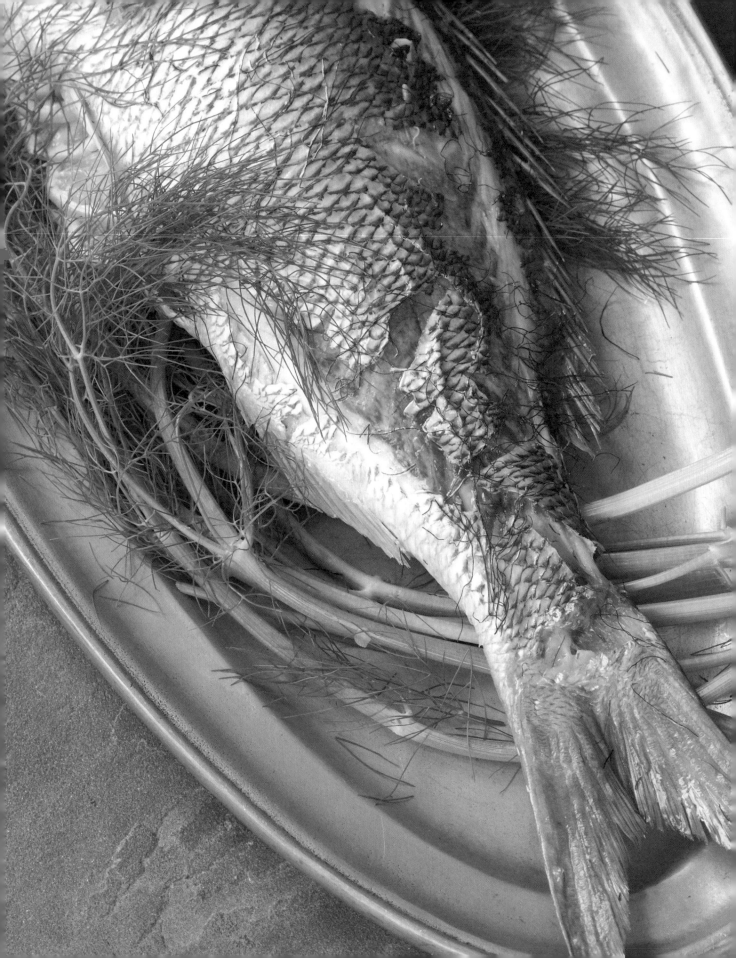

[6]

FISH AND SHELLFISH

The recipes in this chapter range from the extraordinarily simple (Cornmeal-Dusted Panfried Trout and Sand Dabs Meunière) to the extravagantly complex (Lobster Pot Pie and Rich Fish Stew with Lobster, Shrimp, Clams, Mussels, Sea Bass, and White Beans). The complex recipes take time but they're well worth your effort. There are some fun, messy dishes here too, like the Shrimp Boil with Pickled Onions and Corn on the Cob on page 180 and the Dungeness Crabs in Spicy Scallion Butter on page 183, dishes that are great for big, informal gatherings. For small dinners there's nothing better than a roasted or grilled whole fish (page 193–194), easy to make and always visually dramatic (and no, the eyes are not looking at you; it is dead).

Fish is one of the most delicate and perishable foods to cook. It's one of those foods I'll always order in a good restaurant but never in a mediocre restaurant. Cooking times are critical. Find a reliable supplier, and use fish quickly once you've bought it. That old adage about not having fish or visitors in the house for more than three days is true, except the limit (for both) should really be two days. Frozen fish is often fresher than so-called fresh fish because it's frozen on the boats right after it's caught. Fishing boats can go out for a week, and if the fish is not gutted immediately and stored, in slush ice, at 32°F, it will deteriorate. By the time it gets to you it will be far from fresh. Reliable suppliers are so important because they will have reliable suppliers themselves and they will know the provenance of the fish.

I can't discuss fish without expressing my environmental concerns. Many of our wild fish populations are collapsing and in danger of disappearing due to overfishing and habitat destruction. In the restaurant we stick with fish that are relatively abundant. We only buy wild salmon from Alaska, where the fisheries follow sustainable practices. Farmed salmon is an ecological disaster. Chilean sea bass is a delicious slow-growing fish that is being wiped out by poaching. Farmed trout, on the other hand, is acceptable because it's raised in closed systems, which limits environmental impact. Bluefin is the finest tuna there is, but it's now close to extinction, so we use other types such as big eye and yellowfin. We don't worry too much about shellfish—clams, mussels, and oysters—because they're farmed in an ecologically neutral fashion. We buy wild shrimp rather than farmed shrimp raised in former Southeast Asian mangrove swamps that have been destroyed by the shrimp farming, leaving the low-lying coastal areas an easy target for flooding from hurricanes.

You can't be perfect all the time, and we don't have the depth of knowledge or the space to go into all the best choices here, but I encourage you to read and ask questions so you can shop responsibly. True environmental change will come through the marketplace.

rich fish stew with lobster, shrimp, clams, mussels, sea bass, and white beans [makes 8 servings]

This fish stew falls into the bouillabaisse family of fish stews, except it's a bit more over the top because of the lobster. It's complex, and the stock takes some work, but it's worth it. Make this for a fantastic dinner party and you will solidify your reputation as a great cook for the rest of your life. Once you've made the stock, which takes time, there are only a few things to do and watch out for: Make sure the clams and mussels are well cleaned and purged so you don't get sand (see page 83); cook the seafood in the order listed and not too long; and buy impeccably fresh fish. The trick to getting the right texture for the broth is using the toasted bread.

[STOCK]

2	1½-pound lobsters
3	tablespoons canola oil
1	large onion, coarsely chopped
1	medium carrot, peeled and coarsely chopped
2	stalks celery, coarsely chopped
½	small fennel bulb, diced and rinsed
1	leek, white and light green parts only, sliced and rinsed of sand
	Kosher salt
1	14-ounce can tomatoes, with juice
	Generous pinch of saffron
1	head of garlic, cut in half horizontally
1	pound white-fleshed fish bones and heads, soaked in cold water and rinsed until the water runs clean
1	cup dry white wine
	A bouquet garni (page 66) made with the leek greens, well washed, 2 bay leaves, 1 small dried red chile, a handful each of tarragon, parsley, and thyme sprigs, and 1 large basil sprig
½	teaspoon cracked black peppercorns
2	quarts water or lobster cooking water (or a combination)
3	slices whole wheat country bread, toasted

[STEW]

¾	pound White Rose or Yukon Gold potatoes, steamed or roasted until just tender and cut into 1-inch chunks, or fingerling potatoes, steamed or roasted (skin on) and cut on the diagonal into 1-inch slices
1	15-ounce can white beans, drained and rinsed
1	pound white-fleshed fish, such as sea bass, snapper, or halibut, cut into 8 or 16 pieces
24	clams, purged (page 83)
24	mussels, purged (page 83)
16	shrimp, shelled and deveined
2	tablespoons chopped fresh flat-leaf parsley
	Toasted baguette slices and Rouille (page 175), for garnish

1. Steam the lobsters. Bring 1 quart water to a boil in a large pot and add the lobsters, holding them by the tails, head down, and dropping them in head first. Cover tightly. Steam for 12 minutes. Meanwhile, fill a large bowl with ice water. Using tongs, remove the lobsters from the pot and chill in the ice water. Drain. Measure out the liquid in the cooking pot and add water to make 2 quarts. Set aside.

2. Break off the lobster claws and tails, crack them open, and remove the meat. Try to keep the claws intact. Remove the tomalley (the green stuff inside) and any bright red roe from the bodies and save for another purpose, such as tomalley butter (see page 174). Cut the tails into 1-inch pieces. Refrigerate the lobster meat in a covered container. Cut the lobster bodies into quarters using a sharp, heavy knife.

3. Place all the shells and the cut-up bodies in a heavy-duty jumbo food bag. Put the bag inside another plastic bag, and put this into a paper bag or wrap in a towel. This is a job to do outside if you can. Otherwise, lay several layers of newspaper on your kitchen floor. Using a meat pounder, a heavy rolling pin, a mallet, or a hammer, break up the shells in the bag. The volume will reduce considerably.

4. In a large, heavy pot, heat the canola oil over high heat until rippling, just below smoking. Add the broken-up lobster bodies and shells and all the juices in the bag. Cook, stirring often, until the color is a dark brick red and the bottom of the pan is coated with a lobster glaze, 6 to 7 minutes. Add the onion, carrot, celery, fennel, leek, and ½ teaspoon salt and stir, scraping the bottom of the pan so it doesn't scorch. Lower the heat to medium and cook, stirring and scraping often, until the vegetables begin to soften, about 6 minutes.

5. Add the tomatoes, saffron, garlic, and 1 teaspoon salt, and continue to cook, stirring often, until the tomatoes have cooked down and glazed the other ingredients, about 8 minutes. Add the fish bones and 1 cup white wine, and cook, covered, for 5 to 7 more minutes, until some of the wine has evaporated and the fish bones have turned opaque. Add the bouquet garni, stir together, and add the pepper, 2 quarts liquid you set aside, and the bread. Bring to a simmer, reduce the heat, cover, and simmer 30 minutes, or until the garlic is very soft and any fish adhering to the bones is falling off.

6. Strain the soup, preferably through a metal conical strainer that has a pestle, into another pot or bowl. Push as much through the strainer as you can, crushing the ingredients, then dump the contents of the strainer back into the soup pot. Add the strained liquid and bring back to a boil. Boil 5 minutes, stirring occasionally and taking care that the solids don't stick to the bottom of the pot and burn. This will seem redundant, but its result is a final extraction of flavor and it does make a difference.

7. Strain the soup a second time and mash the solids again with a pestle. Using a rubber spatula, scrape the contents on the outside of the strainer into the soup. Then put the soup through a fine strainer (if you don't have a fine strainer, line a medium strainer with cheesecloth). Return to the pot. If there is any juice in the bowl in which you refrigerated your lobster pieces, add to the soup. Taste and adjust the seasoning. Be generous with the pepper. The broth should have a rich flavor and a substantial texture (that's what the bread was for).

8. Add the potatoes and white beans to the soup and bring back to a simmer. Shortly before serving the soup, have the soup at a simmer and add the fish pieces. Simmer 5 minutes, and add the clams, mussels, shrimp, and lobster meat with any juices in the bowl. Cook 3 to 5 minutes, until the clams and mussels open up and the shrimp is pink and opaque. Stir in the parsley. Taste and adjust the seasonings one more time.

9. To serve, ladle some broth with potatoes and white beans into each bowl. Add to each bowl 1 or 2 pieces of fish (depending on how you cut it up), a few pieces of lobster, 3 clams, 3 mussels, and 2 shrimp. Garnish with a couple of croutons topped with rouille or tomalley butter, and serve.

[TOMALLEY BUTTER, makes 4 tablespoons]
Serve this on croutons as hors d'oeuvres.

> Reserved tomalley from 2 lobsters
> 4 tablespoons (½ stick) unsalted butter, at room temperature
> Kosher salt and freshly squeezed lemon juice

Place the tomalley in a bowl and blend in the butter with a fork or a pestle. When the mixture is well blended, season to taste with salt and a few drops of lemon juice. Spread on thin slices of baguette and serve. Or cover and chill until shortly before serving.

rouille [makes 1¾ cups]

Another member of the garlic branch of the mayonnaise family, rouille is a pungent, burnt orange (the word means "rust" in French) aïoli that is most often served as a condiment with fish stews like bouillabaisse. The classic Provençal rouille gets its spice from a small cayenne pepper. I round out the spicy flavor with roasted sweet red pepper, preferably intensely sweet canned Spanish piquillo peppers, available in specialty markets. Use a roasted red bell pepper if piquillos are not to be found.

5	fat garlic cloves, skin on
½	ounce crustless baguette, broken up into pieces (about ¼ cup, tightly packed)
2	teaspoons white wine vinegar
	Generous pinch of saffron, crushed between your thumb and fingers (about ½ teaspoon crushed)
¾	cup plus 1 tablespoon extra virgin olive oil
2	roasted piquillo peppers or ¼ roasted large red bell pepper (optional)
½	dried cayenne pepper or small dried chile (preferably Japanese), broken up
	Kosher salt
¾	cup plus 1 teaspoon canola oil
1	tablespoon warm water (more as needed)
1	large egg yolk
1	teaspoon freshly squeezed lemon juice
	Pinch of cayenne

1. Peel one of the garlic cloves, cut in half, and remove the shoot. Set aside.

2. Bring a small pot of lightly salted water to a boil and add the remaining 4 garlic cloves. Boil 2 minutes, drain, and transfer to a bowl of ice water. Allow to cool completely, then peel, cut in half, and remove the shoots. Set aside.

3. In a small bowl, toss the bread with the vinegar and let sit while you prepare the remaining ingredients.

4. Heat a small frying pan over medium-high heat and add the saffron. Shake the saffron in the pan until it begins to smell fragrant, about 1 minute. Transfer to a small bowl. Return the frying pan to the heat and add 1 tablespoon olive oil. When the oil is hot, add the roasted peppers. Cook, stirring occasionally, for about 5 minutes, until lightly browned. Add the dried hot pepper and continue to cook for about 30 seconds, just until the pepper changes color slightly. Remove from the heat and transfer, with the oil, to the bowl with the saffron.

5. Place the raw and the blanched garlic cloves in a mortar. Add ½ teaspoon salt and 1 teaspoon canola oil. Mash to a paste; don't pound the garlic, but grind it against the sides and bottom of the bowl. Add the peppers and saffron, with the oil, and continue to mash together. Add the bread and 1 tablespoon of warm water, and continue to mash until the mixture is smooth.

6. Add the egg yolk and mix together thoroughly. Slowly begin to drizzle in the remaining ¾ cup canola oil, stirring constantly with the pestle. When you've added about a third of the canola oil and the mixture has begun to emulsify, scrape the mixture into a medium bowl and switch to a whisk. Wet a dish towel and wrap it around the base of the bowl so the bowl doesn't move while you whisk.

7. Continue to add the remaining canola oil while whisking constantly. When all of the canola oil has been added, drizzle in the remaining ¾ cup of olive oil, whisking all the while. Once the mixture has emulsified you can add the oil a little more quickly. Add any remaining vinegar, lemon juice, and cayenne. Taste and adjust the seasoning. Transfer to a covered container and refrigerate until ready to serve.

[ROASTED RED PEPPERS]
Light a gas burner or a griddle and place the pepper directly over the heat. Turn, using tongs, as the pepper chars, until it is uniformly charred. If you have an electric stove, preheat the broiler and line a baking sheet with foil. Place the peppers on the foil and place under the broiler, close to the heat element. Check every few minutes, turning the peppers as they char. Place the peppers in a bowl and cover the bowl tightly with plastic or a plate, and allow them to cool.

Holding the pepper over a bowl to catch the juices, pull off the skin. Tear in half, still holding the pepper over the bowl, remove the seeds and membranes, and transfer to another bowl. Strain in the juice. If not using right away, toss with extra virgin olive oil and refrigerate, covered.

lobster pot pie [makes 10 servings]

If you can make a chicken pot pie, you can make a lobster pot pie. It's almost as easy and it will raise your stock with friends and family. Since the dish requires making a lobster stock as in the previous recipe, you will find this much easier to make if you do most of the work the day before you wish to serve it. Everything through step 8 can be done ahead. Refrigerate, covered, until you assemble the pie. Reheat the vegetables gently before assembling.

I like to cut the vegetables into interesting shapes for this. It makes it fun for me, and it adds body and texture to the finished dish. I cut the carrots and celery into oblique slices, which means cutting on the diagonal, then turning the vegetable 120 degrees and cutting on the diagonal again. The resulting cut has diagonal edges going in the opposite directions.

[LOBSTER AND LOBSTER STOCK]
- 3   1½-pound lobsters
- ¼   cup canola oil
- ½   medium onion, coarsely chopped
- ½   head of garlic, cloves cut in half
-     Kosher salt
-     A bouquet garni made with 1 bay leaf and a few sprigs each parsley and thyme (page 66)
-     Freshly ground black pepper

[VEGETABLES]
- 6   tablespoons (¾ stick) unsalted butter
- 1   large or 2 medium carrots (about 5 ounces), peeled and cut into ½-inch oblique slices (page 81, or see above)
- 3   stalks celery heart (about 3 ounces), cut into ½-inch oblique slices (page 81, or see above)
- 2   ounces baby oyster mushrooms or button mushrooms, washed, trimmed, and quartered
- 1   small fennel bulb (about 4 ounces), trimmed, cored, diced, and rinsed
- 2   White Rose or Yukon Gold potatoes (about 10 ounces), peeled and cut in ½-inch dice

- 1   medium red onion, cut in ½-inch dice
-     Kosher salt
- 4   ounces thin green beans (haricots verts), blanched in boiling salted water for 4 minutes, then transferred to ice water, drained, and trimmed

[SAUCE]
- 3   tablespoons unsalted butter
- 4   tablespoons all-purpose flour
- 1   cup heavy cream
- 1   tablespoon dry sherry
-     Kosher salt and freshly ground black pepper

[TO FINISH]
- 1   tablespoon chopped fresh tarragon
- 1   tablespoon chopped fresh flat-leaf parsley
- ½   teaspoon freshly ground black pepper
- ¾   batch Savory Flaky Dough (page 53), enough to cover a 3-quart baking dish, or the equivalent amount of frozen puff pastry
-     Egg wash made with 1 large egg yolk beaten with 1 tablespoon water

1. Steam the lobsters. Bring 1 quart water to a boil in a large pot and add the lobsters, holding them by the tails, head down, and dropping them in head first. Cover tightly and steam for 10 minutes. Remove from the water, using tongs, and chill in a bowl of ice water. Drain. Measure out the liquid in the cooking pot and add water to make 2 quarts. Set aside.

2. Break off the lobster claws and tails, crack them, and remove the meat. Try to keep the claws intact. Remove the tomalley and any red roe and save for another purpose, such as tomalley butter (see page 174). Cut the tail meat into 1-inch pieces. Refrigerate the meat in a covered container. Cut the lobster bodies into quarters using a sharp, heavy knife.

3. Place all the shells and the cut-up bodies in a heavy-duty jumbo food bag. Put the bag inside another plastic bag, and put this into a paper bag or wrap in a towel. This is a job to do outside if you can. Otherwise, lay several layers of newspaper on your kitchen floor. Using a meat pounder, a heavy rolling pin, a mallet, or a hammer, break up the shells in the bag. The volume will reduce considerably.

4. In a large, heavy pot, heat the canola oil over high heat until rippling, just below smoking. Add the broken-up lobster bodies and shells and all the juices in the bag. Cook, stirring often, until the color is a dark brick red and the bottom of the pan is coated with a lobster glaze, 6 to 7 minutes. Add the onion, garlic, any juices that have accumulated in the bowl in which you put the lobster pieces, and ½ teaspoon salt. Cook, stirring often, until the onion is tender and the mixture fragrant, about 6 or 7 minutes. Stir often and watch closely so the mixture doesn't burn on the bottom of the pan. Add the 2 quarts liquid you set aside and the bouquet garni, and bring to a boil. Reduce the heat, cover, and simmer 30 minutes.

5. Strain the broth, preferably through a metal conical strainer that has a pestle, into another pot or bowl. Push as much through the strainer as you can, then dump the contents of the strainer back into the soup pot. Add the strained liquid and bring back to a boil. Boil 5 minutes, stirring occasionally and taking care that the solids don't stick to the bottom of the pot and burn. This is the final flavor extraction and does make a difference.

6. Strain through a medium strainer and mash the lobster shells against the strainer to get the maximum flavor out of them. Strain again through a fine strainer or a cheesecloth-lined strainer. Season to taste with salt and freshly ground pepper, and set aside 2½ cups. Freeze the rest in 2-cup or 1-quart containers.

7. Prepare the vegetables. Cook the carrots, celery, mushrooms, fennel, potatoes, and onion. It's most efficient to have 2 pans going at once here, but you can do them one at a time in one pan as well; it will just take longer. For each vegetable, heat 1 tablespoon butter over medium heat in a small or medium skillet and add the vegetable with ⅛ teaspoon salt. Cook each vegetable until lightly browned and tender, and transfer to a large bowl with a slotted spoon. Carrots and onions will take about 8 minutes, potatoes 12 to 15 minutes, celery about 6, mushrooms and fennel about 6 minutes. Set aside, along with the green beans.

8. Make the sauce. In a heavy, medium saucepan over medium heat, melt the butter and add the flour. Cook, stirring, until the mixture is very slightly colored and has the texture of wet sand at low tide. Whisk in the reserved 2½ cups lobster stock and bring to a simmer, whisking constantly and being careful that the mixture doesn't stick to the sides or bottom of the pan. Simmer 10 minutes, stirring often. In a separate small saucepan, heat the cream to a simmer and whisk into the sauce. Add the sherry. Taste and adjust the seasonings.

9. Preheat the oven to 425°F. Toss together the vegetables with the tarragon, parsley, and ½ teaspoon pepper. Taste and adjust the salt. Butter a 3-quart baking dish inside and out. Spoon a layer of sauce over the bottom of the dish. Top with the vegetables. Lay the lobster meat over the top, and pour on the remaining sauce. Roll out the pastry and lay over the filling, extending over the top of the dish. Crimp the pastry tightly over the edges of the dish. Brush with egg wash and cut small slits in the pastry to allow steam to escape.

10. Place the baking dish on a baking sheet (to catch drips) and place in the oven. Bake 15 minutes. Turn the heat down to 400°F and bake for another 15 minutes, or until the top is golden brown and the pot pie is bubbling. Remove from the heat and allow to sit for 5 to 10 minutes before serving.

lobster newburg [makes 6 servings]

This is an old American classic. The ingredients in the original dish—vast amounts of butter and cream, egg yolks and lobster, and virtually no vegetables—tell us that it comes from the turn of the last century and was a dish for the wealthy customers who frequented hotels like Delmonico's in New York City, where the dish was created. The dish is quite easy. You do not have to make a lobster stock for the sauce (but please do use the shells and bodies to make a stock for your freezer); the juices from the cooked lobster add sufficient flavor to the cream. I've added vegetables to the dish, not only because they stretch it but also because I like the contrast of textures, shapes, and flavors.

3	1½-pound lobsters
4	tablespoons (½ stick) unsalted butter
⅓	cup dry sherry or Madeira
¾	pound White Rose or Yukon Gold potatoes, steamed, peeled, and cut in ½-inch dice
6	ounces carrots, peeled, cut oblique (page 81), and steamed, roasted, or simmered in butter until tender
½	pound medium asparagus, tough bases snapped off, then steamed for 5 minutes and cut in 1-inch lengths
	Kosher salt and freshly ground black pepper
2	teaspoons finely chopped shallots
1½	cups heavy cream
4	large egg yolks
	Pinch of cayenne (optional)
1	teaspoon freshly squeezed lemon juice (optional)
1	tablespoon chopped fresh flat-leaf parsley or chervil

1. Bring 1 quart of water to a boil in a large pot. Drop in the lobsters, holding them by the tails, head down, cover tightly, and steam for 10 minutes. Transfer to an ice bath, and when cool enough to handle, break off the claws and tails, crack the shells, and remove the meat, trying to keep the claws intact. Cut the tails into 1-inch pieces and set aside in a bowl with the claws. Refrigerate the bodies and shells, and use for lobster stock (page 173).

2. Preheat the oven to 325°F. Heat the butter in a large, heavy saucepan over medium heat and add the lobster and any liquid sitting in the bowl with the lobster meat. Cook, stirring, for 2 to 3 minutes, until the lobster is coated with butter. Add the sherry and continue to cook for another

2 to 3 minutes, or until the lobster is thoroughly cooked. Remove the lobster with a slotted spoon and arrange in a 3-quart gratin dish with the potatoes, carrots, and asparagus. Season with salt and pepper.

3. Add the shallots and the cream to the pan and bring to a boil. Reduce the heat slightly and boil until the mixture has reduced by half. Meanwhile, beat the egg yolks in a bowl. Remove the saucepan from the heat and making sure it's not boiling, whisk about ½ cup into the egg yolks. Whisk this mixture back into the saucepan, scraping it all out of the bowl with a rubber spatula. Return to medium-low heat and heat, stirring constantly with a rubber spatula, until the mixture coats the front and back of your spatula like custard and leaves a wake when you run a finger down the middle of the spatula. Do not allow it to simmer or the eggs will curdle. If you see this beginning to happen, remove from the heat immediately and beat vigorously with a whisk. Remove from the heat and stir in the cayenne and lemon juice. Taste and adjust the salt. Pour over the lobster and vegetables. Heat through in the oven for 10 minutes. Sprinkle with parsley or chervil and serve.

[WHEN CREAM BUBBLES UP]
Make sure you use a large saucepan for this, as the cream will double in volume when it is at the boil and can easily boil over. Keeping a whisk in the pan will help prevent this, as the bubbles break quickly against the wires of the whisk. If you see the bubbling liquid approaching the edges of the pan, remove the pan immediately from the heat and whisk like crazy.

roasted clams with garlic, tomatoes, rouille, and rustic bread

[makes 4 servings]

Recipes can't get simpler than this one, which we've served as both starter and main course. It's a dish that's made for late summer, when tomatoes are at their peak and clams are plump and delicious. The only time-consuming element of this dish is making the rouille, which should be made with a mortar and pestle.

1	large or 2 medium tomatoes (about 14 ounces), peeled
2	tablespoons olive oil, plus oil for brushing the bread
1½	pounds small clams, such as Manila, purged (page 83)
2	plump garlic cloves, cut in half, green shoots removed, then cut in thin, lengthwise slivers
6	ounces crusty country bread, such as ciabatta, cut in ½-inch-thick slices
½	cup Rouille (page 175)
1	tablespoon finely chopped fresh flat-leaf parsley

1. Cut the tomatoes into fillets by quartering and cutting the outside flesh away from the inner core of seeds. Set aside the core (later on you'll use it for rubbing the toasted bread) and cut the fillets into medium dice. You should have 1 scant cup of diced tomato (preparing the tomatoes like this may seem unnecessary to you, but it makes the dish much prettier.)

2. Preheat the oven to 400°F. Heat 2 tablespoons olive oil in a large, heavy skillet over high heat. When the oil is just short of smoking, add the clams. Shake the pan to distribute the clams evenly. Sprinkle the tomatoes and garlic slivers evenly over the clams, cover the pan, and place in the oven. Roast for 5 minutes, or until the clams have opened up.

3. Meanwhile, toast the bread lightly, brush with olive oil, and rub with the core of the tomato. Top with rouille, and distribute among 4 wide bowls.

4. When the clams have opened up, remove from the heat and divide among the 4 bowls, along with the tomatoes, garlic, and broth from the pan. Garnish with parsley and serve.

VARIATION
Substitute mussels for the clams.

shrimp boil with pickled onions and corn on the cob

[makes 6 servings]

This is a big messy meal for a big messy crowd, and it's easy. You don't have to spend hours in the kitchen peeling shrimp (your guests do that after they're cooked). Spread newspapers on the table for this summer meal with southern flavors. Put out finger bowls, and make sure your guests have plenty of napkins.

[COURT BOUILLON]

1	tablespoon canola oil
½	medium or ¼ large onion, sliced
2	garlic cloves, halved, green shoots removed, and coarsely chopped
1	stalk celery, sliced
1	bay leaf
1	small dried red chile (preferably Japanese)
	Handful of parsley sprigs
1	thyme sprig
½	cup dry white wine
2	quarts water
2	teaspoons kosher salt
½	teaspoon cracked black peppercorns
2	tablespoons white wine vinegar

[SPICE MIX]

1	tablespoon coriander seeds
1	teaspoon mustard seeds
1	teaspoon white peppercorns
1	teaspoon fennel seeds
¾	teaspoon celery seeds
¼	teaspoon cayenne

[TO SERVE]

2	pounds medium shrimp, in the shell
½	cup (1 stick) unsalted butter, at room temperature
1	teaspoon kosher salt
2	tablespoons chopped fresh flat-leaf parsley
2	cups Pickled Red Onions (page 235)
	Steamed corn on the cob

1. Make the court bouillon: Heat the canola oil in a large saucepan or soup pot over medium heat and add the onion, garlic, celery, bay leaf, chile, parsley, and thyme. Cook gently, stirring often, until the onion is tender, about 5 minutes, and add the wine. When the wine comes to a boil, add the water, salt, pepper, and vinegar. Bring to a boil, reduce the heat, and simmer 15 to 20 minutes, until fragrant. Strain and return to the pot.

2. Meanwhile, make the spice mix: Toast the coriander seeds, mustard seeds, white peppercorns, and fennel seeds in a small frying pan over medium-high heat until they smell fragrant and a bit like popcorn. Add the celery seeds and cayenne and stir together for a few seconds. Remove from the heat and transfer to a bowl. Allow them to cool for 5 minutes, then grind in a spice mill.

3. Shortly before serving, bring the court bouillon back to a boil. Add the shrimp and cook for about 2½ minutes, until bright pink. Transfer to a bowl using a slotted spoon or skimmer and toss immediately with the butter, spices, and salt to taste. Add the parsley, toss again, and serve, with pickled onions and corn on the cob.

steamed clams or mussels and new potatoes with grilled corn and green beans [makes 4 to 6 servings]

I always use clams for this in the summer; it's a clambake type of dish. But it's equally delicious if you use mussels. You can use flat Romano green beans or regular green beans. The shellfish is steamed over a fragrant vegetable ragout (grilling the corn adds wonderful depth of flavor to it), contributing its wonderful juice to the mix. I like to use fingerling potatoes. They have a perfect texture, and look pretty sliced on the diagonal into thick slices. When you dice the onion, carrot, and celery, try to cut the pieces about the size of the corn kernels.

3	ears of corn, husked
2	teaspoons canola oil
3	tablespoons extra virgin olive oil
½	large onion (about 6 ounces), diced
1	medium carrot, peeled and diced
2	stalks celery, diced
2	plump garlic cloves, halved, green shoots removed, and minced
2	ounces thick-cut bacon, diced
1	fresh flat-leaf parsley sprig, plus 2 tablespoons minced fresh flat-leaf parsley
1	tarragon sprig
1	pound fingerling potatoes or other small waxy potatoes, steamed until tender and sliced ½ inch thick (on the diagonal if using fingerlings)
	Kosher salt
1½	cups Chicken Stock (page 66 or commercial) or water
6	ounces Romano beans or other green beans, trimmed and cut into 1-inch lengths
2	pounds clams or 1½ pounds mussels, purged (page 83)
2	tablespoons unsalted butter
	Freshly ground black pepper
1	to 2 teaspoons freshly squeezed lemon juice (to taste)

1. Prepare a medium-hot grill or heat a cast-iron skillet over medium-high heat. Rub the corn lightly with canola oil and grill, turning frequently, until lightly colored, 10 to 15 minutes. Remove from the heat and allow to cool slightly, then slice off the kernels and set aside. Don't throw away the cobs.

2. Heat 2 tablespoons of the olive oil over medium heat in a wide, deep, lidded frying pan or Dutch oven and add the onion, carrot, and celery. Cook gently, stirring often, until the vegetables begin to soften, about 5 minutes. Add the garlic, bacon, parsley sprig, and tarragon. Continue to cook until the mixture is soft, another 5 to 10 minutes, and add the remaining tablespoon of olive oil, the potatoes, the stripped corncobs, and 1 teaspoon salt. Cook 5 minutes, stirring a few times, and add the chicken stock or water. Bring to a simmer, cover, and simmer 5 minutes. Remove the corncobs and the herb sprigs, add the green beans, cover, and cook 5 to 8 minutes, until the beans are tender. Stir in the corn kernels.

3. Lay the clams or mussels on top of the vegetables. Cover and cook until they open up, 4 to 5 minutes. When the bivalves have opened, use tongs to remove them to a bowl. Return the ragout to the heat, and stir in the butter, salt and pepper to taste, lemon juice, and minced parsley. Taste and adjust the seasonings.

4. Spoon about three-fourths of the ragout onto a very large platter or into a wide bowl. Toss the clams or mussels with the remaining ragout and place them over the ragout on the platter. Scrape any liquid and ragout remaining in the pan over the top, and serve.

[NOTE] You can make this through step 2 several hours ahead of serving. Cover and set aside. Shortly before serving, bring back to a simmer and proceed with step 3. If you have leftovers, remove the clams or mussels from the shells and add to the ragout. Reheat gently in a wide pan.

dungeness crab in spicy scallion butter [makes 4 servings]

This is another big, messy dish that you should eat wearing a big cheap logo T-shirt, preferably outside. Don't bother with napkins; pass out towels. It's inspired by a classic sweet and pungent, spicy and buttery dish I ate in Singapore, called black pepper crab. I loved the dish, but I didn't like the preprocessed black pepper that most of the Singapore chefs used. This version has fresher flavors. If you don't want to cook your Dungeness crab or can only find it precooked and cracked, you can still make the dish. The sauce will lack some depth of flavor because you won't have the crab juices to work with, but it will still be pungent and messy.

1	recipe court bouillon (page 180)
2	Dungeness crabs
3	tablespoons canola oil or Mild Chili Oil (recipe follows)
¼	cup minced shallots
2	tablespoons minced fresh ginger
2	tablespoons minced garlic
	Kosher salt
1½	teaspoons freshly ground black pepper
½	cup dry white wine
2	teaspoons Vietnamese or Thai chili sauce, such as Red Rooster brand
4	tablespoons (½ stick) unsalted butter
1½	cups chopped spring onions or scallions, white and light green parts only
2	tablespoons chopped fresh flat-leaf parsley

1. Bring the court bouillon to a boil and add the crabs. Cook 10 minutes and transfer to a bowl of ice water. Allow to cool, then drain. Break off the carapace, then remove the gills and the tail and discard. Separate out the tomalley and juice and set aside. Break off the legs and claws. Crack the legs and claws with a nutcracker or a small hammer. Cut the body into large chunks. Strain the tomalley and innards and keep the juice. Reserve 1 cup of the court bouillon.

2. Heat a large pan over high heat and add the chili oil. When the oil is rippling, add the crab pieces and cook, stirring, for 2 to 3 minutes, until they're bright pink. Turn the heat down to medium and add the shallots, ginger, and garlic. Stir together for a minute and add ½ teaspoon salt and the pepper. Stir together and add the white wine. Bring to a boil and cook for 2 minutes, then add the strained crab juice, the reserved court bouillon or 1 cup water, and the chili sauce. Simmer for 3 minutes. Taste and adjust the seasoning, then lift the crab out of the pan and onto a large platter.

3. Add the butter, spring onions, and parsley to the pan and swirl together for 1 minute. Pour over the crab, and serve. Make sure everyone has crab picks and finger bowls.

[MILD CHILI OIL, makes 1 cup]
I use this oil when I make Dungeness Crab in Spicy Scallion Butter (above), but it's great for a multitude of other dishes, such as salads and stir-fries, when you want a bit of spice. Be sure to strain out the chiles before using.

1 cup canola oil
4 dried red chiles, broken in half

Combine the oil and chiles in a small saucepan and heat over medium-high heat until the chiles just begin to sizzle. Remove from the heat and allow the chiles to steep for 1 hour before using. Transfer to a jar and refrigerate. You can keep the oil for several weeks in the refrigerator.

cornmeal-crusted pan-fried trout [makes 4 servings]

This is real campfire food, and utterly satisfying. If you go on a fishing trip, just bring a pan, cornmeal, oil, salt, and pepper and you can make it every night. Otherwise, make sure you get really fresh trout. You could also make the dish with thin salmon or sea trout escalopes. Whatever fish you use, have all of your ingredients ready and within reach before you start, because the cooking goes quickly and you need to focus on cooking the fish properly so it will stay moist. Remember to turn on your fan before you cook the fish.

4	small trout, scaled, heads removed, boned, and butterflied, pinbones removed (The fish department should do this. Make sure the tail and skin are intact, and the two fillets are joined at the tail.)
	Kosher salt and freshly ground black pepper
6	tablespoons fine cornmeal (if you only have polenta or coarse cornmeal, you can grind it to a fine powder in a clean spice mill)
1/4	cup all-purpose flour
1	tablespoon plus 1 teaspoon finely chopped fresh flat-leaf parsley
1/4	cup canola oil
1	tablespoon plus 1 teaspoon butter
	Lemon wedges, for serving

1. Heat a large, heavy cast-iron skillet over medium-high heat.

2. Open up the trout, pat dry, and season with salt and pepper. Mix together the cornmeal, flour, 1 teaspoon salt, 1/2 teaspoon pepper, and the parsley in a wide bowl.

3. Dip the trout into the cornmeal mix on the cut side only. Make sure it is thoroughly coated. If not cooking right away, place the fish on a platter in one layer, uncovered, in the refrigerator.

4. Add 2 tablespoons canola oil to the hot pan and when it is just below smoking, carefully add 1 or 2 trout—however many will fit in your pan—skin side up. After 1 minute, add 2 teaspoons butter to the pan. Watch the skin, and when you see it beginning to dimple and curl (this will take about 2 minutes), turn the fish. Cook on the skin side for 30 seconds to a minute, just until the fish begins to curl. Remove from the pan and keep warm in a low oven while you repeat with the remaining oil, butter, and fish. Serve hot, with lemon wedges.

[NOTE] If you can cook only one fish at a time, you will be able to do the first two without adding more oil.

sautéed halibut crusted with seasoned bread crumbs [makes 6 servings]

You can't do better than properly fried fish. The job may be a little messy, but the results are worth it. Correctly done, the crust is crisp and delicious, with no sign of grease, and the fish within is moist and flavorful. You need nothing more than lemon for this, though a side of Horseradish Mashed Potatoes (page 202) wouldn't hurt. Coleslaw (page 34) also goes well with fish prepared this way.

12	ounces country bread, such as ciabatta, with the crusts removed (weigh after removing crust), broken up into approximately 1-inch pieces
3	tablespoons minced fresh flat-leaf parsley
3	tablespoons minced celery leaves
2	large garlic cloves, cut in half, green shoots removed, minced
3	large eggs
⅓	cup heavy cream
	Kosher salt
1½	cups all-purpose flour
6	6-ounce halibut fillets
	Freshly ground black pepper
2	tablespoons canola oil
1	tablespoon unsalted butter
	Lemon wedges, for serving
	Horseradish Mashed Potatoes (page 202)

1. Preheat the oven to 350°F. Place the broken-up bread on a baking sheet and bake for 30 minutes, or until crisp all the way through. Remove from the heat and allow to cool for 20 minutes. Transfer to a food processor fitted with the steel blade. Pulse until the bread has broken down into coarse bread crumbs, about the coarseness of cornmeal. If some pieces don't break down in the food processor, it's because they are still slightly moist. Pick those out and discard. You will have more bread crumbs than you need, but it's better than not having enough.

2. Measure out 1½ cups of bread crumbs and toss with the herbs and garlic in a wide bowl. Set aside.

3. Beat together the eggs and cream in a wide bowl. Add a generous pinch of salt. Place the flour in another wide bowl (you will also have more flour than you need, but it's easier to coat the fish if you have an abundance).

4. Season the fish fillets generously on both sides with salt and pepper. Cover a platter or a baking sheet with parchment paper. Dredge each halibut fillet in the flour, using your left hand if you're right handed and your right hand if you're left handed. Gently shake the fillet to remove excess flour, then dredge in the egg/cream mixture, and finally in the herbed bread crumbs. Pick up the fillet with your dominant hand and place on the parchment. Allow to sit for 30 minutes in the refrigerator so that the coating adheres and dries (this also gives you time to clean up). Meanwhile, preheat the oven to 450°F. Using this method, only one hand, your dominant one, gets messy. It's much easier to work that way.

5. Heat the canola oil in a cast-iron skillet over medium-high heat. When the oil is rippling, add the fish fillets (you will probably have to do this in batches) and cook for 2 minutes. Add the butter to the pan and turn the fillets over. Place in the oven and roast 5 to 10 minutes, depending on the thickness of the fillets. To test for doneness, gently squeeze the sides of the fillets. If they are soft, the fish is still raw in the middle. The fish is done if the sides are firm (but not hard—then it's overdone) and yield just a little to the touch. Remove from the heat. Serve with lemon wedges and horseradish mashed potatoes

VARIATION / SAUTÉED SNAPPER CRUSTED WITH SEASONED BREAD CRUMBS

Other, more delicate fillets, such as red snapper or cod, can also be prepared this way. You will not have to finish cooking the fish in the oven for these thinner types of fish. Follow the recipe as written, but do not preheat the oven. In step 5, after you have turned the fillets over, cook for another 2 minutes. The fish will be ready.

sand dabs meunière [makes 4 servings]

This is the California version of the classic French sole meunière. Sand dabs, a West Coast sole, are smaller than Dover sole. It is an incredibly delicate fish in both flavor and texture. I prefer to cook them on the bone, and even on the bone, you won't need to cook them for more than 2 minutes per side. It's essential that you get your pan nice and hot, and use enough oil so the fish crisps and cooks quickly. If the pan isn't hot enough, the surface of the fish will turn gummy instead of crisp and brown.

1½	to 2 pounds sand dabs (about 8 sand dabs), cleaned and scaled
	Kosher salt and freshly ground black pepper
¼	cup all-purpose flour
2	tablespoons canola oil
4	tablespoons (½ stick) unsalted butter
1	tablespoon plus 1 teaspoon freshly squeezed lemon juice
1	whole lemon, peeled, supremed (see below), and chopped
2	tablespoons chopped fresh flat-leaf parsley

[CITRUS SUPREMES]

When a recipe calls for supremes from a lemon, orange, or grapefruit, it is referring to the fruit without the membranes. To "supreme" a citrus fruit, cut both ends off, then cut away the skin and pith by standing the fruit on one end and cutting down the sides with a sharp knife. Then hold the fruit above a bowl to catch the juices, and using a paring knife, saw just inside each membrane to cut away the fruit. Once you've cut away the fruit, squeeze the membranes in your fist over the bowl to extract the last of the juice.

1. Have all of your ingredients ready by the stove. This recipe is very quick, so everything should be within reach. Heat a heavy frying pan over medium-high heat. A well-seasoned cast-iron skillet works best. Meanwhile, season each fish fillet with kosher salt and pepper, and dredge lightly in the flour. Add the canola oil and when it is just below smoking, add half the fish, or as many as can comfortably fit into the pan without crowding it. Cook for 1½ to 2 minutes, until browned, then turn over and cook another 1½ to 2 minutes (depending on the size of the fish), or until the fish is nicely browned on both sides. Remove to a warm platter. Repeat with the next batch of fish, until all have been cooked.

2. Remove the pan from the heat and pour out the fat. Add the butter and a pinch of salt. Allow the butter to foam and turn golden (this will happen quickly), and add the lemon juice and pulp, and the parsley. Stir together, then pour over the fish. Serve at once.

seared salmon fillets wrapped in basil leaves [makes 4 servings]

This is a beautiful way to use those huge basil leaves you sometimes get. The leaves are quickly softened in boiling water, then layered over the top side of salmon (or ocean trout) fillets. They crisp up when the fillets are cooked, but they maintain their beautiful emerald green color. Make sure to remove the skin from your fillets if they come with the skin on, and to serve the fish immediately so the basil leaves stay crisp.

4   skinless 6-ounce salmon or ocean trout fillets
2   tablespoons plus 2 teaspoons canola oil
    Kosher salt and freshly ground black pepper
    A few sprigs fresh basil, preferably with
        extra-large leaves
1   tablespoon unsalted butter
2   tablespoons Basil or Parsley Pesto (page 59)

1. Heat a heavy frying pan over medium-high heat. Bring a small saucepan of water to a boil. Fill a medium bowl with ice water. Brush each salmon fillet with ½ teaspoon canola oil and salt and pepper both sides generously.

2. Dip the basil sprigs in the boiling water for a few seconds only to soften the leaves, and immediately transfer to the bowl of ice water. Drain on paper towels. Carefully remove the thick stem and shave the vein from the bottom of each leaf.

3. Cover the top of each fillet with basil leaves, vein side down.

4. Add 2 tablespoons canola oil to the hot pan. The oil should not smoke but your hand should feel the heat when you hold it above the pan. Place the salmon fillets in the pan, basil side down. Cook for 2½ minutes, then turn the fillets over and add the butter to the pan. Cook for another 2½ minutes, or until the fillets are firm. Carefully remove from the pan and serve at once, garnishing each serving with a spoonful of basil or parsley pesto.

[HOW TO THAW FROZEN FISH]
Do not remove it from the package. Place it in the refrigerator and let it thaw slowly. It may take a day or more, depending on how cold your refrigerator is and how cold the freezer your fish is coming from is. If you need it faster, thaw it by running it under cold water in the package. Do not use warm water; it will cause the fish to lose flavor and texture, and poses a possible health hazard.

monkfish ragout with mussels and pancetta [makes 4 servings]

Unlike the elaborate rich fish stew on page 173, this is not a tomato- or lobster stock–based stew from the bouillabaisse family. It's easy and quick, and just as delicious. Shellfish and pork always go well together (and not just because they're both forbidden by kosher law). Make sure to remove the mussels from the pan as soon as they've opened so that they don't continue to cook. Overcooked mussels are rubbery and awful.

1½	pounds monkfish fillet, cut in 1-inch chunks
	Kosher salt and freshly ground black pepper
¼	pound pancetta, cut in 1 x ¼-inch strips
1	tablespoon extra virgin olive oil
2	tablespoons water
½	cup dry white wine
¼	cup minced shallots
1	fat garlic clove, halved, green shoots removed, and minced
2	thyme sprigs
1	pound mussels, purged (page 83)
2	cups Chicken Stock (page 66), or 1 cup canned broth and 1 cup water
	Generous pinch of saffron
1	cup shelled fresh English peas (about ¾ pound unshelled)
2	tablespoons unsalted butter
2	tablespoons minced fresh flat-leaf parsley

1. Season the fish generously with salt and pepper and set aside.

2. Combine the pancetta, olive oil, and water in a wide saucepan and bring to a simmer over medium heat. Cover and simmer for 8 to 10 minutes, until the pancetta softens and has colored slightly around the edges. Add the wine, shallots, garlic, and thyme and bring to a boil. Add the mussels, cover, and cook for 3 to 4 minutes, or until the mussels have just opened. Remove from the heat and immediately remove the mussels from the pan, using tongs and tipping them over the pan as you do so you don't lose any juices. Remove the mussels from the shells, rinse briefly, and set aside in a small bowl (discard the shells).

3. Add the chicken stock (or broth and water) and the saffron to the pan and bring to a simmer. Season to taste with salt, then add the fish and the peas. Cover, turn down the heat, and simmer for 5 to 10 minutes, until the fish is opaque and firm all the way through. Taste the broth and adjust the seasonings. Stir in the mussels along with the butter and parsley. Season to taste with salt and pepper, heat through, and divide among wide soup plates.

monkfish osso buco with risotto milanese and gremolata

[makes 4 servings]

One day I was looking at a large monkfish and it occurred to me that monkfish tail looks something like a veal shank. I wondered if I could use monkfish for osso buco, the classic Italian braised veal shank seasoned with gremolata and served with risotto Milanese. I tried it out, and it worked. When you order the fish, specify to the fishmonger that you want the bone in. Do not get the monkfish slices from the narrow end of the tail. Make sure they're at least 2½ inches in diameter.

7	cups Chicken Stock (page 66)
	Kosher salt
8	1- to 1½-inch-thick slices monkfish, preferably with the bone in (about 2 pounds with the bone, 1½ pounds without), at least 2½ inches in diameter
	Freshly ground black pepper
2	tablespoons canola oil
1	tablespoon extra virgin olive oil
1½	cups arborio or Carnaroli rice
	A generous pinch of saffron (about ½ teaspoon)
½	cup finely chopped onions or shallots
1	fat garlic clove, cut in half, green shoot removed, then sliced
1	cup finely diced peeled tomatoes (fresh or canned)
½	cup dry white wine
1	tablespoon unsalted butter

[GREMOLATA]

1	teaspoon finely chopped lemon zest
½	teaspoon finely chopped orange zest
1	teaspoon finely minced garlic
2	tablespoons finely minced fresh flat-leaf parsley

1. Place the chicken stock in a saucepan and bring to a simmer. Season well with salt.

2. Season the fish generously with salt and pepper. Heat a wide saucepan over medium-high heat and add the canola oil. When it is hot—you can feel the heat when you hold your hand above it—add the monkfish pieces, cut side down. Work in batches so you don't crowd the pan. Sear for 2 to 3 minutes on each side, until lightly colored, and transfer to a platter or a baking sheet.

3. Preheat the oven to 400°F. Turn the burner heat to medium and add the olive oil to the pan. Add the rice and stir constantly over the heat, until the rice begins to smell toasty, like popcorn, and the kernels are opaque. Crush the saffron threads between your fingers and stir into the rice, along with 1 teaspoon salt. Add the onions or shallots and garlic and continue to stir for 1 to 2 minutes, scraping

the bottom of the pan to deglaze. Add the tomatoes and continue to stir and scrape the pan for about 3 minutes. Reduce the burner heat to medium-low. Add the wine and stir until it has been absorbed by the rice.

4. Begin ladling in the simmering stock. It should just cover the rice and should immediately begin to bubble, though not too hard. If it is boiling hard, turn down the heat a bit more. Stir until just about absorbed, and add another ladleful. Stir often and continue to add stock whenever you see that there is not much left in the saucepan. Gradually the mixture will become creamy.

5. After about 25 minutes, the rice should be cooked al dente and the mixture should be creamy. *Al dente* means "toothy" in Italian, so it should be just firm to the tooth in the center of the grain. Taste and adjust the seasoning. Continue to add stock and cook if necessary. It should not take more than 30 minutes. Be careful not to let the rice stick to the bottom of the pan.

6. When the rice is al dente and the mixture creamy, cover the rice one more time with stock. Making sure that you can see the stock bubbling, place the monkfish fillets on top of the rice and tip in any liquid that has gathered on the platter. Cover and place in the preheated oven for 10 minutes.

7. Meanwhile, make the gremolata. Combine all of the ingredients on a cutting board and mince together. Set aside in a small bowl.

8. After 10 minutes, remove the fish and rice from the oven. The fish should be opaque and firm all the way through. If it is not, return to the oven for another 5 minutes. Take the fish off the rice. If the rice is not creamy, stir in another ladle or two of stock. Stir in the butter. Spoon the rice onto a platter. Top with the fish. Sprinkle on the gremolata, and serve.

VARIATION

Add 1 cup cooked peas or cooked pearl onions (or ½ cup each) to the rice when you stir in the final ladleful of stock.

whole roast fish [makes 4 servings]

This is one of the easiest dishes you will ever make. Seriously, a hamburger has more components. The tricky part is filleting the fish after it's cooked (see the photos and captions on the following page; the technique applies to all vertical fish). It really is too bad that whole fish are hard to come by in most markets. The one exception is Asian markets, where fresh whole fish are easy to find. To choose the freshest fish, look at the eyes, which should be clear and not at all sunken, and the scales, which should be shiny. If they allow you, press on the flesh; it should be firm and spring back; your finger should leave no indentation. If there are any tears in the midsection over the rib bones, the fish is not fresh. I like to use a firm, white-fleshed fish such as porgy, sea bass, or snapper for this. Have the fish department clean and scale the fish for you.

2 1½-pound whole fish, such as porgy, sea bass,
      or snapper, cleaned and scaled
      Extra virgin olive oil, for brushing the fish
      Kosher salt and freshly ground black pepper
4   paper-thin lemon slices, cut in half and seeded
2   large tarragon sprigs
½   cup tightly packed tarragon leaves
2   tablespoons pastis or absinthe
      Fleur de sel

[NOTE] Do not sprinkle the pastis or absinthe on the fish when it is on the grill. They can contain up to 50 percent alcohol and could cause a dangerous flare-up.

1. Preheat the oven to 450°F. Brush the fish with olive oil and season inside and out with salt and pepper. Place 2 lemon slices inside each fish's belly with 1 large tarragon sprig.

2. Oil a rack that fits inside a baking pan or sheet pan. Place the fish on the rack and cover the fish with the tarragon leaves. Drizzle 1 tablespoon olive oil over the leaves. Roast 20 to 25 minutes, until the fish separates from the bones at the fleshiest part of the dorsal fin.

3. Remove the pan or baking sheet from the oven and drizzle the pastis or absinthe over the fish. Return to the oven for 1 to 2 minutes (to cook off the raw alcohol flavor).

4. Using 2 spatulas, transfer the fish to a serving platter and scrape off and discard the tarragon. Drizzle on a few drops of extra virgin olive oil and sprinkle with fleur de sel. Fillet and serve.

VARIATION / ROAST FISH WITH FENNEL

Substitute wild fennel fronds for the tarragon. Place a frond in the fish's belly and place a bed of fronds on top of and underneath the fish in the baking dish.

(continues)

TOP LEFT Make an incision down to the bone from top to bottom right behind the head and the front fin.
MIDDLE Make an incision down to the bone from top to bottom about 1 inch in front of the tail.
BOTTOM With the tip of your knife, make an incision from head to tail along the belly.

[HOW TO FILLET A WHOLE COOKED FISH]

1. With the tip of your knife, make an incision down to the bone from top to bottom right behind the head and right in front of the tail.

2. With the tip of your knife, make an incision from head to tail along the backbone and along the belly, right above the edge of the belly. If you wish to remove the skin, lift it off, using a flat fish knife or your fingers.

3. With the tip of your knife, cut down the center of the fish to the bone, from the head to the tail. If the fish is small, serve one portion from the top half and one from the bottom half, easing the fish off the bone with your knife and onto a spatula. If the fish is large, divide the top and bottom into sections and slide onto the spatula.

4. Lift the head or the tail of the fish away from the bottom half, easing the flesh off the bone, and gently pull off the entire skeleton. Pick off any bones you see, and divide the bottom half of the fish into portions.

[GRILLED WHOLE FISH]

Substitute thyme sprigs or wild fennel fronds for the tarragon sprigs. Omit the tarragon leaves. Prepare a medium-hot grill. Soak a generous handful of thyme sprigs or wild fennel fronds in water for 10 minutes. Spread them over the grill, away from the direct heat of the coals and covering a swath about the size of the fish. Place the fish, presentation side down, on top of the thyme or fennel. Cover the other side with moistened thyme or fennel sprigs. Cover the grill and grill 10 minutes. Uncover and carefully turn the fish over. Cover again and grill 8 minutes, or until the flesh separates from the bone easily at the thickest part or the dorsal fin. Remove the fish from the grill and transfer to a platter. Discard the thyme or fennel. Drizzle on a few drops of extra virgin olive oil and a few drops of lemon juice, pastis, or absinthe, sprinkle with fleur de sel, and serve.

[GRILLING TIPS]

1. You don't need a huge fancy grill (most of the recipes in this book that involve grilling can be done on a hibachi). But I do recommend using a solid fuel grill rather than a gas grill, mainly because you can distribute the charcoal (or wood) in such a way that you have a choice of temperatures, with hotter areas and cooler areas. It's more difficult to achieve this range with a gas grill.

2. Get a good grill brush and use it to keep the grill clean; your food will not stick to a clean grate if you don't try to fiddle with it too soon.

3. When you put food down on a hot grill, the first thing that happens is that it sticks. Patience is required. Do not try to move or turn the food until you can see that it will lift away easily.

4. Sear food on the hottest part of the grill, then move it away from the direct heat to cook through.

5. Always grill food on its presentation side first.

6. If your recipe instructs you to cover the grill and you want a really intense smoky flavor, use a large stainless bowl (buy one and dedicate it to this job only, as it will very quickly be charred black) to cover the food.

TOP LEFT With the tip of your knife, make an incision from head to tail along the top edge of the fish.
TOP RIGHT With the tip of your knife, cut down the center of the fish to the bone, from the head to the tail.
MIDDLE LEFT Divide into 4 sections.
MIDDLE Using a spatula, ease the sections off the bone.
MIDDLE RIGHT Cut off the tail with kitchen scissors and gently lift off the skeleton.
BOTTOM LEFT Trim away the edges and small bones along the belly and top edge.
BOTTOM RIGHT Divide the bottom half of the fish into 4 portions.

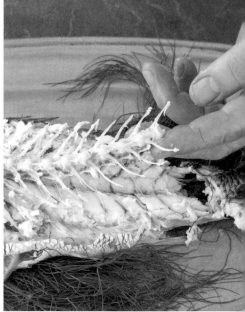

sturgeon or salmon in a red wine sauce [makes 6 servings]

This is based on a classic French matelote, a fish stew made with river fish—often eel—and red wine. We've done it at the restaurant with sturgeon, salmon, and trout. Monkfish also works well. I think of the dish as a winter fish stew, with rich, complex flavors. It's a convenient dish for entertaining, because you can have everything prepared ahead of time, then cook the fish in the red wine sauce at the last moment. Instead of the fish stock you can use half chicken broth and half water. Fish stock is preferable, but you can buy chicken broth at the store.

¼ pound bacon (about 4 strips), cut crosswise in ¼-inch strips

2 tablespoons water

1 tablespoon all-purpose flour

½ medium onion, sliced crosswise against the grain
  Kosher salt
  A bouquet garni made with a few sprigs each parsley and thyme, a bay leaf, 2 garlic cloves, halved and green shoots removed, and 1½ teaspoons peppercorns (page 66)

2 cups red wine, such as Pinot Noir

2 cups Chicken Stock (page 66), or 1 cup canned broth and 1 cup water

8 pearl onions, blanched and peeled, or small spring onions (bulbs only)

1 tablespoon unsalted butter

3 ounces wild mushrooms, cut in ½-inch-thick slices or separated into small clumps (depending on the type of mushroom)
  Freshly ground black pepper

2 pounds sturgeon, monkfish, salmon, or trout fillets
  Minced fresh flat-leaf parsley, for garnish

1. Combine the bacon with the water in a large saucepan over medium heat and cook, stirring from time to time, until the bacon is lightly browned, 5 to 8 minutes. Add the flour and cook, stirring, for a minute, then add the onion and ½ teaspoon salt. Cook, stirring often, until tender, about 5 to 8 minutes. Add the bouquet garni and the wine and bring to a boil, stirring the bottom of the pan with a wooden spoon to deglaze. Add the stock (or broth and water), bring to a simmer, cover, reduce the heat, and simmer 30 minutes, stirring often. Strain through a medium strainer and set aside.

2. Meanwhile, make a small slit with a paring knife in the ends of the pearl or spring onions. Heat the butter in a wide, lidded skillet over medium heat and add the onions and ½ teaspoon salt. Cook, stirring often, until beginning to color, 3 to 4 minutes, then add the mushrooms. Cover and cook over medium-low heat until tender, about 5 minutes. Stir from time to time and add 1 tablespoon of water if the pan dries out and the vegetables begin to stick. Taste and adjust the salt. When tender, add the strained red wine sauce and simmer 5 minutes.

3. Taste the wine sauce and add salt and pepper as needed. Remove from the heat if not serving right away. Shortly before serving, bring the sauce to a simmer. Season the fish fillets with salt and pepper and add to the sauce. They should be barely covered with the sauce. Cover and cook gently, being careful not to allow the sauce to boil, until cooked through but not falling apart, about 8 to 10 minutes for sturgeon or monkfish, 5 minutes for salmon, 3 minutes for trout fillets. Taste the sauce again and adjust the seasonings.

4. Remove the fish to a warm platter and spoon some of the sauce, with the onions and mushrooms over and around the fish. Sprinkle with parsley, and serve with boiled potatoes or fresh noodles.

[NOTE] If serving with noodles (I recommend pappardelle or wide egg noodles), mound the cooked noodles on a large platter. Arrange the fish fillets on top of the noodles and spoon on a generous amount of sauce. Sprinkle with parsley and serve.

tuna confit [makes 1½ pounds, about 6 servings]

This tuna confit is tuna that has been cooked very slowly in extra virgin olive oil; it's what great canned tuna should be. The fish is submerged in the oil, and the oil brought slowly to 140ºF, where it must remain throughout the cooking time, about 30 minutes for one 1½-pound piece of fish. Since the temperature won't be even, you need to gently circulate it by moving the pan or stirring it carefully with a small spoon. A thermometer is essential for this recipe. If the temperature goes above 140°F, it won't be a pretty picture. The albumin, a protein in the fish, will ooze from the tuna, covering it with a white film that looks like cottage cheese, and the tuna will be tough and dry. But keep it at or just below 140°F and you'll have satiny, succulent fish that you'll want to keep on hand as a staple item in the refrigerator.

1½	pounds thick yellowfin or albacore tuna steaks (or a single 1½-pound piece, cut in 1½-inch-thick steaks)
1	to 2 teaspoons kosher salt (to taste)
½	large onion, sliced
	Leaves from a few fresh flat-leaf parsley sprigs
1½	cups extra virgin olive oil

1. Season the fish generously on both sides with salt. Place on a plate, baking sheet, or in a wide bowl and cover with the onion and parsley. Cover with plastic wrap and refrigerate for 1 hour.

2. In a small saucepan (though large enough to accommodate the oil and the tuna), heat the olive oil over very low heat. Insert a thermometer and when the oil reaches 140°F, place the tuna in it with the onion. Keep the oil at 140°F and leave the tuna in it for 30 minutes. The tuna should turn gray but there should be no white protein streaks. Remove from the heat, cover, and refrigerate the tuna in the oil. It will keep well for 2 weeks.

oyster po' boys [makes 4 servings]

This is a New Orleans classic, a fried oyster and coleslaw sandwich on a soft roll (don't use a hard roll; when you bite into it everything will squeeze out onto your lap). You can make this with jarred shucked oysters, which will be less expensive and require less work.

½   cup (1 stick) unsalted butter
4   soft rolls, split open (a good-quality hamburger bun will do perfectly)
¾   cup all-purpose flour, approximately
12   to 16 shucked medium oysters
1½   cups Celery Remoulade (page 34) or Coleslaw (page 34)
½   cup Remoulade Sauce (page 34)

1. Heat a heavy frying pan over medium-high heat and add half the butter. Place the bread, cut side down, in the pan and fry in the butter until lightly browned. Remove from the pan.

2. Place about ¾ cup flour in a bowl and toss the oysters in the flour. Transfer the floured oysters to a strainer and tap the strainer against the bowl to release the flour. You will not use up the flour (the oysters should just be lightly coated and not gummy), but it's easier to do this with the quantity called for.

3. Heat the remaining butter over medium-high heat. When it stops foaming and is turning light brown, add the oysters. Cook for about 1 minute on each side, until lightly browned. Remove from the heat.

4. Top the bottom half of each roll with about ⅓ cup celery remoulade or coleslaw (or a little more) and lay 3 to 4 oysters on top. Place a teaspoon of remoulade sauce on each oyster, top with the other half of the roll, and eat immediately.

fish and (onion ring) chips [makes 6 servings]

Deep-frying is something to do only occasionally in your home kitchen. It can make a mess and you always have at least two quarts of oil to dispose of at the end. But if you do this well you'll discover why the British love fish and chips as much as Americans love hamburgers. Use an electric deep fryer so that you can keep the temperature constant, and use fresh, lean white-fleshed fish, like halibut, cod, black cod, or sea bass. You can also use snapper as long as the fillets are thick; too thin and they'll fall apart. Rather than French fries, I serve batter-fried onion rings with my batter-fried fish.

[BATTER]

1½	cups cornstarch
1½	cups all-purpose flour
1½	teaspoons salt (regular, not kosher)
1½	teaspoons baking soda
1½	teaspoons baking powder
1½	cups (1 bottle) dark beer
1½	cup plus 2 tablespoons club soda

[ONIONS AND THE FISH]

2	large, firm red onions, preferably flat, wide ones
1½	cups malt vinegar, plus additional for serving
	Kosher salt and freshly ground pepper
2	quarts canola oil, for deep frying (more as needed, depending on the size of your fryer)
12	½- to 1-inch- thick white-fleshed fish fillets, such as halibut, black cod, cod, sea bass, or snapper, 2 to 3 ounces each
1	cup all-purpose flour
	Tartar sauce (page 34), lemon wedges, and malt vinegar for serving

1. Make the batter. Sift the cornstarch, flour, salt, baking soda, and baking powder into a large bowl. Add the beer and whisk together well. Whisk in the sparkling water. Test the batter by plunging a spoon into it and pulling it out. There should be a thin coating of batter adhering to the spoon after the excess drips off. Fill a larger bowl with ice and water and set the bowl with the batter in it to chill and keep very cold.

2. Peel and cut the onions crosswise against the grain into ¼-inch-thick rings. Discard center slices that are not rings. Place the malt vinegar in a large bowl and gently toss the onions in the vinegar to coat, taking care not to break them. Cover and chill for 30 minutes.

3. Remove the fish fillets from the refrigerator and pat them very dry with paper towels. Season on both sides with kosher salt and pepper, and return to the refrigerator.

4. Heat the oil in a deep-fryer, preferably one with a basket, to 350°F to 375°F. Stir together ½ teaspoon salt and 1 cup all-purpose flour. Drain the onions and dry thoroughly on paper towels. A handful at a time, gently toss with the flour, then lift out and tap off excess flour. Dip into the batter, then carefully place in the hot oil. Deep-fry until the coating is deep brown, turning the rings over with tongs or a deep-fry skimmer to ensure even browning. Remove from the oil, allowing the excess oil to drip back into the fryer, and drain on newspapers, paper towels, or a rack. Continue to cook all of the onion rings in this fashion, making sure to bring the oil back up to at least 350°F between batches. Transfer to a large newspaper- or brown paper–lined bowl or platter (or make newspaper cones).

5. Deep-fry the fish. Make sure the oil is at 350° to 375°F. Lightly coat the fish fillets with flour, then dip into the batter and add to the deep-fryer, in batches. If your batter begins to thicken noticeably (from the flour coating on the onions and fish), add a tablespoon of sparkling water. Cook until deep brown, turning the fillets over once. Remove from the oil and drain on newspapers, paper towels, or a rack. Transfer to a platter, surround with onion rings and lemon wedges, and serve, with tartar sauce and malt vinegar for dipping.

[NOTE] The soda water in the batter contributes to the leavening, resulting in a light, crispy batter.

[7]
SIDE DISHES

There are two types of side dishes in this chapter: vegetable side dishes and starches—potatoes, rice, and other dishes of that nature. Some diet fads equate starches with the spawn of Satan. I like calling a starch a starch, and find that a meal without a side dish from this food group can feel incomplete and insubstantial. We need mild-tasting potato and grain dishes to balance the strong forward flavors of rich meats and stews, to absorb juices and gravies, and to round out many of our menus.

At Campanile (and other restaurants as well) it's often the side vegetables that sell an entrée, and I take pains to choose the best produce I can find. Every Wednesday morning you will find me walking through the farmers' market in Santa Monica, looking at produce and talking to the farmers I've gotten to know over the years. I never know exactly what I'm going to buy before I go; I see what looks good and then decide. Produce is variable; on a given day at the same market I've had transcendent peas and awful peas from the same area, grown by different farmers. This is the way to decide what to cook for dinner. Look and, if possible, taste. Even if you buy your vegetables at the supermarket, see what looks good, then decide what to cook.

There's a range of side dishes here. Some are complex and take time. Others couldn't be simpler. There are many in between. Two dishes, Long-Cooked Greens and Long-Cooked Green Beans with Bacon on pages 230, are inspired by traditional dishes from the American South. They require little in the way of labor, but a lot of time on the stove. You may wonder why I enjoy cooking these carefully chosen vegetables for so long, but when you experience the richness of long-cooked greens and taste the long-cooked green beans with bacon and their sweet juices, you'll see why the dishes appeal to me.

Whether you choose to cook a simple dish or a complex one, all vegetables deserve your full attention. No matter how they are cooked, they should be cooked long enough to bring out their flavor. If Simone Beck, the famous French cooking teacher and co-author with Julia Child of *Mastering the Art of French Cooking*, were alive today, she would be very happy to see that the age of undercooked nouvelle cuisine vegetables is long gone. In the '70s she reprimanded me for serving her crunchy green beans. "We are not rabbits!" she sputtered, and the beans went back to the kitchen to be cooked properly so she could actually taste them.

I don't think I loved vegetables as a kid as much as I do now, but I can thank my mother for getting me on the path at a young age. She would say "Eat your vegetables or no dessert!" So I always did. Today the produce is so much better; if it had been this good when I was a kid, I might not have needed the ice cream at the end of the stick.

mashed potatoes, finally revealed [makes 4 to 6 servings]

We chefs all lie about our mashed potatoes. We don't tell you we've used 1½ pounds of cream and butter with 1¾ pounds of potatoes. You don't need to know. Mashed potatoes are one of those very simple dishes that require some work and technique. The results when you do them right are spectacular. You will never again need to bring anything else to a potluck. Cream, butter, and a good sieve are essential, and so is a double boiler for heating them. This will create some extra dirty dishes and take more time than other methods, but do it this way anyhow.

2	pounds russet potatoes, peeled and cut in 2-inch chunks (1¾ pounds peeled)
4	fat garlic cloves, cut in half, green shoots removed
1½	cups heavy cream
1½	cups (3 sticks) unsalted butter
1	teaspoon kosher salt

1. Place the potatoes and garlic in a steamer basket above boiling water, cover, and steam for 25 minutes, until very tender.

2. Meanwhile, combine the cream, ¾ cup (1½ sticks) of the butter, and the salt in a medium saucepan and heat until the cream simmers and the butter melts.

3. When the potatoes are tender, put through a ricer or the medium blade of a food mill. Add the cream mixture and mix together well. Then press through a flat tamis or a large strainer, using a rubber spatula or a pestle to press the mixture into a stainless steel bowl that will rest in a saucepan without touching the bottom.

4. Make a double boiler by filling a saucepan with 1 inch of water and placing the bowl in it. The bottom of the bowl should not touch the water. Bring the water to a simmer over medium heat. Stir the potatoes as they heat. Cut the remaining ¾ cup butter into pieces and, using a whisk or a rubber spatula, beat into the hot puree until combined. Continue to heat the potatoes over the simmering water, stirring often, until hot and silky. Taste, adjust the seasoning, and serve.

VARIATION / HORSERADISH MASHED POTATOES
Just before serving, whisk in 1 tablespoon grated fresh horseradish for every cup of mashed potatoes.

mashed potatoes with cantal and mozzarella cheese

[makes 6 servings]

This is an adaptation of a French classic, pommes aligot, which is made with fresh Cantal cheese curds. When we make the dish, we combine Cantal and fresh mozzarella cheese; the Cantal gives the mashed potatoes the authentic flavor, and the mozzarella gives it the authentic stringy consistency. You have to serve this immediately, while the cheese is still stringy in the hot mashed potatoes. If it cools, the texture will become grainy and rubbery. If it does cool down, you can restore the texture by reheating it in a double boiler and again beating vigorously with a whisk or a rubber spatula. This is very similar to the recipe for mashed potatoes, but because of the cheese, you use less butter and replace the cream with milk.

2	pounds russet potatoes, peeled and cut in 2-inch chunks (1¾ pounds peeled)
3	fat garlic cloves, cut in half, green shoots removed
1½	cups whole milk
½	cup (1 stick) unsalted butter, cut into pieces
1½	teaspoons kosher salt
6	ounces Cantal cheese, grated (about 1½ cups tightly packed)
6	ounces fresh mozzarella cheese, cut into small pieces (about 1½ cups)

1. Place the potatoes and garlic in a steamer basket above boiling water, cover, and steam for 25 minutes, or until very tender.

2. Meanwhile, combine the milk, butter, and salt in a medium saucepan and heat until the milk simmers and the butter melts.

3. When the potatoes are tender, put through a ricer or the medium blade of a food mill. Add the milk mixture and mix together. Then press through a flat tamis or a large strainer, using a rubber spatula or a pestle to press the mixture into a stainless steel bowl that will rest in a saucepan without touching the bottom.

4. Make a double boiler by filling a saucepan with 1 inch of water and placing the bowl in it. The bottom of the bowl should not touch the water. Bring the water to a simmer over medium heat. When the potatoes are hot, gradually stir in the cheese, a handful at a time, beginning with the Cantal and stirring after each addition. When all of the cheese has been added, beat vigorously until the cheese has melted and the potatoes are smooth and elastic, stretching like rubber bands when you lift the spoon. Serve immediately.

roasted fingerling potatoes [makes 4 servings]

Simple roasted fingerling potatoes, named after their shape (need we say more?), are a staple in the restaurant. We use them in many dishes, as will you. Rose Finn, Russian Banana, and La Ratte are all excellent varieties of fingerling potatoes. They are all young, small, dense, and delicious.

1¼   to 1½ pounds fingerling potatoes, scrubbed
2   tablespoons extra virgin olive oil
      Kosher salt and freshly ground black pepper
      A few sprigs or 1 tablespoon chopped rosemary
         or thyme (optional)

1. Preheat the oven to 425°F. Place the potatoes in a baking dish and toss with the oil, salt, and pepper. Make sure the potatoes are well coated with oil and the baking dish is also well oiled. Add the herbs, if desired. Cover the baking dish and place in the oven for 45 minutes. Check the potatoes. They should be tender all the way through when pierced with a knife, but still a little firm. If they are not, give them another 10 minutes.

2. Remove from the oven and allow to cool in the pan before serving.

parsleyed potatoes [makes 4 servings]

In France, parsleyed potatoes are simple steamed potatoes tossed with butter and parsley. I like to brown the steamed potatoes lightly in the butter so that the edges are slightly crisp. Parsleyed potatoes go with a range of meat and fish dishes, from simple roasts to more complex braises and stews.

1 ½ pounds Yukon Gold potatoes, peeled and cut in half
2 tablespoons unsalted butter
2 tablespoons finely chopped fresh flat-leaf parsley
 Kosher salt

1. Steam the potatoes until tender, about 20 to 30 minutes depending on the size of the potatoes. Remove from the heat and allow to cool and dry out for about 5 minutes, then cut in thick (¾-inch) slices.

2. Heat a heavy skillet over medium-high heat and add the butter. When the butter has ceased foaming and has begun to color lightly, add the potatoes and turn the heat to medium. Cook on one side until crusty and lightly browned, about 5 minutes, then turn over and cook on the other side until crusty and lightly browned. Add the parsley and salt, toss together for a minute, and serve.

gratin dauphinoise [makes 6 servings]

This classic, rich potato gratin is all about potatoes, cream, and butter. The other ingredients—garlic, herbs, cheese—should be used with restraint to infuse and accent the main ingredients. Make sure to slice the potatoes uniformly so they cook evenly. If you have a mandoline it will make the slicing much easier.

1	garlic clove, cut in quarters, green shoot removed
2½	pounds russet potatoes, peeled and sliced ¼ inch thick
1½	to 2 teaspoons kosher salt (more to taste)
	Freshly ground white pepper
4	ounces Gruyère cheese, grated (1 cup tightly packed)
4	tablespoons (½ stick) unsalted butter, melted
1¼	cups heavy cream
1	cup whole milk
4	small thyme sprigs

1. Preheat the oven to 375°F. Rub the inside of a 2-quart gratin dish with the cut side of a garlic clove. Toss the potatoes in a bowl with the salt, pepper, half the cheese, and the melted butter. Place in the gratin dish in an even layer. Mix together the cream and milk and pour over the potatoes. Press the potatoes down into the liquid. Tuck a quarter clove of garlic and a thyme sprig into the corners of the baking dish.

2. Bake the gratin for 45 minutes. Remove from the oven and gently press the potatoes down into the liquid, using the back of a spoon. Sprinkle the remaining cheese over the top and bake for another 30 to 45 minutes, until nicely browned. Remove from the heat and allow to sit for 10 to 15 minutes before serving.

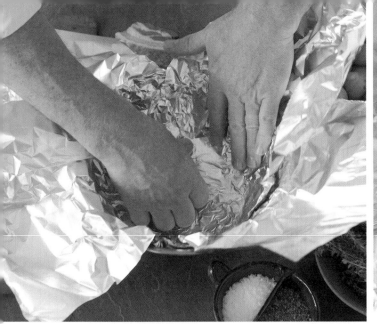

campfire potatoes [makes 8 servings]

We've had campfire potatoes on our family menus many times over the years, and we're constantly tweaking the recipe. They go with all sorts of dishes. The dish is called campfire potatoes because it was conceived as a dish you could make by just throwing potatoes wrapped in foil into a campfire. You can make them in a Weber grill, too, or in the oven. You'll always have the smoky flavor if you use the bacon. You can set this dish up hours before you're ready to cook it, and throw it on the fire or in the oven 45 minutes before dinner.

2	pounds Yukon Gold potatoes, scrubbed and cut into 2-inch chunks, or smaller potatoes such as fingerlings, scrubbed and left whole or cut in half
1	tablespoon slivered sage leaves
2	teaspoons fresh thyme leaves or summer savory leaves
1½	to 2 teaspoons kosher salt (to taste)
½	teaspoon freshly ground black pepper
¼	cup extra virgin olive oil
6	garlic cloves, unpeeled
1	strip thick-cut bacon (optional)

1. Preheat the oven to 450°F or prepare a medium fire in a charcoal grill. Toss all the ingredients except the bacon together in a large bowl.

2. Line another large bowl with a large piece of heavy-duty foil, shiny side down, leaving at least 6 inches of overhang on both sides of the bowl. Turn the bowl and line with another sheet. Turn the bowl and line with one more sheet. If you don't have heavy-duty foil, use five layers of regular foil and make sure there are no cracks in the packet.

3. Place the piece of bacon on the foil and top with the potatoes, making sure to scrape all the oil and herbs from the bowl. Fold the edges of the top sheet of foil in loosely over the potatoes and crimp together. Repeat with the other 2 sheets. Make sure the packet is tightly sealed and no oil can drip out. Lift the whole package out of the bowl and place on a baking sheet if roasting in the oven.

4. If using the grill, set the packet right into the coals. If using the oven, place in the oven. Roast for 45 minutes, turning the packet over halfway through. Remove from the heat and allow the packet to sit for 5 to 10 minutes before opening. Carefully cut open and dump the contents, except the bacon, into a large serving dish. If desired, cut the bacon into strips and sprinkle over the top. Serve at once.

TOP LEFT Line a large bowl with 3 overlapping sheets of heavy-duty foil, shiny side down, leaving at least 6 inches of overhang on all sides of the bowl.
TOP RIGHT Place the bacon on the foil at the bottom of the bowl.
MIDDLE LEFT Top with the seasoned potatoes, making sure to scrape all of the oil, garlic, and herbs from the bowl.
MIDDLE Fold the edges of the top sheet of foil in loosely over the potatoes and crimp together.
MIDDLE RIGHT Repeat with the other 2 sheets.
BOTTOM LEFT Make sure the packet is tightly sealed and no oil can drip out.
BOTTOM RIGHT Lift the whole package out of the bowl and place on a baking sheet if roasting in the oven. If using the grill, set the packet right into the coals.

VARIATION / CAMPFIRE POTATOES WITH ARTICHOKES
Use 1½ pounds potatoes, prepared as above, and ½ pound baby artichokes, trimmed (page 26) and cut in half. Proceed with the recipe.

pommes boulangère [makes 6 servings]

Pommes Boulangère, loosely translated as "potatoes from the bakery," got their name because decades ago in French villages the bakery housed the only oven in town. In the morning, when the baker's bread came out of the wood-fired oven and the oven was still hot, families would bring dishes like this simple potato gratin that required long, slow baking, pop them in the oven, and come back to retrieve them in time for lunch or dinner.

2	ounces thick-cut bacon, cut in ¼-inch strips
4	tablespoons (½ stick) unsalted butter
½	medium onion, cut in half and sliced across the grain
1	large leek, white and light green part, sliced and cleaned (page 54)
	Kosher salt
2	fat garlic cloves, cut in half, green shoots removed, and sliced thin, plus 1 clove, just cut in half, green shoot removed
2	pounds Yukon Gold, White Rose, or Red Rose potatoes, peeled and sliced ¼ inch thick
	Freshly ground black pepper
¾	cup chicken stock or broth
¾	cup beef stock or broth
1	large thyme sprig
1	bay leaf
2	ounces Gruyère cheese, grated (½ cup tightly packed)

1. Preheat the oven to 375°F. Combine the bacon and 1 tablespoon butter in a heavy saucepan or skillet and cook over medium heat until the bacon renders its fat and begins to color. Add another tablespoon of butter, the onion, leek, and ½ teaspoon salt, and cook, stirring, until the onion is tender but not colored, about 8 minutes. Add the sliced garlic and continue to cook, stirring often, for another few minutes, until the ingredients are fragrant. Remove from the heat and add the remaining butter, and stir until it melts.

2. Rub a 2-quart gratin dish with the cut clove of garlic. Toss the potatoes in a large bowl with 2 teaspoons salt, a generous amount of freshly ground pepper, and the onion mixture. Place in an even layer in the gratin dish. Combine the chicken and beef stock and add to the dish. Place the thyme sprig and the bay leaf on top. Place in the oven.

3. Bake for 45 to 60 minutes, until the liquid is almost absorbed. Remove from the oven and gently press the potatoes down into the liquid, using the back of a spoon. Remove the bay leaf and thyme sprig. Sprinkle the cheese over the top and bake for another 15 to 20 minutes, until nicely browned on the top and sides. Allow to sit for at least 10 to 15 minutes before serving.

spaetzle [makes 6 to 8 servings]

This is the easiest fresh pasta you'll ever make. Spaetzle are very small dumplings, made from a batter, not a dough. The batter is passed through the holes of a colander or a perforated pan (or, if you live in Germany or Austria and make spaetzle all the time, a sort of ricer called a spaetzler), and falls by small droplets into a pot of boiling salted water, where it quickly cooks up into tasty little dumplings. Spaetzle is great with stews (like the Beef Goulash on page 121) and as a side dish with meat. Try it also with the Smothered Pork Chops on page 145. It's important to chill the spaetzle before sautéing. If you go straight from boiling to sautéing you will have a gummy mess.

8	large eggs
⅓	cup whole milk, plus a bit more if needed
	Salt (use regular salt, which dissolves in the batter better than kosher salt)
1	teaspoon freshly ground black pepper
	Small pinch of freshly grated nutmeg (more or less to taste)
3	cups all-purpose flour, plus a bit more if needed
1	tablespoon canola oil (if not serving right away)
4	tablespoons (½ stick) unsalted butter (more to taste)

1. Combine the eggs, milk, 2½ teaspoons salt, the pepper, and nutmeg in a large stainless steel bowl or the bowl of a standing mixer fitted with the paddle, and beat together well.

2. Add the flour, and with the paddle attachment or by hand, beat vigorously for 5 minutes to aerate it and develop the gluten. The batter is ready when it blisters. Add milk if the batter seems too thick. If large bubbles slowly come up to the surface and pop, the batter is the right consistency. If no bubbles occur, you need to add a little more flour. If bubbles appear but they can't rise, the batter is too stiff and needs some more liquid.

3. Let the batter rest for 10 minutes or longer. Meanwhile, bring 4 quarts of water to a boil in a large, wide saucepan or pot and add 4 teaspoons salt. Fill a large bowl with ice and water and set a strainer or colander in the water.

4. Put a few spoonfuls of batter at a time through a perforated pan or a colander into the pot and cook just until the dumplings rise to the surface. Remove from the water with a spider or a slotted spoon and transfer directly to the strainer in the ice water. When all of the spaetzle have been cooked and cooled in the ice bath, stir and drain well. If not using right away, toss with 1 tablespoon canola oil.

5. Just before serving, heat the butter over medium-high heat in a large, wide frying pan and add the spaetzle. Sauté for a few minutes, until lightly browned, taste and add salt and pepper if desired, and serve.

VARIATION / SPAETZLE WITH WILTED SPINACH
To the above recipe add:

6	ounces baby spinach (1 bag), washed
	Kosher salt
1	fat garlic clove, halved, green shoot removed, and minced
	Freshly ground black pepper

Make the spaetzle as directed. Heat the butter in the frying pan over medium-high heat and add the spinach and ½ teaspoon salt. Cook, stirring, until the spinach wilts. Add the garlic and stir for a minute, then remove from the heat, transfer the spinach and garlic to a bowl, and allow to cool. Squeeze out excess water with your hands and roughly chop. Cook the spaetzle following the instructions in the recipe, but just before it's done, add the chopped spinach and garlic and stir together for a couple of minutes. Taste and add salt and pepper if desired, and serve.

polenta with butter and parmesan cheese [makes 4 to 6 servings]

We love serving polenta at the restaurant. It goes equally well with meat or fish, and it's as comforting as mashed potatoes but not as rich. Polenta is the way Italians eat corn; made from ground field corn, it resembles coarse-ground cornmeal. When you cook it slowly in milk and water, the resulting dish is creamy and rich, especially after you add the butter and Parmesan. If you serve this to friends from the American South, just call it grits (it'll save on arguments).

2 cups plus 2 tablespoons whole milk
2 cups plus 2 tablespoons water
1¾ teaspoons kosher salt
1 fresh sage sprig
1 cup medium polenta
4 tablespoons (½ stick) unsalted butter
2 ounces Parmesan cheese, grated
(½ cup tightly packed)

1. Combine the milk, water, salt, and sage in a large, heavy saucepan and bring to a simmer over medium heat. Very slowly stream in the polenta, stirring constantly with a wooden spoon or a whisk. Turn the heat to low and simmer, stirring often and scraping the bottom and sides of the pan with a wooden spoon, until the polenta is thick and creamy and the spoon stands up when it is stuck in the middle, 20 to 30 minutes. Remove the sage. After about 15 minutes, taste for salt and add a pinch more if you think it's necessary.

2. Remove the polenta from the heat and immediately stir in the butter and Parmesan. Butter a 2-quart baking dish and scrape in the polenta. Serve at once, or cover tightly and chill overnight. You can reheat the polenta in a double boiler (see Mashed Potatoes, Finally Revealed, page 202). It will not be as smooth.

VARIATION / FRIED POLENTA TRIANGLES

These must be served hot and crisp. The trick is to get them brown and crisp without burning the cheese. Keep the heat moderate rather than high once the pan gets hot.

1. Increase the polenta in the recipe to 1⅓ cups and cook as directed. Once cooked, scrape into a small sheet pan or baking dish in a layer about ¾ inch thick, and chill.

2. When the polenta is cold and stiff, cut into 3-inch triangles. Line a baking sheet with parchment and place the triangles on it. Chill for 1 hour or longer.

3. Heat 2 tablespoons extra virgin olive oil in a large, heavy skillet over medium-high heat. Lightly dredge the polenta triangles in all-purpose flour. Add 1 tablespoon unsalted butter to the pan, and when it stops foaming, carefully add as many polenta triangles as you can add without crowding the pan. Turn the heat to medium and cook for a minute or two, until golden. Carefully turn over with a spatula, and cook on the other side until golden. Carefully remove from the pan and drain briefly on paper towels. Repeat with the remaining polenta triangles. Serve hot. If not serving right away, place on a rack over a baking sheet and keep warm in a low oven.

grits with bacon, cheddar cheese, and butter [makes 6 servings]

Grits made from dried hominy is a true Southern dish, yet they have much in common with polenta. Unless you use quick-cooking grits (and you can for this recipe, but don't use instant), cooking them is a long, slow process. On their own, grits are the blandest of foods, but they offer the cook a blank canvas for adding other ingredients, like the bacon and cheese in this dish.

2	ounces bacon, cut crosswise in ¼-inch-wide strips
4	cups plus 1 tablespoon water
1½	teaspoons kosher salt
1	cup regular or quick grits (but not instant)
1	cup whole milk
4	ounces aged, medium-sharp cheddar cheese, grated (1 cup tightly packed)
3	tablespoons unsalted butter
	Freshly ground black pepper

1. Combine the bacon and 1 tablespoon water in a heavy 3-quart saucepan and cook over medium-high heat until the bacon is lightly browned and beginning to crisp, about 5 minutes. Remove the bacon from the pan and set aside on paper towels. Leave the fat in the pan. Add the remaining 4 cups water and the salt and bring to a boil, scraping the bottom of the pan with a wooden spoon.

2. When the water is boiling, turn the heat to medium and slowly stream in the grits, stirring constantly. Turn the heat to low, cover, and simmer until the water is absorbed. This will take anywhere from 10 to 45 minutes, depending on what kind of grits you are using (stone-ground old-fashioned grits will take the longest; the box will indicate the amount of time needed). Stir often to prevent the grits from sticking to the bottom of the pot and burning.

3. When all of the water has been absorbed, stir the milk into the grits and simmer, uncovered, until the grits are creamy, about 10 minutes. Stir and scrape the bottom of the pan often. Add the bacon and the cheese and stir until the cheese has melted. Stir in the butter. Taste and adjust the seasonings, adding salt and pepper as desired. Serve hot.

rice pilaf with aromatic spices [makes 4 servings]

Rice pilaf isn't much more complicated than plain steamed rice, but it is far more delicious. We enhance ours with cumin seeds, coriander seeds, garlic, and a pinch of saffron. Sometimes, to vary the texture, we stir in some cooked farro.

1	tablespoon extra virgin olive oil
1	cup basmati or long-grain rice
½	medium onion, chopped
¾	teaspoon kosher salt
2	garlic cloves, halved, green shoots removed, and minced
¾	teaspoon cumin seeds, toasted and ground (page 33)
¾	teaspoon coriander seeds, toasted and ground (page 33)
2	cups Chicken Stock (page 66 or commercial), or 1 cup chicken broth and 1 cup water
	Pinch of saffron
1	to 2 tablespoons chopped fresh flat-leaf parsley

1. Heat the olive oil over medium heat in a large, heavy saucepan or Dutch oven and add the rice. Cook, stirring constantly, until it is opaque and begins to smell like popcorn, and stir in the onion and salt. Cook, stirring often, until the onion is tender, about 3 to 5 minutes. Add the garlic, stir together for about half a minute, and stir in the cumin and coriander. Cook for a couple of minutes, until the ingredients begin to smell fragrant, and stir in the 2 cups chicken stock (or 1 cup each chicken broth and water), and the saffron. Bring to a simmer, then reduce the heat, cover, and simmer 15 minutes, or until the liquid has been absorbed.

2. Remove the pan from the heat, cover it with a clean dish towel, and place the lid over the towel. Let sit undisturbed for 15 to 20 minutes. The excess water will be absorbed or will evaporate. The rice will steam and should be fluffy. Toss with the parsley, and serve.

VARIATION
Stir ½ cup cooked farro (page 217) into the pilaf.

COUSCOUS [makes 6 generous servings]

We serve couscous with Moroccan-inspired stews like the lamb tagine on page 137, but also as a side dish stand-in for potatoes, rice, or other grains. Couscous has been previously steamed and dried. It requires reconstituting, them steaming in a covered dish in the oven.

2	cups couscous
1	teaspoon salt (kosher or regular)
2½	cups Chicken Stock (page 66) or water, or a combination (more if necessary)
2	tablespoons unsalted butter

1. Place the couscous in a bowl and mix with the salt. Heat the stock or water until warm and pour over the couscous. There should be enough liquid to cover the couscous by ½ inch. Add more if needed. Let the couscous soak up the liquid for 20 minutes, stirring or tossing with spoons or moistened hands every 5 minutes, to prevent the grains from clumping. Taste and adjust the salt.

2. Preheat the oven to 325°F. Lightly oil a 2- or 3-quart baking dish and spoon the couscous into the dish. Dot the top with butter. Cover tightly and place in the oven for 20 minutes. Uncover, toss the grains again, and serve.

yorkshire pudding [makes 6 servings]

Traditionally, Yorkshire pudding was a batter poured into a pan that was placed under a joint of meat roasting on a spit in an open fireplace. It caught the dripping fat and cooked at the same time. This pudding is simple, ephemeral, and delicious. It derives its flavor from the fat. This one gets its character from roast beef, but you could also make Yorkshire pudding with drippings from a roast leg of lamb or with clarified butter. Whatever fat you do use, you can have the batter made up ahead, but bake the Yorkshire puddings right before serving. They are like savory popovers or dense soufflés, and will collapse very soon after being removed from the oven.

½ cup hot roast beef drippings (page 131)
4 large eggs
2 cups whole milk
1 teaspoon kosher salt
2 cups all-purpose flour, sifted

1. Preheat the oven to 450°F. Brush 12 large muffin tin cups with dripping. Place 2 teaspoons of the hot drippings into each cup and place in the oven while you mix the ingredients.

2. In a medium bowl, beat the eggs with the milk and salt. Add the flour and beat well to combine.

3. Remove the muffin tins from the oven. The fat should just be starting to smoke. Pour ⅓ cup batter mixture into each cup. Return immediately to the oven and bake 15 to 20 minutes, until puffed and brown. Serve at once.

barley and farro [makes 4 to 6 servings]

These two grains are hearty and chewy, and stand up to robust meat dishes like the Braised Lamb Shanks on page 135. They can both stand in for rice, potatoes, or noodles.

[PEARL BARLEY]

1	cup pearl barley
3	cups chicken stock
¾	teaspoon kosher salt

Combine the barley, stock, and salt in a medium saucepan and bring to a boil. Reduce the heat to low, cover, and simmer 30 to 40 minutes, until the barley is tender. If all the liquid has not been absorbed when the barley is tender, drain.

[FARRO]

Farro is a type of whole wheat berry. Some cooks recommend soaking farro to shorten the cooking time.

1	cup farro
1	teaspoon salt
4	cups water or chicken stock

Combine the farro, salt, and water or chicken stock in a medium saucepan and bring to a boil. Reduce the heat, cover, and simmer 40 to 50 minutes, until cooked through and chewy. Remove from the heat and allow the grains to swell in the cooking water for 10 minutes, then drain.

[NOTE] If you substitute American wheat berries for the farro, soak the berries for 8 hours or overnight and cook as directed. You can also soak farro for 1 or 2 hours, and the cooking time will be a little shorter.

campanile beans [makes 4 to 6 servings]

Beans are one of my favorite foods; I like to have them on hand in the refrigerator so I can snack on them. We cook different types of beans at Campanile—flageolets, cannellini, Peruvanas (white beans not unlike cannellini beans), and pintos. Our formula is pretty much the same for all of them.

1 tablespoon extra virgin olive oil

2 ounces bacon in 1 piece or thick-cut bacon, cut in ¼-inch strips

1 medium or ½ large onion, chopped

4 garlic cloves, cut in half, green shoots removed, and sliced

Kosher salt

A bouquet garni made with a bay leaf, a few sprigs each thyme and savory, a handful of parsley sprigs, and 2 or 3 celery tops (page 66)

1 pound dried beans, washed, picked over, and soaked for 6 hours or overnight in water to cover by 2 inches

1 cup Chicken Stock (page 66, or commercial)

1. Heat the olive oil in a large, heavy casserole over medium heat and add the bacon. Cook until the bacon renders some fat, 3 to 4 minutes, and add the onion. Cook, stirring often, until tender, about 5 minutes, and add the garlic. Stir together for about a minute, until the garlic is fragrant, and add 2 teaspoons salt, the bouquet garni, the beans with their soaking liquid, and the chicken stock. Because the beans will have absorbed a great deal of their soaking water, add enough water to cover the beans by 3 inches. Bring to a boil. Skim off any foam that rises. Cover, reduce the heat, and simmer gently for 1½ to 2 hours, until the beans are tender and the broth is delicious.

2. Taste and adjust the seasonings. Remove from the heat. Remove the bouquet garni, and the bacon if desired, and discard. Serve immediately or refrigerate and serve later, cold, hot, or at room temperature, whenever the urge strikes.

[NOTE] You can make a vegetarian version of this by omitting the bacon and the chicken stock.

ratatouille [makes 6 servings]

I wish I always had ratatouille on hand in the refrigerator. The "secret" is to cook everything separately, combine them, and stew them together briefly, then let them rest. Most of the time required by this recipe is in the peeling and cutting. Once you have the ingredients prepared and organized, the cooking doesn't take long. Use a half-sheet pan to line up your vegetables, and another one for the finished vegetables. The vegetables are sliced thickly so they maintain their integrity as they cook.

2	pounds eggplant (2 large), sliced ½ inch thick
	Kosher salt
2	pounds tomatoes, peeled (page 90)
I	pound red bell peppers, or a combination of red and yellow peppers (not green), stemmed, seeded, and sliced ½ inch thick
½	pound yellow squash (preferably yellow zucchini), sliced ½ inch thick
I	pound zucchini, sliced ½ inch thick
I ½	pounds onions, cut in half and sliced with the grain
6	garlic cloves, halved, green shoots removed, and sliced
I	to 2 teaspoons fresh thyme leaves, or ½ to I teaspoon dried thyme
	Extra virgin olive oil, as needed (about ½ cup)
2	ounces (on the stem) fresh basil, leaves stemmed and cut crosswise into ½-inch-wide strips
	Freshly ground black pepper
	Pinch of cayenne

1. Sprinkle the eggplant slices generously with salt. Place on a rack above a half-sheet pan and set the timer for 20 minutes. Turn the slices over and salt the other side. Let sit for another 20 minutes. Rinse well and pat dry.

2. Meanwhile, cut the tomatoes in half across the equator. Place a strainer above a bowl and squeeze out the seeds and juice from the tomatoes. Press the pulp through the strainer and discard the seeds. Cut the tomatoes into 1-inch pieces and set aside the juice for later.

3. Place the vegetables in neat rows on a half-sheet pan or in a large baking dish. Have another empty half-sheet pan or baking dish next to the stove.

4. Heat a large, heavy skillet over high heat and add 2 table-spoons olive oil. When the oil is very hot but not smoking,

add the peppers and toss together. Add about ¼ teaspoon salt, or more to taste, and cook, stirring occasionally, until the peppers are seared and softened, 8 to 10 minutes. Remove from the heat and scrape out onto the empty baking sheet in a pile, so the heat of the peppers allows them to continue to wilt.

5. Heat another tablespoon of olive oil over medium-high heat in the skillet and add the yellow squash in an even layer. Season with salt. Cook on one side until golden brown, 2 to 3 minutes. Using tongs, turn the squash rounds over and cook until golden brown on the other side, 2 to 3 minutes. The squash should be softened by this time. Leave a little longer if it isn't. Remove from the pan and place next to the peppers on the baking sheet.

6. Heat 2 tablespoons olive oil in the skillet and add the zucchini in a single layer. Do this is batches if all of your zucchini won't fit in a single layer. Season with salt and cook on each side until golden brown on the outside and tender inside, about 2 to 3 minutes per side. Transfer to the baking sheet.

7. Add another tablespoon of oil to the pan and add the onions. Turn the heat down to medium and cook until seared on the edges and beginning to soften, about 6 minutes. Add the garlic, thyme, and ¼ teaspoon salt and stir together. Cover and cook, stirring often, until tender, another 5 to 10 minutes.

8. Meanwhile, heat another skillet over medium-high heat and add 2 tablespoons olive oil and a single layer of the rinsed and patted dry eggplant rounds. Cook on both sides until nicely browned, about 4 minutes per side. Continue with the remaining eggplant rounds, adding a tablespoon of oil as necessary. Transfer to the baking sheet, allow to cool slightly, and cut in ½-inch squares. Set the skillet aside.

(continues)

(You cook the eggplant in a separate skillet because, unlike other vegetables, the glaze at the bottom of the pan after cooking eggplant can be quite bitter.)

9. When the onions are tender, add the tomato water to the pan and turn up the heat. Stir and deglaze the bottom of the pan and reduce the liquid for 2 to 3 minutes. Add the tomatoes and stir together. Cover the pan and cook 5 minutes, just until they begin to soften.

10. Stir all the cooked vegetables back into the pan, along with the basil, salt and pepper to taste, and a pinch of cayenne. Gently toss the vegetables together, reduce the heat, cover, and simmer gently for 10 to 15 minutes, until the vegetables are tender and fragrant but still hold their shape, and there's plenty of liquid in the pan.

11. Place a colander over a bowl and, with a rubber spatula, scrape the ratatouille into the colander. Allow to drain for 10 minutes. Transfer the juice back to the pan. Spoon the ratatouille into the bowl.

12. Bring the liquid to a boil and reduce to a syrupy consistency over high heat. Pour back into the ratatouille and fold together gently. This concentrates the flavor without overcooking the vegetables. Taste and adjust the seasoning. For the best flavor, refrigerate overnight and reheat gently, or serve cold.

eggplant and tomato confit [makes 6 servings]

Eggplant, tomatoes, garlic, and onions: That may taste like Provence to some, but to me it tastes like California. As this long-simmering combination cooks down, the vegetables slowly caramelize and take on an almost jamlike intensity. I serve the dish most often with lamb, but it really goes with anything—chicken, meat, or fish. You can also serve it on its own as a first course, and use the leftovers as a topping for bruschetta.

2	pounds eggplant, preferably small Japanese eggplants
	Kosher salt
2	pounds tomatoes, peeled, or one 28-ounce can, with juice
6	tablespoons extra virgin olive oil
1	medium onion, roughly chopped
4	large garlic cloves, halved, green shoots removed
	Cracked black peppercorns
4	large basil sprigs

1. Sprinkle the eggplant slices generously with salt. Place on a rack above a half-sheet pan and set the timer for 20 minutes. Turn the slices over and salt the other side. Let sit for another 20 minutes. Rinse well and pat dry. Cut into 1 x 1 x ½-inch dice.

2. Cut the tomatoes in half and squeeze over a strainer set over a bowl to remove the seeds and retain the juice. Press the pulp against the strainer to extract the juice. Discard the seeds and retain the juice. Coarsely chop the tomatoes.

3. Heat 2 tablespoons of oil in a large, heavy skillet (a nonstick one works well here) over medium heat and add the onion and ½ teaspoon salt. Cook, stirring, until tender but not colored, about 5 minutes. Add 2 more tablespoons of oil and add the eggplant and garlic. Cook, stirring, until the eggplant has softened, about 10 minutes. Add the tomatoes, about ¼ teaspoon pepper, the basil sprigs, and 1 teaspoon salt and cook, stirring, until the mixture begins to simmer. Add 2 more tablespoons of oil. Turn the heat to very low and cook, stirring often to prevent the mixture from sticking to the bottom of the pan, for 1 hour, or until there is no liquid left in the pan and the mixture is just beginning to stick. Taste and adjust the seasonings. Serve at room temperature. This will taste even better the next day.

braised fennel [makes 6 servings]

Fennel is a delicious winter vegetable that goes especially well with fish. This is a very forgiving dish to cook, and easy to make ahead and reheat the next day.

4	plump, heavy fennel bulbs, trimmed and cut in half lengthwise (about 2 pounds)
¼	cup extra virgin olive oil
½	medium onion, sliced
1	stalk celery, diced
4	garlic cloves, halved, green shoots removed, and sliced
1	lemon, the ends removed, then sliced very thin
3	thyme sprigs
1	bay leaf
1	cup Chicken Stock (page 66, or commercial)
1	teaspoon kosher salt
¼	teaspoon freshly ground black pepper
1	tablespoon finely chopped fresh flat-leaf parsley

1. Preheat the oven to 325°F. Bring a large pot of generously salted water to a boil and drop in the fennel. Boil until partially cooked, about 5 minutes. Drain.

2. Heat 2 tablespoons of olive oil in a flameproof casserole or Dutch oven over medium heat and add the onion and celery. Cook, stirring, until the vegetables soften but do not color, about 5 minutes, then add the garlic. Stir together for a minute, until fragrant, and add the fennel and the remaining ingredients except the parsley. Bring to a simmer on top of the stove, cover, and place in the oven. Braise for 40 minutes, or until the fennel is thoroughly tender but still holds its shape and the liquid has reduced.

3. Using tongs, remove the fennel from the pot and place on a cutting board. Allow to cool for 5 minutes, then, using a carving fork or a towel to steady the bulbs, cut the halved bulbs lengthwise into quarters or thirds, depending on the size. Transfer to a baking dish or gratin dish, overlapping the slices. Strain the liquid in the casserole and pour over the fennel.

4. Return the fennel to the oven and heat through. Sprinkle with parsley and serve warm or at room temperature.

VARIATION / BRAISED CELERY HEARTS
Substitute 3 celery hearts, cut in half lengthwise and ends trimmed, for the fennel. Blanch for 3 minutes only in step 1. Follow the recipe through step 3 but do not return to the oven. Instead, transfer to a platter. Sprinkle with fleur de sel and freshly ground pepper. Drizzle on some of the braising liquid or about ½ cup Basic Lemon Vinaigrette (page 16), sprinkle with parsley, and serve. Or refrigerate and serve cold (but not too cold) or at room temperature.

braised endive [makes 4 servings]

I love the way bitter endive contrasts with the sweet tarragon and onion in this braise. It's not a difficult dish, but you have to keep a few things in mind when you cook endive. If you sear them too much, they'll be bitter beyond belief, and if you overcook them in the braise, they'll be mushy and stringy. Your knife should just slide into the base when they're done.

4   Belgian endive, ends trimmed, torn or brown outer leaves removed, cut in half lengthwise
    Kosher salt and freshly ground black pepper
¼   cup extra virgin olive oil
½   medium onion, sliced across the grain
¼   cup dry white wine
1   teaspoon fresh whole tarragon leaves (from 1 large sprig)
½   lemon, ends removed, then cut in thin slices
1   tablespoon finely chopped fresh flat-leaf parsley
    A few drops of freshly squeezed lemon juice

1. Sprinkle the endive with salt and pepper. Heat a pan over high heat and when very hot, add 2 tablespoons of olive oil. Turn the heat down to medium and add the endive, cut side down. Sear just until golden brown, about 4 minutes. Remove from the pan and set aside. Add another tablespoon of olive oil and the onion. Add ½ teaspoon salt and cook until the onion is tender and lightly colored, about 5 to 8 minutes. Add the white wine and bring to a boil.

2. Spread the onion out over the bottom of the pan and return the endive to the pan, cut side up, with their butt ends in toward the middle of the pan. Cover with the tarragon leaves and the lemon slices. Cover the pan and turn the heat to low. Cook 10 minutes. Using tongs, remove the endive from the pan, and arrange on a platter. Add the remaining olive oil to the pan along with a pinch of salt and pepper, raise the heat, and continue to cook, stirring often, until the onion has cooked down almost to a marmalade, about 10 minutes. Stir in the parsley and a few drops of lemon juice, and spread over the endive. Serve warm or at room temperature.

braised spring carrots with leeks [makes 4 servings]

Spring carrots are tender and sweet, and this is an easy, impressive dish to make with them. In our farmers' markets you can find yellow, purple, and red carrots as well as the orange ones. They're very pretty, but tempting as they look, most are too fibrous, so stick to the orange ones for this. The Nantes variety is best. If you want to make this dish with regular carrots, quarter the fat ends and cut the thin ends in half lengthwise, then cut them into 4-inch lengths.

3	tablespoons extra virgin olive oil
½	pound leeks or (preferably) baby leeks, white and light green part only, root ends cut away, cut in thin lengthwise strips and cleaned (page 54)
¾	teaspoon kosher salt
1	garlic clove, halved, green shoot removed, and minced
1	pound small, tender spring carrots, peeled
½	cup water
2	teaspoons freshly squeezed lemon juice
1	tablespoon chopped fresh chervil
2	teaspoons chopped fresh tarragon

1. Heat 2 tablespoons of the olive oil in a lidded skillet over medium heat and add the leeks and a pinch of the salt. Cook gently until tender but not colored, about 5 minutes. Add the garlic and cook, stirring, until fragrant, 30 seconds to a minute. Add the carrots in as few layers as possible, the water, and the salt and bring to a simmer. Cover and simmer gently 15 to 20 minutes, until the carrots are tender when pierced with a knife. Remove the carrots from the pan and transfer to a platter.

2. Increase the heat to high and reduce the liquid that remains in the pan by half. Stir in the remaining tablespoon of olive oil, lemon juice, chervil, and tarragon. Taste and adjust the salt. Spoon the contents of the pan over the carrots. Serve hot, or allow to cool and serve at room temperature. You can also chill this overnight and bring to room temperature before serving.

roasted asparagus [makes 4 servings]

Roasting at high heat intensifies the flavor of asparagus. Do not try this method with thin stalks; they should be no smaller than your index finger. Serve the asparagus plain or, when cool, with Remoulade Sauce (page 34). Make sure to turn on your fan or your smoke alarms will go off.

1   pound medium-thick asparagus, woody ends broken off
2   tablespoons extra virgin olive oil
½   teaspoon kosher salt
    Pinch of freshly ground black pepper
    Leaves from 4 fresh thyme sprigs

1. Preheat the oven to 450°F.

2. Place the asparagus on a baking sheet in a single layer and drizzle with the olive oil, making sure to rub the oil over each stalk. Sprinkle with the salt, pepper, and thyme.

3. Place in the oven for 10 minutes, until the asparagus is just beginning to wrinkle and color. Remove from the heat and immediately transfer the asparagus to a serving dish. Pour the juices from the pan with the thyme over the asparagus. Serve hot, or allow to cool and serve with remoulade sauce if desired.

VARIATION / STEAMED ASPARAGUS WITH HOLLANDAISE SAUCE
Instead of roasting the asparagus, steam it for 5 minutes and serve it with this classic Hollandaise sauce.

[HOLLANDAISE SAUCE]
2   tablespoons minced shallot
2   tablespoons white wine vinegar
½   cup dry white wine
1   large or extra-large egg yolk
1   cup (2 sticks) unsalted butter, melted and hot (but not scalding)
½   teaspoon freshly squeezed lemon juice
    Pinch of cayenne
¼   teaspoon kosher salt

1. Combine the shallot, vinegar, and wine in a small saucepan and bring to a boil over medium heat. Boil until the mixture is reduced to ¼ cup. Set aside to cool.

2. Bring 1 cup of water to a boil in the bottom of a double boiler, which you can fashion out of a saucepan and a bowl that sits on the top. The bottom of the bowl should not touch the water.

3. Transfer the wine mixture to the bowl and add the egg yolk. Whisk together over the simmering water. Keep the heat at medium-low and whisk continually. From time to time, test the temperature of the mixture with the back of your middle finger, at the knuckle, where it is most sensitive to heat. When the mixture is hot and thick (but not so hot that the egg curdles), remove from the heat.

4. Moisten a towel, make a ring with it on your work surface, and set the bowl on the ring. This will keep it from spinning and walking away from you as you whisk. Gradually whisk in the butter, a small ladleful at a time. The mixture should emulsify and become glossy. When all the butter has been added, whisk in the lemon juice, cayenne, and salt. Allow it to sit for 5 minutes so the salt dissolves. Taste and adjust the seasoning.

[NOTE] If the sauce begins to curdle around the edges while you're making it, immediately remove the bowl from the heat and add ½ teaspoon of cold water to drop the temperature.

roasted beets [makes 4 to 6 servings]

Every few days we roast beets in the restaurant. We go through them quickly, as they go into salads and side dishes. If you think you don't like beets, chances are you've never tried them roasted. You don't have to worry about peeling these until they're cooked, at which point the skins will slide off.

2   pounds beets
2   tablespoons olive oil
     Kosher salt and freshly ground black pepper
     Chopped chives, for serving

1. Preheat the oven to 450°F. Cut the tops off the beets, about ½ inch from the bottom of the stems. Set aside for another purpose. Scrub the beets under running water, then dry and place in a bowl. Toss with the olive oil and a generous amount of salt and pepper.

2. Place the beets in a baking dish. Cover tightly and bake in the preheated oven for 1 hour for large beets, 45 minutes for medium. They are done if a small, sharp knife slides into them easily. Remove from the oven, uncover, and allow to cool in the pan. To peel, cut off the ends and rub off the skins with paper towels. Wear plastic gloves if you don't want your hands to get red. Serve tossed with more olive oil, salt, pepper, and chopped chives.

charred rapini with warm bacon vinaigrette [makes 4 servings]

This rich, sharp, and smoky dish makes a great accompaniment for meats, particularly beef and duck. You can substitute other sturdy greens here, like kale. Rapini is also known as broccoli rabe.

1½ pounds rapini (2 bunches)
Kosher salt
1 recipe Warm Bacon Vinaigrette (page 20)
1 tablespoon canola oil
Freshly ground black pepper
3 tablespoons almonds (about 36 almonds), toasted (page 16) and coarsely chopped

1. Trim the ends from the rapini. Wash in several rinses of water while you bring a large pot of generously salted water to a boil. Fill a bowl with ice water.

2. Blanch the rapini for 1 minute in the boiling water. Using a slotted spoon or skimmer, transfer to the bowl of ice water, then drain and squeeze out the excess water.

3. Make the bacon vinaigrette, then remove the bacon with a slotted spoon and set it aside. Keep the vinaigrette warm in the pan.

4. In a large, heavy skillet, heat the canola oil over high heat until just about smoking. Add the blanched rapini and sear until it is lightly colored, 5 to 6 minutes. Season with salt and pepper and stir in the bacon from the dressing.

5. Heat the chopped toasted almonds in the pan with the dressing. Spoon over the rapini and serve.

VARIATION
You can make this with other sturdy greens, such as kale. Remove the leaves from the stems and chop coarsely. Proceed with the recipe above.

creamed spinach [makes 4 servings]

Steak and creamed spinach go together like Republicans and martinis (or Democrats and Chardonnay). We don't limit our creamed spinach to steak, though. Weigh the spinach after removing the stems but before washing. One pound of spinach is a surprisingly large amount that cooks down to a surprisingly small amount. So don't estimate.

1	pound spinach leaves without the stems, washed in 2 changes of water
2	tablespoons unsalted butter
2	tablespoons finely chopped shallot
2	tablespoons all-purpose flour
1¼	cups whole milk
	Kosher salt and freshly ground black pepper
	Pinch of freshly ground nutmeg (optional)
2	tablespoons heavy cream, as needed

1. Bring a large pot of generously salted water to a boil and add the spinach. Blanch for 30 seconds, then transfer to a bowl of ice water. Drain and, taking the spinach up by the handful, squeeze dry. Finely chop the spinach and set aside.

2. In a medium saucepan over medium heat, melt the butter and add the shallot. Cook, stirring, until tender, 3 to 5 minutes, and stir in the flour. Cook, stirring, for several minutes, until the roux begins to color slightly, and take off the heat. Whisk in the milk all at once. Return to the heat and heat, stirring constantly, until the mixture simmers and thickens. Turn the heat to low and simmer, stirring or whisking often, for 15 minutes. Stir the bottom and sides of the pan often with a rubber spatula or wooden spoon so that the sauce doesn't stick and scorch. There should be no floury taste.

3. Add ½ teaspoon salt and pepper to taste, and stir in the spinach and a touch of nutmeg if desired. Taste and add more salt and pepper as desired. Thin with 2 tablespoons cream, or more to taste. Simmer very gently for 5 to 10 minutes, stirring often, and serve.

swiss chard gratin [makes 6 to 8 servings]

This rich gratin—what we would call a casserole—is packed with Swiss chard, both the leaves and the ribs. It goes well with meat or fish, and a vegetarian might make a meal of it. It does require some time to prepare all the elements, but it can be assembled hours before baking, so it's a do-ahead dish.

1	cup béchamel (page 111)
2	large bunches Swiss chard, preferably with wide ribs (about 2 pounds)
2	tablespoons unsalted butter
1	tablespoon extra virgin olive oil
1	medium onion, cut in half and sliced crosswise Kosher salt
2	garlic cloves, halved, green shoots removed, and roughly chopped Freshly ground black pepper
4	ounces Gruyère cheese, grated (1 cup, tightly packed)
2	ounces Parmesan cheese, grated (½ cup tightly packed)
⅓	cup bread crumbs, preferably Herbed Garlic Bread Crumbs (page 18)

1. Make the béchamel, following the directions on page 111. Measure out 1 cup and set aside.

2. Butter a 2-quart gratin dish. Thoroughly wash the Swiss chard, then cut the ribs out from the leaves. Stack the leaves and cut in ½-inch-wide ribbons. Slice the ribs ¼ inch thick and set aside separately.

3. Heat 1 tablespoon of the butter and the olive oil in a large, heavy frying pan over medium heat and add the onion, the ribs from the chard, and ½ teaspoon salt. Cook gently, stirring often, until very tender, about 10 minutes. Add the garlic and continue to cook, stirring often, for another minute or two. Add a few grinds of pepper.

4. Add as much of the chard as will fit in the pan, stir together, and cover the pan for 1 minute. Uncover and stir again, then add the remaining chard. Cover for 1 minute. If all the chard still doesn't fit into the pan, do this a third time. Stir and continue to cook, stirring often, until all the greens have wilted and any liquid has evaporated, 10 to 15 minutes. Season to taste with salt and pepper and remove from the heat. Stir in the béchamel, the Gruyère, and half the Parmesan, and scrape into the gratin dish. Allow to cool at least 30 minutes. (This is when you can set it aside in the refrigerator for hours, even overnight, covered well, before baking.)

5. Preheat the oven to 400°F. Mix together the remaining Parmesan with the bread crumbs and sprinkle over the cooled gratin mixture. Dot with the remaining tablespoon of butter. Bake 40 to 45 minutes, until bubbling and nicely browned on the top and sides. Remove from the heat, allow to sit for at least 10 minutes, and serve.

long-cooked greens [makes 4 to 6 servings]

This is the Southern way with greens, and I love the deep flavor they develop when they cook for this long. If you buy greens with the stems on, you'll need about 2 pounds. If you buy the convenient 1-pound bags of stemmed, cleaned, and chopped greens, you will only need one bag.

1	1-pound bag cleaned stemmed greens, or 2 pounds greens on the stem, such as chard, kale, or collard greens
5	tablespoons extra virgin olive oil
1	medium onion or ½ large onion, cut in half, then sliced across the grain
1	to 2 teaspoons kosher salt
1	dried red chile preferably Japanese
2	to 4 garlic cloves, halved, green shoots removed, and sliced
1	ham hock or 4 ounces salt pork (optional)
½	cup water, as needed
	Freshly ground black pepper

1. Stem the greens and wash thoroughly in 2 changes of water (packaged greens only require 1 change). If using Swiss chard, retain the ribs and slice on the diagonal, about ¼ inch thick.

2. Heat 2 tablespoons of the olive oil in a large, lidded skillet or saucepan over medium heat and add the chard stems and onion, along with ½ teaspoon salt. Cook gently until softened, about 5 minutes, and add as many of the greens as will fit in the pan. Cover and wait a few minutes, until the greens wilt and collapse. Continue to add more greens, cover and wilt until all the greens have been added. Add another ½ teaspoon salt, the chile, the garlic, and optional ham hock or salt pork and bring the mixture to a simmer (add a small amount of water if necessary). Turn the heat to low, cover, and simmer 30 minutes, stirring every 10 minutes or so and checking to make sure there is liquid in the pan. If the pan dries out, add ½ cup water. Uncover the pan, add the remaining 2 tablespoons olive oil, and continue to cook another 30 minutes, stirring often, until the liquid in the pan has reduced to a thin film at the bottom. While the greens are simmering, uncovered, they should not be submerged, but should be braising in about ½ inch of liquid. Add more water if necessary. They will lose their dark green color and turn more of a khaki color.

3. Add the remaining tablespoon of olive oil. Simmer another 10 minutes, until the greens are very tender. If there is too much liquid in the pot for you to serve this neatly as a side dish, increase the heat to boil some of it off before serving. Adjust the seasonings and serve.

long-cooked green beans with bacon [makes 4 servings]

When green beans are cooked for 20 minutes, they lose their bright green color and firm texture, but they take on a sweet flavor that is altogether different from beans that are cooked for 5 minutes. They're like a different vegetable, and they're quite delicious, especially when they're cooked Southern style with bacon. Use Blue Lake, Romano, or any other fresh, firm, dense green bean.

1	pound green beans
2	ounces thick-cut bacon, cut in 1-inch pieces
2	tablespoons extra virgin olive oil
½	large or 1 medium onion, sliced across the grain
	Kosher salt
2	garlic cloves, halved, green shoots removed, and sliced
1	cup water
2	teaspoons red wine vinegar

1. Bring a large pot of generously salted water to a boil and add the green beans. Fill a bowl with ice and water. Blanch for 3 minutes and transfer to the bowl of ice water. Allow to cool, then drain and trim away the stem ends. Set aside.

2. Combine the bacon and olive oil in a wide, lidded frying pan or saucepan over medium heat and cook until the bacon has rendered some of its fat, about 3 minutes. Add the onion and ½ teaspoon salt and cook gently for about 5 minutes, stirring often, until the onion is tender. Add the garlic and cook, stirring often, until fragrant, 30 seconds to a minute. Add the blanched beans and 1 cup water, bring to a simmer, cover, and simmer over low heat for 20 minutes. The beans will be tender and their color will be a muted green.

3. Turn up the heat and reduce the liquid in the pan until it has a syrupy consistency. Sprinkle in the vinegar, taste, and adjust the seasoning. Serve warm.

grilled corn with herb butter [makes 6 servings]

This uniquely American grilled corn is one of my favorite dishes. The sweet corn is balanced by the pungent butter and the smokiness of the charred husks. When you grill sweet corn, if you husk it and put it directly on the grill it will burn quickly because there's so much sugar in the kernels. So a few layers of the husk are left on, but the silk is taken out. Do this by pulling off the outer layers, carefully peeling back the inner layers, and pulling out the silk. Then rub the corn with garlic and herb butter, fold the husk back up over the corn, and tie it at the ends and in the middle. This is a bit messy, but not difficult. The corn takes very little grilling skill, but it does take some grill space, so plan accordingly.

1	medium or fat garlic clove, cut in half, green shoot removed
¼	teaspoon salt
½	to ¾ cup (1 to 1½ sticks) unsalted butter, softened
2	to 3 tablespoons finely minced fresh herbs, such as fresh flat-leaf parsley, tarragon, basil, chervil, chives
6	to 12 ears of corn (as desired)

1. In a mortar and pestle, combine the garlic and salt and mash the garlic to a smooth paste. Blend in the butter and the herbs. Taste and adjust the seasoning. Transfer to a bowl, or if using as a spread, place on a sheet of parchment or plastic and roll up into a cylinder. Chill if not using right away, but bring to room temperature when you're ready to prepare the corn.

2. Light a medium-hot grill while you prepare your corn. Remove the outer leaves of the husk, leaving 2 layers. Gently pull down the remaining leaves and pull off the silk. Rub a tablespoon of herb butter over the corn, and fold the husks back up, covering the buttered corn.

3. Cut 12 to 24 pieces of butcher's string about 6 inches long and moisten them with water. Tie the cobs at the top and midway down with the wet string. (You can also tear strips from the discarded leaves, tie them together, and use them for tying up the corn; this takes longer but it's pretty.)

4. Place the corn on the side of the grill with the base toward the heat and the tip away from it, and grill until the corn is uniformly charred, turning the ears often. This could take anywhere from 10 to 20 minutes, depending on the heat of your grill. Remove from the grill and cut away the strings. Serve hot, with more herb butter, if desired.

creamed corn [makes 3 cups, serving 6]

I have vivid taste memories of the canned creamed corn my mother used to serve when I was a kid. I loved it. But canned creamed corn can't compare to the fresh version. When you grate the corn it releases so much of its own "cream" that you need no cream for the recipe. You can make variations by adding sweet, tender fresh herbs like tarragon, chervil, or chives.

8	large ears of corn, husks removed
5	tablespoons unsalted butter
2	tablespoons minced shallot (optional)
	Kosher salt

1. Grate the corn on the medium holes of a box grater.

2. Melt the butter in a medium saucepan over medium heat and add the shallot, if using. Cook, stirring, until tender and fragrant, about 2 to 3 minutes, and add the corn and ½ teaspoon salt. Cook slowly for 5 to 10 minutes, until sweet and creamy. Taste and adjust the salt. Remove from the heat. Serve hot.

[GRATING CORN ON A BOX GRATER]
Here's a little trick I learned from Rosie, a prep cook at Campanile. When you are grating corn on a box grater, wrap the grater in plastic wrap so you don't get splashed by all the spray that occurs when you're grating. Wrap several layers around the grater, then, with scissors, cut away the wrap from the side you are using.

Organic corn on the cob, which is the only kind we use, might have a worm or two nestled into the top of the ear. Remember, the farmer did not use pesticides. You'll find them when you shuck the corn. This is nothing to worry about; they aren't dirty or poisonous. Chop off the end of the ear with the worm and keep the corn.

springtime succotash with fava beans and sweet peppers

[makes 8 generous servings]

There's a short period of time at our farmers' markets when we can get both sweet corn and fava beans. Once all of the vegetables for this colorful succotash are prepared, the cooking goes very quickly. It's important to mince the red pepper very small (see below) and to rinse it so it doesn't discolor the mix.

2	heaping cups shelled fava beans
6	ears of corn, husks removed
1	tablespoon canola oil
3	tablespoons unsalted butter
	Kosher salt
1	bunch scallions, trimmed and sliced on the diagonal, about ⅛ inch thick
1	large red bell pepper, very finely diced, rinsed with cold water, and drained on paper towels
2	garlic cloves, halved, green shoots removed, and minced
3	tablespoons crumbled cooked bacon
1	tablespoon chopped fresh tarragon
	Freshly ground black pepper

1. Bring a large pot of salted water to a boil. Prepare a bowl of ice water. Add the fava beans to the boiling water. Boil 2 minutes and transfer, using a skimmer, to the ice water. Allow the beans to cool in the water, then drain. Skin the favas, using your thumbnail to open up the skin at the spot where the bean is attached to the pod, then gently squeeze out the bean. You should have about 1¼ cups. Set aside.

2. Blanch the corn in the boiling water for 2 minutes, and cool in the ice bath. With a sharp knife, slice the kernels from the cobs.

3. Heat the canola oil in a large, heavy skillet over medium-high heat and add the corn. Cook, stirring, for 2 minutes, and add 2 tablespoons of the butter and 1¼ teaspoons salt. Stir together for about half a minute and add the scallions and shelled favas. Cook, stirring, for 2 minutes, until the scallions are tender, then add the finely diced red peppers and the garlic. Cook, stirring, for a minute, and stir in the bacon and the tarragon. Taste and adjust the salt. Add pepper if desired. Stir in the remaining tablespoon of butter, and serve.

pickled red onions [makes I quart]

Keep these on hand as a staple item to use whenever you need a condiment, side dish, or quick garnish. Their sharpness makes them great with spicy and fatty meat dishes (like the Spicy Pulled Pork on page 144 or the shrimp boil on page 180), and they're also a perfect condiment for cold poached fish. Slice some up for sandwiches, or add to any salad.

2	pounds (2 large) red onions, sliced in rings
I	garlic clove, halved, green shoot removed, and sliced
I	teaspoon mustard seeds
I	bay leaf
I	quart water
2	cups white wine vinegar (7% acidity)
I ½	teaspoons coarse sea salt
½	cup sugar

1. Bring a large pot of water to a boil. Fill a bowl with ice and water. When the water comes to a boil, add the sliced onions. Blanch 30 seconds. Transfer to the ice bath, cool, and drain. Set aside in a separate bowl with the sliced garlic, mustard seeds, and bay leaf.

2. Combine the water, vinegar, coarse salt, and sugar in a saucepan and bring to a simmer. When the salt and sugar have dissolved, remove from the heat and pour over the onions. Weight the onions with a small plate so they remain completely submerged. Cover with plastic wrap and refrigerate for 3 days.

3. Transfer the onions to a sterilized wide-mouth jar and fill with the pickling solution. Close the jar and refrigerate. You can use the onions in a day, or refrigerate for up to 3 weeks.

refrigerator pickles [makes I quart]

These quick cucumber pickles are meant to be eaten within a few days, though they'll keep for a couple of weeks. They're really more of a condiment than a side dish, meant to accompany Southern meals like fried chicken (page 156), shrimp boil (page 180), or fried fish. Put them in big meaty sandwiches, or serve them on a relish tray with burgers.

I	pound Japanese cucumbers, sliced on the diagonal about ¼ inch thick
I	tablespoon plus I teaspoon coarse sea salt
½	large or I medium onion, thickly sliced
¾	cup white wine vinegar
¾	cup water
3	tablespoons sugar
I	teaspoon mustard seeds
I	garlic clove, halved, green shoot removed, and sliced

1. Place the sliced cucumbers in a bowl, salt with I teaspoon of the salt, and let sit 15 to 30 minutes. Pour off the water that accumulates in the bowl.

2. Meanwhile, cover the sliced onion with cold water and let sit for 5 to 10 minutes. Drain and rinse.

3. Combine the remaining salt, the vinegar, water, sugar, mustard seeds, onion, and garlic in a saucepan and bring to a simmer. Simmer until the sugar has dissolved, and pour over the cucumbers. Make sure everything is submerged. If it isn't, add a little water as necessary. Weight with a small plate. Cover well and refrigerate for I to 2 days before serving. These will last 2 to 3 weeks in the refrigerator.

green tomato relish [makes 2 cups]

This looks like pickle relish, but the resemblance ends there. This one is savory and pungent with capers, with a hint of anchovy. It's great with cold meats or fish, and with the spicy shrimp boil on page 180. Try it on a hamburger or hot dog instead of regular relish. It will keep for several weeks in the refrigerator, a great way to use up your last crop of tomatoes after the weather has cooled.

2	teaspoons kosher salt
2	tablespoons capers, rinsed and finely chopped
½	cup minced onion, soaked for 5 minutes in cold water, then drained, rinsed, and drained again on paper towels
3	tablespoons extra virgin olive oil
2	teaspoons sugar
½	teaspoon dried oregano
2	teaspoons finely chopped lemon zest
1	anchovy fillet, minced
¾	pound green tomatoes, finely diced

1. Thoroughly combine all the ingredients except the tomatoes and allow the mixture to rest and "marry" for 30 minutes.

2. Fold the mixture into the finely diced green tomatoes and allow to rest for at least 1 hour before serving.

[8]
DESSERTS

We don't do "fancy" desserts at Campanile——you won't find chiles, meat, fish, or poultry in our confections, or pulled sugar towers that are impossible to eat. We stick with comforting, straightforward desserts, especially on our Monday Night Family Dinner menus. We're inspired by the marvelous fruit we find at the farmers' market (if I didn't love chocolate so much I think I'd ban it from the menu between June and October), and by the desserts we remember from our childhood, like Boston Cream Pie and Devil's Food Layer Cake with White Mountain Frosting. I call the latter "archeology recipes," because they're imprinted in our early childhood taste memory (though we try to make them a little better and fresher than the ones we remember). They come up on our Monday Night Family Dinner menus because they pair so well with the other traditional dishes and we don't have to wonder whether people will like them.

You don't have to be a pastry chef to make the desserts in this chapter. I'm particularly fond of homemade ice cream, which is why the first seven recipes are ice creams. I make it at home in a cheap green plastic electric ice cream maker, the ice and rock salt type, that I bought at Target. You won't need anything fancier than that. My most vivid early taste memory is of eating hand-cranked fresh peach ice cream one summer day at a picnic when I was in high school. The mashed peaches were macerated in sugar and nutmeg, then folded into freshly cranked vanilla ice cream. It was so good we ate it right out of the can the minute it was ready without waiting to pack it in the freezer. And we ate it until it was gone.

There are desserts in this chapter that you'll only make during the summer, like that peach ice cream, or the Plum Compote or the Roasted Figs. But others, especially the classics like Chocolate Pudding with Whipped Cream, can be done at any time of year. You may love to make desserts for your family, or you may only make them when you entertain, but whatever you choose will not be difficult and I hope it will have a permanent place in your home.

vanilla ice cream [makes 1⅓ quarts]

Of course you can buy perfectly good vanilla ice cream, but I like ours better because it's not as sweet as commercial brands. Master it and you'll not only have a great vanilla ice cream but also an ice cream base for most of the ice creams we make at Campanile. There are many simple, reasonably priced electric ice cream makers on the market that are perfect for these small batches. Despite all of these convenient new machines, I still think the best machines are the ones that use ice and rock salt and make a horrendous grinding sound as they operate. If you use this type of ice cream maker, you'll definitely want to run it outside or in an unoccupied room, with the machine sitting in a much larger bucket and the door closed.

2½	cups whole milk
2	cups heavy cream
2	vanilla beans, split and scraped
8	large egg yolks
⅔	cup sugar
	Pinch of salt

1. Combine the milk, cream, and vanilla bean seeds and pod in a heavy, medium saucepan over medium heat and bring to a simmer. Immediately remove from the heat and cover the pan with plastic wrap. Allow the mixture to steep for 15 minutes.

2. Fill a large bowl with water and ice, and set a medium bowl in it. In a medium bowl, beat together the egg yolks, sugar, and salt until the egg yolks are very frothy and thick.

3. Bring the milk mixture back to a simmer over medium heat and remove from the heat. Making sure the liquid is not boiling, whisking constantly, slowly pour ½ cup of it into the egg yolks. Using a heatproof rubber spatula, scrape the now-tempered egg yolks into the saucepan with the milk and cream, whisking constantly. Place the saucepan over medium-low heat and insert a thermometer. Stir constantly with a rubber spatula, moving the spatula in a figure 8 and scraping the sides and bottom of the pan, until the mixture thickens and coats the spatula, and reaches 170°F. Run your finger down the middle of the spatula. The sauce should not run back into the canal created by your finger.

4. Immediately remove from the heat and continue to stir for 1 minute, then strain through a medium strainer into the bowl set in the ice bath. Allow to cool, stirring often, to 40°F. At this point you can refrigerate the base (which is a custard sauce) for up to 2 days.

5. Place a 2-quart container for storing the ice cream in the freezer. Meanwhile, freeze the ice cream base in an ice cream maker, following the manufacturer's instructions. Scrape into the chilled container, and place in the freezer for at least 2 hours, until packed.

6. Allow to soften in the refrigerator for 15 to 30 minutes before serving

VARIATION / GELATO AFFOGATO
Gelato affogato is vanilla ice cream with a shot of espresso poured over the top. Place 2 scoops of vanilla ice cream in each bowl. Pour a shot of hot regular or decaf espresso over each serving and serve at once.

pistachio ice cream [makes 1⅓ quarts]

This was my father's favorite ice cream flavor. Pistachios are nutty, sweet, and floral at the same time. You can find pistachio paste in Middle Eastern markets and gourmet markets that sell pastry ingredients.

	Vanilla Ice Cream Base (page 240), hot from the stove
1	cup whole pistachios, lightly toasted (page 16), cooled, and ground in a food processor fitted with the steel blade
¼	cup pistachio paste
¼	teaspoon almond extract
1	teaspoon dark rum
1	tablespoon freshly squeezed lemon juice

1. Make the vanilla ice cream base following the instructions on page 240, and scrape into a bowl without straining. While the sauce is still hot, stir in the ground pistachios, pistachio paste, almond extract, rum, and lemon juice. Combine well. Place the bowl in an ice bath (a large bowl filled with ice water) and cool for 30 minutes, stirring occasionally. Meanwhile, chill a 2-quart storage container in the freezer.

2. Strain the ice cream base into another bowl, pressing against the strainer to extract all the liquid from the ground nuts. Freeze in an ice cream maker following the manufacturer's instructions. Scrape into the chilled container and freeze for at least 2 hours. Allow to soften in the refrigerator for 15 to 30 minutes before serving.

chocolate chip ice cream [makes 1⅓ quarts]

This vanilla ice cream, with chocolate chips and flecks, is called "straciatella" in Italian ice cream shops. You make it by drizzling warm chocolate sauce into vanilla ice cream as it is just finishing its spin in an ice cream maker. The sauce seizes and breaks up into little bits as it hits the cold ice cream. There's a wonderful contrast of soft and hard textures, and bitter chocolate and sweet vanilla flavors.

	Vanilla Ice Cream Base (page 240)
8	ounces bittersweet chocolate (70%), finely chopped

1. Make the vanilla ice cream base as directed, and begin to freeze in an ice cream maker, following the manufacturer's directions. Meanwhile, chill a 2-quart storage container in the freezer. While the ice cream is freezing, melt the chocolate in a double boiler or in a microwave at 50 percent power. When the ice cream has reached the desired texture, continue running the machine while you drizzle in the chocolate in a very fine stream. Lift it from the bowl on a rubber spatula and let it drizzle from the spatula into the ice cream machine. If you are using the ice and rock salt type of machine, you will have to stop the machine, open it, and drizzle in one-third of the chocolate. Close the machine and restart, let run for a minute or two, then repeat two more times.

2. When all the chocolate has been added, scrape into the chilled container and freeze for at least 2 hours. Allow to soften in the refrigerator for 15 to 30 minutes before serving.

strawberry ice cream [makes 2 quarts]

Use only ripe strawberries for this, and don't omit the sugar and maceration stage. To macerate means the same thing as to marinate. The sugar prevents the strawberries from getting too icy and hard. Frozen strawberries work well too, but read the ingredient list, as the packager might already have sugar or corn syrup and citric acid added.

Vanilla Ice Cream Base (page 240)
2   pints strawberries, hulled and quartered
3   tablespoons sugar
1   tablespoon freshly squeezed lemon juice

1. Make the vanilla ice cream base as directed, and chill in an ice bath.

2. Toss the strawberries with the sugar and lemon juice and allow to macerate for 30 minutes. Transfer to a food processor fitted with the steel blade or to a blender, and pulse to blend coarsely. Don't leave large chunks because they will become very hard when they freeze.

3. Fold the strawberries into the ice cream base and freeze as directed in an ice cream freezer, following the manufacturer's directions. Meanwhile, chill a 2-quart storage container in the freezer.

4. Scrape the ice cream into the chilled container and freeze for 2 hours or longer. Allow to soften in the refrigerator for 15 to 30 minutes before serving.

peach ice cream [makes 2 quarts]

Peach ice cream was the first freshly made ice cream I ever tasted, in the early '70s when I was in high school in Santa Rosa in northern California. At a picnic someone made fresh hand-cranked vanilla ice cream, and at the end they threw in roughly chunked fresh peaches macerated in sugar and vanilla extract. It was one of my first taste revelations, and it remains one of my strongest.

Vanilla Ice Cream Base (page 240)
1 recipe Peach Compote (page 258)

1. Make the vanilla ice cream base as directed, and chill in an ice bath.

2. Fold the peach compote into the ice cream base and freeze as directed in an ice cream freezer. Meanwhile, chill a 2-quart storage container in the freezer.

3. Scrape the ice cream into the chilled container and freeze for 2 hours or longer. Allow to soften in the refrigerator for 15 to 30 minutes before serving.

peach swirl ice cream [makes 1½ quarts]

You can make this ice cream with the homemade vanilla ice cream on page 240, or you can use commercial ice cream, which will be sweeter.

1 quart Vanilla Ice Cream (page 240) or commercial
2 cups Peach Compote (page 258)

Soften the ice cream in the refrigerator for 30 minutes, or until it can easily be spooned out of its container. Chill a 2-quart storage container in the freezer. Mash the peaches in the compote with a fork or a potato masher so the mixture will spread more easily in between the layers of ice cream. Place a layer of vanilla ice cream in the bottom of the container. Spoon on a thin layer of peach compote and top with another layer of vanilla ice cream. Continue alternating the layers (the ice cream layers should be thicker than the compote layers) until you fill the container. Cover with a sheet of plastic wrap, then a lid, and freeze.

VARIATION / PLUM SWIRL ICE CREAM
Substitute Plum Compote (page 259) for the peach compote.

dulce de leche ice cream [makes 1¼ quarts]

This sweet, rich Mexican-style ice cream gets its unique flavor from the dulce de leche, also known as leche quemada. Dulce de leche is caramelized sweetened condensed milk. You can make it at home by simmering a can of sweetened condensed milk in a pan of water for 2 hours (see below). This caramelizes the sugars in the milk without losing water content. Since the caramelized milk is so sweet, very little sugar is required for the ice cream. In fact, for a little acidity, we temper it by adding crème fraîche to the mix.

1	cup whole milk
1	cup heavy cream
1	3-inch cinnamon stick
1	teaspoon pure vanilla extract
5	large egg yolks
3	tablespoons sugar
	Pinch of salt
1	14-ounce can dulce de leche (see below)
¾	cup crème fraîche

[TO MAKE DULCE DE LECHE]
Place an unopened can of sweetened condensed milk in a medium saucepan, and fill the saucepan with water. Lie the can down on its side if you need to, to make sure it is submerged in the water. Bring to a boil over medium-high heat, then reduce the heat to low. Cover and simmer for 2 hours, checking regularly to make sure the can is submerged in the simmering water and adding water as necessary. Remove from the water and allow to cool before using.

1. Combine the milk, cream, cinnamon stick, and vanilla in a heavy, medium saucepan over medium heat and bring to a simmer. Immediately remove from the heat and cover the pan with plastic wrap. Allow the mixture to steep for 15 minutes.

2. Fill a large bowl with water and ice, and set a medium bowl in it. In a medium bowl, beat together the egg yolks, sugar, and salt until the egg yolks are very frothy and thick.

3. Bring the milk mixture back to a simmer over medium heat and remove from the heat. Making sure the liquid is not boiling, whisking constantly, slowly pour ½ cup of it into the egg yolks. Using a heatproof rubber spatula, scrape the now-tempered egg yolks into the saucepan with the milk and cream, whisking constantly. Place the saucepan over medium-low heat and insert a thermometer. Stir constantly with a rubber spatula, moving the spatula in a figure 8 and scraping the sides and bottom of the pan, until the mixture thickens and coats the spatula, and reaches 170°F. Run your finger down the middle of the spatula. The sauce should not run back into the canal created by your finger.

4. Immediately remove from the heat and continue to stir for 1 minute, then whisk in the dulce de leche and the crème fraîche. Strain through a medium strainer into the bowl set in the ice bath. Allow to cool, stirring often, to 40°F.

5. Place a 2-quart container in your freezer. Freeze the ice cream base in an ice cream maker, following the manufacturer's instructions. Scrape into the chilled container and freeze for at least 2 hours. Allow to soften in the refrigerator for 15 minutes before serving.

oro blanco sorbet [makes 1¼ quarts]

This sorbet may be the simplest recipe in this book. It's also great made as a granita. The Oro Blanco grapefruit is my favorite grapefruit. Its flavor is bright and clean, not too sweet, with just a hint of bitterness. Try sprinkling ½ teaspoon of good white rum over each portion just before serving.

¾   cup sugar
¾   cup water
⅓   cup light corn syrup
2   tablespoons finely chopped grapefruit zest
1   quart strained freshly squeezed Oro Blanco
     grapefruit juice
1   tablespoon freshly squeezed lemon juice

1. Combine the sugar and water in a medium saucepan and bring to a boil. Reduce the heat and simmer until all the sugar has dissolved. Stir in the corn syrup and the grapefruit zest and remove from the heat. Allow to steep and cool for 15 to 30 minutes (you can cool the mixture in an ice bath). Strain into the grapefruit juice. Stir in the lemon juice.

2. Place a 2-quart container in the freezer. Freeze the sorbet mixture in an ice cream maker following the manufacturer's instructions. Scrape into the cold container, and freeze for at least 2 hours to pack. Allow to soften for 15 minutes in the refrigerator before serving.

grasshopper pie [makes on 9-inch pie]

The traditional grasshopper pie is a green pie in an Oreo cookie crust, a "white trash" cooking sort of dish, made with marshmallow fluff and topped with Reddi-Wip. We've made it much better with homemade vanilla ice cream, now green and minty with the addition of only ¼ cup of crème de menthe. The secret to gussying up any recipe is to use good ingredients, freshly and properly made. Changing the quality does not necessarily change the character of a dish; it's still a little "white trash."

[CRUST]

1½	cups chocolate cookie crumbs, made from the wafer part of Oreo cookies or other chocolate wafers
2	ounces bittersweet chocolate, cut in ¼-inch pieces
6	tablespoons (¾ stick) unsalted butter, melted and hot
½	teaspoon pure vanilla extract

[PIE]

½	recipe Vanilla Ice Cream Base (page 240)
¼	cup green crème de menthe
	Whipped cream, for serving (optional)

1. Make the crust: Put the chocolate cookie crumbs and chocolate in the bowl of a food processor fitted with the steel blade and process until the chocolate is finely grated. With the machine running, add the melted butter and vanilla, and process until evenly incorporated.

2. Transfer the mixture to a buttered 9-inch pie or tart pan and press evenly into the bottom and sides of the pan. It helps to place a piece of plastic wrap over the mixture and press on that so your hands don't get sticky and covered with the mixture. Place in the freezer.

3. Whisk together the vanilla ice cream base and crème de menthe, and freeze in an ice cream maker, following the manufacturer's instructions. Spread the ice cream in the piecrust, and place in the freezer until solid.

4. Thirty minutes before serving the pie, transfer to the refrigerator. Use a serrated knife dipped into hot water to slice the pie and serve. Top each serving with whipped cream, if desired.

chocolate pudding with whipped cream [makes 8 servings]

If Jell-O Pudding could fantasize about becoming something great, this would be it. Lighter and less intense than pots de crème (page 250), the creamy, comforting pudding with a whisper of mint added to the chocolate is very popular at the restaurant. We serve it in whiskey glasses. Note how little peppermint extract is needed here. You have to use this ingredient with caution. Mint is delicious right up to the point where it turns awful.

4	cups whole milk
I	cup sugar
	Pinch of salt
⅓	cup Dutch process cocoa powder
⅓	cup cornstarch
3	large egg yolks
2	ounces bittersweet chocolate (70%), finely chopped
2	tablespoons unsalted butter, cut in small pieces
2	teaspoons pure vanilla extract
¼	teaspoon peppermint extract
	Whipped cream or Whipped Crème Fraîche (recipe follows) for serving

1. In a large saucepan, combine the milk, ½ cup of sugar, and the salt and bring to a boil over medium heat. Remove from the heat.

2. In a small bowl, combine the remaining ½ cup of sugar, the cocoa powder, and the cornstarch. Sprinkle this slowly into the milk, whisking constantly. Return to the heat and whisk constantly until thick and bubbling. Remove from the heat, make sure the mixture isn't boiling, and one at a time, whisk in the egg yolks, then the chocolate, butter, vanilla, and peppermint extract. Whisk constantly until the chocolate has dissolved. Return to low heat and whisk constantly until the mixture thickens again, being careful that it does not boil, then immediately remove from the heat and strain into a bowl.

3. Spoon into whiskey glasses (the pudding will fill about two-thirds of the glass) and cover with plastic. If you don't want a skin to form, place the plastic directly over the pudding. Chill in the refrigerator for at least 2 hours. Top with a generous spoonful of whipped cream or whipped crème fraîche, and serve.

[WHIPPED CRÈME FRAÎCHE]

3	tablespoons crème fraîche
½	cup heavy cream
2	teaspoons sugar

Combine all of ingredients in a bowl and whip to soft peaks. Refrigerate in a covered bowl until ready to use.

dark chocolate pots de crème with whipped crème fraîche

[makes 6 servings]

This is the easiest fancy dessert you'll ever make. The little chocolate custards—French chocolate pudding—are quite rich, but they're small, and I can't think of a menu where they wouldn't fit. You'll need ramekins for this, straight-sided 4- to 5-ounce porcelain cups without handles, or special pots de crème dishes, which have handles and lids. If you don't want to serve these with the whipped crème fraîche, you can just spoon a little cream over the top or serve plain.

1¾	cups whole milk
½	cup heavy cream
½	cup sugar
½	vanilla bean, split and scraped
4	ounces bittersweet chocolate (70%), finely chopped
2	large eggs
2	large egg yolks
	Pinch of salt
	Whipped Crème Fraîche (page 248)

1. Preheat the oven to 325°F with the rack positioned in the center. Place six 4-ounce ramekins or pots de crème in a baking pan that is higher than the tops of the ramekins.

2. Combine the milk, cream, sugar, and vanilla bean and seeds in a medium saucepan and bring to a simmer over medium heat. Remove from the heat and add the chocolate. Cover with plastic and let steep for 15 minutes. Stir the mixture until the chocolate has melted and is evenly mixed into the cream.

3. Beat together the eggs, egg yolks, and salt in a medium bowl. Return the milk mixture to the heat and bring back to a simmer. Remove from the heat, and making sure the mixture is not boiling, whisk ½ cup of the mixture into the eggs. Whisk the egg mixture back into the pot, adding every last bit with your rubber spatula. Whisk well, then strain through a fine strainer into a bowl or a large Pyrex measuring cup.

4. Fill each ramekin or pot to just below the rim with the mixture. Fill the baking pan with enough hot water to measure two-thirds of the way up the sides of the ramekins. Cover the baking dish with aluminum foil (this is unnecessary if you have ramekins with lids. In that case, just put the lids on the little cups). Poke a small hole in the aluminum foil to let some steam escape (otherwise the condensation will drip into the pots and ruin the custards).

5. Bake 45 minutes, until the custards are just set. They should jiggle slightly. Remove from the oven and allow to cool. Cover the ramekins and refrigerate for at least 2 hours before serving. Serve each pot de crème with 1 to 2 teaspoons whipped crème fraîche. The pots de crème will keep for 2 to 3 days in the refrigerator.

boca negra [makes one 9-inch ring]

Boca negra is a dense, fudgy chocolate pudding cake enriched with a lot of bourbon or brandy. It's an easy dessert to make, but always very impressive. Serve very small slices of this rich dessert.

12	ounces bittersweet chocolate (70%), finely chopped
1	cup (2 sticks) unsalted butter, cut in ½-inch pieces
1⅓	cups sugar
½	cup bourbon or brandy
5	large eggs, at room temperature
1½	tablespoons all-purpose flour
	Whipped Crème Fraîche (page 248), for serving

1. Preheat the oven to 325°F, with the rack in the middle. Butter a 9-inch springform pan and line the outside with foil so that none of the batter leaks out. Place in a roasting pan with sides at least 2 inches high.

2. Combine the chocolate and butter in a microwave-safe bowl and melt at 50 percent power, about 2 minutes. Stir gently with a spatula until the mixture is smooth. Combine 1 cup of sugar and the bourbon or brandy in a small saucepan and bring to a simmer. Stir the mixture just until the sugar dissolves, and remove from the heat. Pour over the chocolate and butter. Tap the bowl against your work surface to submerge the chocolate and butter and stir gently with a rubber spatula until the mixture is smooth.

3. In a standing mixer fitted with the whip attachment, combine the eggs and 3 tablespoons of the remaining sugar and beat on medium-high speed until thick and foamy. Add the melted chocolate mixture and beat together. Combine the flour and remaining sugar and beat in at low speed. Continue to beat until the mixture is silky smooth. Pour into the prepared springform pan, scraping out all of the batter with a rubber spatula.

4. Fill the baking dish with hot water to come halfway up the sides of the springform pan. Place in the oven and bake 40 minutes, until just set. Remove from the oven and remove from the water bath. Allow to cool for 15 minutes, then remove the sides of the springform pan and allow to cool. The cake will be easier to cut if you refrigerate it for 15 to 30 minutes or longer. Serve very thin slices (you should be able to get 20 servings out of one cake) with whipped crème fraîche.

devil's food layer cake with white mountain frosting

[makes one 2-layer cake]

This moist, dark chocolate cake with white icing couldn't be more classic. It's a great chocolate cake to have in your repertoire, and it's easy to make. White Mountain Frosting, also known as seven-minute frosting, is a classic Italian meringue, made by drizzling a hot sugar syrup into beaten egg whites while continuing to beat them. The result is a shiny, marshmallowy confection. Use the best chocolate you can find for the cake.

[CAKE]

1	cup all-purpose flour
1	cup cake flour
2	teaspoons baking soda
½	teaspoon baking powder
½	teaspoon salt
4	ounces bittersweet chocolate (70%), finely chopped
⅓	cup unsweetened cocoa powder, preferably Dutch process
1	cup regular-strength brewed coffee
¾	cup buttermilk
¾	cup canola oil
1	cup granulated sugar
½	cup firmly packed light brown sugar
1	teaspoon pure vanilla extract
3	large eggs, at room temperature

1. Preheat the oven to 350°F with the rack positioned in the middle. Spray two 9 x 2-inch-high cake pans with vegetable oil and line with parchment. Spray the parchment.

2. Sift together the flours, baking soda, baking powder, and salt. Set aside.

3. Place the chocolate and cocoa powder in a bowl. Bring the coffee to just below a simmer and pour over the chocolate. Tap the bowl against your work surface so the chocolate settles into the liquid, and let sit 1 minute. Using a wire whisk, stir gently until the chocolate has melted and the mixture is smooth. Whisk in the buttermilk.

4. In the bowl of a standing mixer fitted with the paddle attachment, mix together the canola oil, sugars, and vanilla. Beat at medium speed for 2 minutes. Scrape down the sides of the bowl. Add the eggs one at a time and beat in at medium-high speed, scraping down the sides of the bowl after each addition. At low speed, in 3 additions, add the flour mixture and the chocolate mixture, alternating the two and scraping down the sides of the bowl after each addition. Mix until just combined. Do not over-mix or the cake will be tough.

5. Divide the batter between the 2 pans, filling the pans two-thirds of the way. Tap gently on your work surface once to disperse air bubbles and even out the batter. Place in the oven on the middle rack. Bake 25 minutes, then switch the pans from back to front and turn them 180°.

(continues)

Bake for another 10 minutes. Test for doneness by lightly touching the top. It should spring back and the sides should be very slightly pulling away from the sides of the pan. If it does not seem done, leave for another 5 minutes and test again. Remove the cakes from the oven and cool on racks in the pans for 15 minutes, then invert onto a rack. Remove the pans and parchments, and cool completely.

6. When the cakes have cooled, use a long knife, an offset serrated knife, or a bread knife to cut away the domes so the cakes have flat, even surfaces. Place one cake on a round or on a plate and cover with the frosting. Place the other cake on top and cover the entire cake with frosting. Dimple the top and sides so it looks like the pictures on cake mix boxes.

[WHITE MOUNTAIN FROSTING makes enough for a large 2–layer cake]

1	cup plus 3 tablespoons sugar
3	tablespoons water
1	tablespoon light corn syrup
3	large egg whites, at room temperature
1/4	teaspoon cream of tartar
1	teaspoon pure vanilla extract

1. Combine 1 cup of sugar, the water, and the corn syrup in a heavy medium saucepan. Cover and place over medium-high heat for 4 minutes, or until the sugar has dissolved and the mixture is simmering. Insert a candy thermometer and boil until the mixture reaches 235°F. Remove from the heat.

2. Meanwhile, begin beating the egg whites in the bowl of a standing mixer fitted with the whisk attachment at medium speed. When they begin to foam, add the cream of tartar and 1 tablespoon of sugar. Continue to beat at medium speed while you slowly add the remaining 2 tablespoons sugar. When the egg whites form soft peaks, begin to slowly drizzle in the hot syrup while you beat at medium speed, drizzling it down the inside of the bowl and being careful not to drizzle it over the beaters. When all the syrup has been added, stop the mixer and scrape down the sides of the bowl. Add the vanilla and beat at high speed until the egg whites are stiff, glossy, and cool. The frosting will have lost quite a bit of volume from when it was just meringue; it will be dense and sticky, but stable and spreadable.

plum trifle [makes 8 to 10 servings]

Pastry chefs often make trifles with leftover cake and preserves. But this is so good, it's worth making from scratch. It's a great summer dish, giving you one more choice of desserts to make with the bounty of plums from your farmers' market. Use a clear glass bowl or trifle dish for this. The beauty of it is seeing the colorful layers through the sides of the dish.

2½ cups whole milk
1 vanilla bean, split and scraped
5 large egg yolks
½ cup sugar
Pinch of salt
4 cups sponge cake (see right; can be stale), broken or cut in approximately 2-inch pieces
2 cups Plum Compote (page 259)
1½ cups heavy cream
Cream sherry
Freshly grated nutmeg

1. Fill a large bowl with water and ice, and set a medium bowl in it. Set aside for later.

2. Combine the milk, vanilla bean seeds, and pod in a heavy, medium saucepan over medium heat and bring to a simmer. Immediately remove from the heat and cover the pan with plastic wrap. Allow the mixture to steep for 15 minutes.

3. In a medium bowl, beat together the egg yolks, sugar, and salt until the egg yolks are frothy and thick.

4. Bring the milk mixture back to a simmer over medium heat and remove from the heat. Making sure that the liquid is not boiling, whisking constantly, slowly stir ½ cup of it into the egg yolks. Pour the now-tempered egg yolks into the saucepan with the milk and cream, whisking constantly. Scrape all of the egg yolk mixture out of the bowl using a heat-proof rubber spatula. Place the saucepan over medium-low heat and insert a thermometer. Stir constantly with a rubber spatula, moving the spatula in a figure 8 and scraping the sides and bottom of the pan, until the mixture thickens and coats the spatula, and reaches 170°F. Run your finger down the middle of the spatula. The sauce should not run back into the canal created by your finger.

5. Immediately remove from the heat and continue to stir for 1 minute, then strain through a medium strainer into the bowl set in the ice bath. Allow to cool to 40°F.

6. Line a flat wide glass bowl (or a trifle dish, a stemmed glass bowl with a flat bottom and straight sides) with a layer of half the cake. Top the cake with half of the plum compote and half the custard sauce. Repeat the layers. Cover with plastic wrap and chill for 1 hour or longer.

7. Beat the cream until it forms soft peaks, and flavor it with cream sherry and nutmeg to taste. Spoon over the trifle, and refrigerate, covered, until ready to serve.

[SPONGE CAKE makes one 9-inch cake]

4 eggs, separated
Scant ¼ teaspoon cream of tartar
⅔ cup sugar
1½ teaspoons pure vanilla extract
1 cup plus 2 tablespons all-purpose flour, sifted

1. Preheat the oven to 350°F. Spray a 9-inch round cake pan with pan spray and line with parchment. Spray the parchment.

2. In the bowl of a standing mixer fitted with the whisk attachment, beat the egg whites on low speed until they form soft peaks. Add the cream of tarter and increase the speed to medium while you gradually add half the sugar, one tablespoon at a time. Beat until the whites form medium-stiff peaks.

3. In a standing mixer fitted with the whip attachment, or in a large bowl with an electric mixer or whisk, beat together the egg yolk and remaining sugar on high speed until the mixture is thick and pale yellow, and holds a ribbon when drizzled from a spatula, about 3 minutes. Beat in the vanilla. Stir in ¼ of the beaten egg whites.

4. Fold the flour into the egg yolks in four additions, alternating with the egg whites.

5. Scrape the batter into the prepared cake pan. Tap once against the work surace to deflate large air bubbles. Bake 15 minutes and rotate the pan. Bake another 10 to 15 minutes, until firm to the touch and a cake tester comes out clean. Remove from oven and allow to cool in the pan on a rack for 1 minute, then invert onto another rack, remove the pan, peel off the parchment, and invert again to cool on the rack.

pâte sucrée [makes two 9-inch shells]

This is the classic sweet dessert pastry dough. You can make it in a standing mixer or in a food processor. Note that you will need to chill the dough for several hours, or up to a day, before rolling out and baking. The dough freezes well; line pans and freeze them, then transfer directly from the freezer to the oven for prebaking without the filling (pastry chefs call this "blind baking"). You don't need weights when you prebake frozen dough right from the freezer.

1	cup (2 sticks) unsalted butter, cut in $\frac{1}{2}$-inch pieces
$2\frac{1}{2}$	cups all-purpose flour
$\frac{1}{2}$	cup sugar
$\frac{1}{8}$	teaspoon salt
2	cold large egg yolks
1	to 2 tablespoons cold heavy cream

[USING A FOOD PROCESSOR]

1. Cut up the butter and place it in the freezer for 15 minutes.

2. Combine the flour, sugar, and salt in the bowl of a food processor fitted with the steel blade and pulse together. Add the butter and pulse until the mixture looks like cornmeal. Beat together the egg yolks and 1 tablespoon of the cream. Turn on the food processor and pour in the mixture in a thin stream. Stop as soon as the dough comes together on the blades. If it does not come together right away, add the second tablespoon of cream.

[USING A MIXER]

1. Cut up the butter and place it in the freezer for 15 minutes.

2. Combine the flour, sugar, and salt in the bowl of a standing mixer and mix at low speed for 1 minute. Add the butter and beat at medium-low speed until the mixture resembles cornmeal. Add the egg yolks and 1 tablespoon of the cream and beat at medium-low speed until the mixture comes together. If the dough feels dry, add the other tablespoon of cream and beat until the dough comes together.

[CHILLING AND SHAPING]

3. Remove from the mixer bowl or food processor, and divide into 2 equal pieces. Place on plastic wrap and flatten to about $\frac{1}{2}$ inch thick. Wrap tightly and refrigerate for at least 4 hours or overnight.

4. To roll out the dough, place one piece at a time on a flat, smooth, lightly floured work surface and tap with a rolling pin just until it is pliable. Roll out to a $\frac{1}{4}$-inch-thick circle. If the dough is sticky, place between sheets of parchment paper or plastic. Store flat between pieces of parchment in the refrigerator or freezer, or line pans, wrap tightly, and store. If you freeze flat pieces, be careful when you handle them as they will break easily. Thaw them before you attempt to line a tart or pie pan.

[PREBAKING]

Preheat the oven to 350°F, with the rack in the lower third. Line the dough with parchment or large coffee filters and fill with dried beans or rice. Bake for 18 minutes. Remove the beans or rice and liner and bake another 15 to 20 minutes, or until a deep golden brown. After this do not use the beans or rice for anything but blind baking other tart shells.

rhubarb and strawberry tart [makes one 9-inch tart]

I never liked rhubarb when I was a kid, probably because it looks like celery. I only came to appreciate it when I grew up. Rhubarb is often paired with strawberries, which are also acidic, but sweeter. In this dessert I love the contrast between the sweet strawberries and streusel topping and the sweet/tart rhubarb. When you work with rhubarb, cut off and discard any leaves; they are mildly toxic.

½	cup plus 2 tablespoons sugar
¼	cup water
½	vanilla bean, split and scraped
⅛	teaspoon ground cinnamon
6	large stalks rhubarb, rinsed and cut in 1-inch pieces
1½	cups rinsed, hulled, and quartered strawberries
1	9-inch Pâte Sucrée, fully baked (page 256)
1	cup Streusel Topping
	Crème fraîche or vanilla ice cream, for serving

1. Make the rhubarb compote: Combine ½ cup of sugar, the water, and vanilla bean and seeds in a heavy saucepan, cover, and slowly bring to a boil over medium heat. Leave the cover on the pot for 5 minutes, then remove the lid. When the syrup begins to turn golden, quickly add the cinnamon and half the rhubarb to it. Cover, reduce the heat to medium-low, and simmer, stirring often, until the rhubarb breaks down completely, about 20 minutes. Add the remaining rhubarb, cover, and simmer until it softens in the slurry, 10 to 15 minutes. Remove from the heat and set aside to cool. Remove the vanilla bean.

2. Toss the strawberries in a bowl with the remaining 2 tablespoons sugar. Allow to macerate for about 15 minutes.

3. Preheat the oven to 350°F, with the rack positioned in the middle. Fill the prebaked tart shell with the rhubarb compote and arrange the strawberries on top. Sprinkle on a layer of streusel topping. It is not necessary to cover the top totally.

4. Bake 20 to 25 minutes, until the streusel is golden brown. Remove from the oven and allow to cool completely before serving. Serve with crème fraîche or vanilla ice cream.

[STREUSEL TOPPING makes 3 cups]

This recipe makes a large batch of streusel topping. We use it to top fruit tarts, like the Rhubarb and Strawberry Tart and crumbles. You can keep it on hand in the freezer for 2 months.

2	cups all-purpose flour
½	cup granulated sugar
1	cup tightly packed light brown sugar
1½	cups rolled oats
2	teaspoons ground cinnamon
¼	teaspoon freshly grated nutmeg
¼	teaspoon salt
¾	cup (1½ sticks) cold unsalted butter, cut in ½-inch pieces

1. In a standing mixer fitted with the paddle attachment, mix together the flour, sugars, oats, cinnamon, nutmeg, and salt on low speed. Add the butter and beat on medium speed until the butter is evenly distributed through the mixture and the streusel has a crumbly texture. This can also be made in a food processor fitted with the steel blade, using the pulse action.

2. Preheat the oven to 350°F. Line a baking sheet with parchment. Spread the streusel topping in an even layer over the parchment and bake 20 minutes, stirring halfway through, or until lightly and evenly browned.

3. Remove from the heat and allow to cool. Store airtight in the freezer.

peach compote [makes 3 cups]

Make this compote during those few weeks in summer when peaches are perfect. Spoon it over ice cream, or use it to make Peach Ice Cream (page 243) or Peach Swirl Ice Cream (page 243). I prefer the old-fashioned peach varieties, which have better flavor but tend to be furrier and smaller than newer types (growers have been hybridizing out the furriness). I also prefer yellow peaches to white peaches; people say the white ones are sweeter, but actually they're just lacking in acidity. The peaches should be ripe but not soft. Press gently on the shoulder of the peach, right around where the stem would be; it should give just a bit.

2½	pounds peaches
½	cup sugar
½	teaspoon pure vanilla extract, or ½ vanilla bean, split and scraped
1	inch cinnamon stick
⅛	teaspoon freshly grated nutmeg
½	cup dry but fruity white wine, such as a Vouvray or Viognier

1. Peel the peaches by blanching for 1 minute in boiling water, then transferring them to a bowl of ice water to cool. Slip off the skins. Cut in half, remove the pits, then cut into 1-inch chunks.

2. Combine the peaches and the remaining ingredients in a heavy, medium saucepan over medium heat and bring to a boil. Cook, stirring often, for 15 minutes, until the liquid has concentrated and the peaches have softened but are mostly intact. Remove from the heat. Remove the cinnamon stick. Allow to cool, transfer to a bowl or container, cover, and chill.

VANILLA BEANS

Vanilla beans are expensive, but they're essential for true vanilla flavor. The long pod is the dried fruit of a variety of orchid. They are so expensive because the flowers open only once a year and must be hand pollinated, and the beans must be very carefully fermented and sun-dried for six months once harvested.

The many tiny seeds and pulp inside the pod give desserts the distinctive vanilla flavor. When you use vanilla beans, split them open by cutting them lengthwise down the middle with the tip of a sharp knife, then scrape out the seeds. The pod does contain aromatic oils, so it should be steeped, along with the seeds and pulp, in the liquid you are using for your vanilla sauce. The pods can be dried and submerged in a jar of sugar or pulverized with the sugar to infuse it with a vanilla aroma, so don't throw them away after you strain them out of a sauce.

There are three types of vanilla bean. The most common, from Madagascar and the Comoros off the coast of Africa, are known as bourbon or bourbon Madagascar beans. My favorite are the plumper Tahitian beans. They are more aromatic, with a higher oil content but fewer seeds. Mexican beans are the rarest vanilla beans, with a distinctive spicy flavor. Any of these beans is suitable for these recipes. Do not buy beans that are dry and brittle; they should be supple, shiny, and aromatic. Keep them well wrapped in plastic, in the refrigerator or in a dark, cool cupboard.

plum compote [makes 2½ cups]

We make this compote throughout the summer, to serve on its own and to use in sorbets, ice creams, trifles, and other desserts. I like to use a combination of Santa Rosa and Elephant Heart plums for this. The Santa Rosas are more flavorful and tannic, and the Elephant Hearts are sweet and complex, with deep, dark red color.

2½	pounds plums
½	cup sugar
½	teaspoon pure vanilla extract, or
	½ vanilla bean, split and scraped
1	inch cinnamon stick
⅛	teaspoon freshly grated nutmeg
1	strip lemon zest, about 1 inch long x ½ inch wide
½	cup fruity red wine, such as a Beaujolais

1. Cut the plums in half, remove the pits, then cut into 1-inch chunks.

2. Combine the plums and the remaining ingredients in a heavy, medium saucepan and bring to a boil. Turn the heat to medium and cook, stirring often, for 15 minutes, until the liquid has concentrated and the plums have softened but are mostly intact. Remove from the heat. Remove the cinnamon stick and lemon zest. Put through a large-holed strainer or a food mill fitted with the medium screen. Allow to cool, transfer to a bowl or container, and chill.

PLUMS

Two common plums in California are Santa Rosa and Elephant Heart. Santa Rosas are small football-shaped plums with dark red/purple skin and golden yellow meat. There's a marked difference in flavor between their sour, tannic skins and sweet pulp, so when you cook them, skin and pulp together, you get a complex flavor. Elephant Hearts have red, juicy meat and a pale greenish-red skin with a sour edge. They're sweet and complex, but the skin isn't as tannic as the Santa Rosas'. If you cook with these you'll get great color without the tannin because the meat is dark purple.

peach melba [makes 4 servings]

When the nineteenth-century opera singer Nellie Melba was dieting, as she often was, she ate melba toast. When she wasn't, she ate Peach Melba, a dessert created for her by Auguste Escoffier at the Savoy Hotel in London. When he brought it to her, he presented it in an ice sculpture of a swan inspired by her performance in *Lohengrin*. I like Peach Melba because it's simple. Many nineteenth-century recipes sound complicated, but the complexity is actually in the presentation (like the ice sculpture of a swan). If any of you want to make the ice sculpture I commend you, but I won't copy you. I'm happy with a simple, perfectly ripe peach poached in a red wine caramel sauce with raspberries, served with vanilla ice cream.

4	ripe but firm freestone peaches
I	cup sugar
3	tablespoons water
I	tablespoon light corn syrup
2	cups dry red wine
	Pinch of black pepper
½	3-inch cinnamon stick
	A small pinch of ground nutmeg
I	juniper berry
3	whole cloves
½	vanilla bean, split
I ½	½-pint baskets raspberries (about 9 ounces)
2	teaspoons grappa (optional)
I	pint vanilla ice cream
20	small amaretti cookies (optional garnish)

I. Fill a large saucepan with water and bring to a boil. Fill a bowl with ice water. When the water comes to a boil, drop in the peaches. Boil 30 seconds to a minute (if they are hard they'll need a minute) and transfer to the ice water. Slip off the skins. Halve the peaches, remove the pits, and set aside.

2. In a clean, medium saucepan, combine the sugar, water, and corn syrup. Stir them together with a very clean spoon, making sure no lumps of dry sugar remain. The consistency should be like wet sand. Brush down the inside of the pan with a little water, using your fingers to feel for stray granules of sugar. Cover the saucepan and place over medium heat for 4 to 5 minutes, until the mixture is boiling. Remove the lid and increase the heat to high. Do not stir. When stray sugar crystals appear on the side of the pan, brush them down with a wet pastry brush.

3. When the mixture begins to turn a golden brown, insert a candy thermometer and lower the heat slightly. Continue to cook until the caramel is the color of medium-dark honey and reaches 325°F. At 325°F, remove the pot from the heat, and let it sit for 2 minutes, until the bubbles subside.

4. Slowly and carefully add the wine to the caramel. The caramel will bubble up and seize, but it will liquefy again when you heat it. Return it to the heat and add the spices and vanilla bean. Bring back to a boil, reduce the heat, and simmer until reduced by half. Remove from the heat and remove the cloves, juniper berry, cinnamon stick, and vanilla bean.

5. Bring the sauce back to a boil, turn the heat to low, and carefully add the peaches, cut side down (you may have to do this in 2 batches). Turn off the heat and cover the pot. Set the timer for 5 minutes. Using tongs, carefully turn the peaches over. Cover and leave to cool in the sauce, then, using tongs, gently transfer the peaches to a large platter. If necessary, repeat this process with the second batch of peaches. Cover and chill.

6. Set aside 16 raspberries. Add the remaining raspberries to the sauce and bring to a simmer. Simmer until the raspberries have burst, about 5 minutes, and crush with the back of a spoon. Remove from the heat and strain through a medium sieve into a bowl. Add the grappa, if using, and set aside.

7. To serve, spoon some of the sauce over a dessert plate or wide bowl. Place 2 peach halves, rounded side down, on the syrup, and add 2 quenelle-shaped scoops of ice cream. Spoon on a little more sauce, dot with raspberries, and serve. If using the garnish, crumble 4 of the cookies into a small bowl. Prepare the plates as above, and garnish each with 4 amaretti. Sprinkle the crumbled amaretti over the top.

plum granita or sorbet [makes 1 quart, 4 to 6 servings]

There's a progression of flavors in this dessert. When you take a spoonful, all you get at first is sweetness; then as it warms up in your mouth, the richness and sharp complexity of the plum flavors and the spices emerge. If you use only Santa Rosas, which are more available than Elephant Hearts, the result will be sharper and more tannic because of the skins. A word of caution: Do not wear a white linen shirt while making this.

2	pounds ripe plums, Elephant Hearts and Santa Rosas if available, quartered (retain the pits)
1	vanilla bean, split and scraped
3	whole cloves
¼	teaspoon cracked black peppercorns
½	cup sugar
	Zest of 1 lemon
2	cups red wine, preferably a light Pinot Noir

1. If you are making granita, place a 9 x 11-inch Pyrex baking dish in the freezer. Place the plums with their pits in a heavy medium saucepan. Add the vanilla bean and seeds, the cloves, pepper, sugar, lemon zest, and 1 cup of wine. Bring to a simmer and simmer 15 minutes, until the plums are very soft.

2. Remove from the heat and add another cup of wine. Let sit for 15 minutes. Pick out the pits with tongs, leaving all the pulp behind. Put through the fine blade of a food mill, or strain through a medium sieve, using a pestle or a rubber spatula to push the mixture through. Strain the mixture again through a fine strainer. You should have about 4 cups.

3. If making sorbet, freeze in an ice cream maker following the manufacturer's directions. If making granita, scrape with the rubber spatula into the chilled baking dish and place back in the freezer. Set the timer for 30 minutes. Using a fork, scrape and mix the frozen ice crystals from the outside of the baking dish into the center. Return to the freezer and set the timer for another 30 minutes. Continue to scrape the mixture with a fork every 30 minutes, until you have a uniform frozen mixture. It should not be frozen solid. If you forget to scrape and the mixture does freeze like an ice cube, cut into chunks and use a food processor fitted with the steel blade to break it up. Transfer to a container and refreeze. Allow to soften for 15 minutes in the refrigerator before serving.

roasted figs [makes 4 to 6 servings]

Roasting figs brings out their sweet jamminess. Don't use overripe figs, or they'll fall apart. Use ever-so-slightly underripe or just-ripe figs. Serve these warm with vanilla ice cream, or at room temperature with a cheese course. They go especially well with blue cheeses.

1	pound fresh figs
¼	cup Port wine
	Tiny pinch of ground pepper
2	teaspoons sugar
1	teaspoon mild honey, such as clover or acacia

1. Preheat the oven to 500°F. Cut the stems off the figs, then make a ½-inch-deep crosshatch across the tops. Choose a baking dish or an ovenproof pan the figs will fit into snugly. Place the figs in the pan, with those that are less ripe on the outside. Pour the port over them, sprinkle with the pepper and sugar, and drizzle on the honey.

2. Place in the oven for 12 to 15 minutes, just until slightly caramelized on top and soft to the touch. The figs should retain their shape.

3. Remove from the oven. Allow to cool slightly in the pan, about 10 minutes. Carefully drain most of the juice into a saucepan and bring to a boil. Boil 1 minute, or until reduced slightly, and pour back over the figs.

concord grape sorbet [makes 1 quart, 4 to 6 servings]

It's amazing to me how Concord grapes can make the best jelly, jam, and sorbet—and the worst wine. I grew up on juice and jam made from this distinctive grape. Like Santa Rosa plums, it's the skins here that have the tannin and color. The seeds are quite bitter, so make sure you strain them out without crushing them.

2	pounds Concord grapes
1	vanilla bean, split and scraped
3	black peppercorns, cracked
½	cup sugar
	Zest of 1 lemon
2	cups red wine, preferably Beaujolais

1. Place the grapes in a heavy medium saucepan. Add the vanilla bean and seeds, black pepper, sugar, lemon zest, and 1½ cups of wine. Bring to a simmer and simmer 10 minutes, just until the grapes burst.

2. Remove from the heat and let stand for 1 minute. Stir in the remaining ½ cup wine and let sit for 15 minutes, occasionally stirring and popping the grapes with the back of your spoon. Put through the fine blade of a food mill, or strain through a medium sieve, using a pestle or a rubber spatula to push the puree through. Try not to crush the seeds; they will give the sorbet a bitter flavor. Strain the mixture again through a fine strainer. You should have about 4 cups.

3. Freeze in an ice cream maker following the manufacturer's directions. You can also make this into a granita (see page 262).

boston cream pie [makes one 9-inch layer cake]

Boston Cream Pie isn't a pie at all—it's a filled cake. But who am I to argue with the city of Boston? You can make the cake and the filling a day before you assemble this. Store it, well sealed, in the refrigerator.

[CAKE]
1½ cups all-purpose flour
1½ teaspoons baking powder
    Pinch of salt
½   cup (1 stick) unsalted butter, softened
¾   cup sugar
3   large eggs, at room temperature
1   teaspoon pure vanilla extract
½   cup whole milk

[PASTRY CREAM]
1⅓ cups whole milk
⅓   cup sugar
1   tablespoon Grand Marnier (optional)
½   vanilla bean, split and scraped, or 1 teaspoon
        pure vanilla extract
    Pinch of salt
2   tablespoons cornstarch
2   large eggs
2   teaspoons unsalted butter, softened

[CHOCOLATE GLAZE]
3   ounces bittersweet (70%) chocolate, finely chopped
4   tablespoons (½ stick) unsalted butter
1   tablespoon light corn syrup

1. Make the cake: Preheat the oven to 350°F, with a rack positioned in the middle. Spray a 9-inch cake pan with pan spray and line with parchment. Spray the parchment. Sift the flour, baking powder, and salt twice and set aside.

2. In the bowl of a standing mixer fitted with the paddle attachment, beat together the butter and sugar on medium speed until very light and fluffy, about 5 minutes. Scrape down the sides of the bowl and the beaters. Beat in the eggs, one at a time, scraping down the bowl and beaters after each addition. Beat in the vanilla. Scrape down the sides of the bowl and the beaters, and begin beating at low speed while you add the milk and the flour mixture, in 3 additions, alternating the dry and wet ingredients. Beat until smooth, but be careful not to overbeat. Scrape into the prepared pan.

3. Bake 30 to 40 minutes, turning the pan 180° halfway through the baking, until the cake springs back when lightly touched in the middle and is beginning to pull away from the

sides of the pan. Remove from the oven and allow the cake to cool in the pan on a rack for 15 minutes. Unmold, remove the parchment, and allow to cool completely, at least 2 hours.

4. Make the pastry cream: In a medium saucepan, combine the milk, 3 tablespoons of sugar, the Grand Marnier (if using), and the vanilla or scraped vanilla bean and seeds, and bring to a simmer over medium heat. While the milk is heating, sift together the remaining sugar, salt, and cornstarch. In a large bowl, whisk the eggs and add the sifted dry ingredients. Whisk until fluffy.

5. When the milk begins to simmer, remove from the heat. Making sure that it is not boiling, whisking constantly, slowly pour the milk into the eggs. Once the milk is incorporated into the eggs, whisk them back into the hot milk. Scrape all the eggs into the milk with a rubber spatula.

6. Return to medium-low heat and immediately begin to rapidly whisk the pastry cream. It will boil and begin to thicken. Continue to whisk for about 3 minutes, until it reaches pudding consistency. If the mixture looks like it's curdling, remove the pan from the heat immediately and whisk rapidly for a few minutes.

7. Remove the pot from the heat and immediately strain it into a clean bowl. Add the butter and stir until it is melted and incorporated. Place a sheet of plastic wrap directly over the pastry cream and refrigerate for 2 hours.

8. Assemble the cake: Split the cake in half horizontally. Place the bottom half on a cake plate or stand. Spread the pastry cream over the cake in an even layer and top with the other half.

9. Make the chocolate glaze: Combine the chocolate, butter, and corn syrup in a bowl and set the bowl over a saucepan with 1 inch of simmering water, taking care that the bottom of the bowl does not touch the water. Stir until the ingredients melt together. Remove from the heat and allow the icing to cool for 10 minutes, until it is almost room temperature. Scrape the icing over the top of the cake and spread with an offset spatula. Serve at room temperature and refrigerate any leftovers.

key lime cheesecake [makes one 9-inch cake]

I spent two days in Key West, Florida, with my wife, Daphne Brogdon, searching for good Key lime pie. We failed. It was all overly sweet, tasting of chemicals, and gummy with cornstarch. For great Key lime flavor, try this cheesecake. Key limes are also known as Mexican limes. They have a lot more seeds than the standard Persian lime, which has almost none, and much better flavor.

1½	cups graham cracker crumbs
2	tablespoons unsalted butter, melted
1	pound cream cheese, softened and at room temperature
¾	cup sugar
3	large or extra-large eggs, at room temperature
3	tablespoons strained freshly squeezed Key lime or Mexican lime juice
1½	teaspoons finely chopped Key lime or Mexican lime zest
1	teaspoon pure vanilla extract
1½	cups crème fraîche

1. Preheat the oven to 350°F. Spray a 9-inch springform pan with pan spray and line the bottom with parchment. Spray the parchment. Wrap the outside of the pan with aluminum foil so no water will leak in from the water bath when you bake the cake.

2. Mix together the graham cracker crumbs and melted butter and spread in an even layer in the bottom of the pan. Press the crumbs down gently. Chill while you mix the filling.

3. In a standing mixer fitted with the paddle attachment, combine the cream cheese and sugar and beat on low speed until smooth, about 2 minutes. Add the eggs, one at a time, scraping down the sides of the bowl and the beaters after each addition. Add the lime juice and zest and the vanilla, and beat until smooth. Add the crème fraîche and beat until smooth. Scrape down the bowl and beaters and beat again for about 30 seconds.

4. Scrape the mixture into the prepared pan. Place the pan in a roasting pan and fill the roasting pan with enough hot water to come halfway up the sides of the springform pan.

5. Place in the oven and bake 1 hour. Turn off the oven and do not open the oven door for 45 minutes. Remove from the oven and remove from the water bath. Take off the aluminum foil from the bottom of the pan. Cool on a rack for 2 hours, then cover and refrigerate for 4 hours or overnight before serving.

6. To serve, run a knife along the inside of the rim of the springform pan and remove the rim. Slice and serve.

peach cobbler with buttermilk drop biscuit topping [makes 8 servings]

This is a classic summer dessert, one that evokes front porches and hand-cranked ice cream. It's a great picnic item that you can make ahead and bring with you (cover it with a clean dish towel so the flies don't get at it). For a really impressive dessert, serve this with the Peach Swirl Ice Cream on page 243.

[TOPPING]

2	cups unbleached all-purpose flour
¼	cup sugar
2	teaspoons baking powder
½	teaspoon baking soda
¼	teaspoon salt
½	cup (1 stick) cold unsalted butter, cut in ½-inch pieces
2	teaspoons finely chopped lemon zest
1	large egg
⅔	cup buttermilk

[PEACH FILLING]

3	pounds ripe but firm yellow peaches
¼	cup sugar
¼	cup tightly packed light brown sugar
1	teaspoon vanilla extract
¼	teaspoon almond extract
⅛	teaspoon freshly grated nutmeg
1	teaspoon cornstarch dissolved in 1 tablespoon fresh lemon juice
2	tablespoons chopped candied ginger

[FOR BRUSHING THE TOP]

2	tablespoons whole milk
1	tablespoon sugar

1. Make the topping: Sift together the flour, sugar, baking powder, baking soda, and salt into the bowl of a standing mixer fitted with the paddle attachment, or into a food processor fitted with the steel blade. Add the butter and lemon zest and mix at low speed for 1 minute (if using the stand mixer) until the butter and flour are broken down into coarse crumbs about the size of broken walnuts. Rub the mixture between your hands to distribute the butter evenly through the flour mixture until the mixture has the consistency of coarse cornmeal. If using a food processor, pulse until you have a coarse, even mixture.

2. In a separate bowl, whisk together the egg and the buttermilk. Add to the flour mixture and beat just until the dough comes together. Transfer to a bowl and refrigerate for 1 hour or longer (preferably overnight).

3. Make the filling: Bring a large saucepan of water to a boil and blanch the peaches, a few at a time, for 1 minute. Transfer to a bowl of ice water and allow to cool. Slip off the skins, cut in half and remove the pits, then cut in 1-inch chunks.

4. In a large bowl, toss together the peaches with all of the filling ingredients. Let sit for 30 minutes. Meanwhile, preheat the oven to 400°F and butter a 2-quart baking dish.

5. Assemble the cobbler: Spoon the peaches with all of their juices into the buttered baking dish. Dollop heaping tablespoons of the topping side by side over the peaches, starting at the outside and finishing in the middle.

6. Place in the oven and bake 20 minutes. Brush lightly with milk and sprinkle with the sugar, and bake another 15 to 20 minutes, until golden brown and shiny. Remove from the heat and allow to cool for 10 minutes or longer before serving. Serve with vanilla ice cream, peach ice cream, or whipped cream.

plum clafoutis [makes 8 servings]

A clafoutis is an easy and impressive dessert to make, with the appeal of a tart but without the crust. It's sort of a cross between a flan and a pancake, and is traditionally baked in a fluted ceramic baking dish. I love to make this with the green plums or green pluots (a cross between a plum and an apricot) that we get at the end of summer. A firm plum that holds its shape is best. There are low, fluted, straight–sided ceramic baking dishes made specifically for clafoutis; they're pretty but not necessary.

1 ¼	pounds plums, pitted and cut in half if small, into quarters or sixths if larger
½	cup sugar
2	tablespoons plum brandy or kirsch
1	cup whole milk
3	large eggs
1	vanilla bean, scraped
1	teaspoon finely chopped orange zest
	Pinch of salt
½	cup all-purpose flour

1. Preheat the oven to 375°F. Butter a 10-inch glass baking dish, a ceramic clafoutis dish, or a round ceramic baking dish. Toss the plums with 1 tablespoon of the sugar and the plum brandy or kirsch. Let sit for 15 minutes. Pour off the liquid from the bowl into a measuring cup. Add milk to make 1 cup liquid.

2. Beat together the eggs and remaining sugar in a large bowl. Add the seeds from the vanilla bean, the orange zest, and the salt. Add the flour and beat together well. Beat in the milk.

3. Arrange the plums, skin side up, in the baking dish. Pour on the batter. Place on a baking sheet in the oven and bake 25 to 30 minutes, until puffed and browned. Serve warm or at room temperature.

CAMPANILE FAMILY DINNER MENUS

[SPRING LAMB]
GREEN BEAN SALAD WITH WALNUTS
LAMB DAUBE
RHUBARB AND STRAWBERRY TART

[WHOLE ROAST FISH]
COLD CUCUMBER AND YOGURT SOUP
WHOLE ROAST FISH WITH ROASTED ASPARAGUS
POLENTA WITH BUTTER AND PARMESAN CHEESE
PEACH ICE CREAM

[SOUTHERN FRIED CHICKEN]
GREEN AND RED TOMATOES WITH RUSSIAN DRESSING
UNABASHED, UNASHAMED SOUTHERN FRIED CHICKEN
LONG-COOKED GREENS
MASHED POTATOES, FINALLY REVEALED
GRASSHOPPER PIE

[VEAL PICCATA]
ROASTED TOMATO SOUP
VEAL PICCATA WITH POMMES BOULANGÈRE
AND LONG-COOKED GREEN BEANS WITH BACON
PLUM GRANITA

[POT AU FEU]
LEEKS VINAIGRETTE
POT AU FEU
DARK CHOCOLATE POTS DE CRÈME WITH
WHIPPED CRÈME FRAÎCHE

[LASAGNE]
GRILLED INSALATA TRICOLORE
LASAGNE BOLOGNESE
GELATO AFFOGATO

[GUINEA HEN]
FRESH SHELL BEAN RAGOUT
GUINEA HEN FRICASSÉE WITH RED WINE,
BACON, AND MUSHROOMS
ROASTED FINGERLING POTATOES
ORO BLANCO SORBET

[VEAL PARMESAN]
CLAMS CASINO
BREADED VEAL SCALOPPINE WITH SMOKED
MOZZARELLA, PARMESAN, AND TOMATO SAUCE
POLENTA WITH BUTTER AND PARMESAN CHEESE
CHARRED RAPINI WITH WARM BACON VINAIGRETTE
CHOCOLATE CHIP ICE CREAM

[STEAK BORDELAISE]
ICEBERG LETTUCE SALAD WITH
ROQUEFORT-BUTTERMILK DRESSING
STEAK BORDELAISE
CREAMED SPINACH AND PARSLEYED POTATOES
BOCA NEGRA

[SAUSAGES BRAISED IN BEER]
LEEK TART WITH CRÈME FRAÎCHE
SAUSAGES BRAISED IN BEER WITH SAUERKRAUT
WARM GERMAN POTATO SALAD
PLUM COMPOTE

[LOBSTER NEWBURG]
BUTTER LETTUCE SALAD WITH STILTON AND WALNUTS
LOBSTER NEWBURG
BOSTON CREAM PIE

[SPAGHETTI WITH MEATBALLS]
BRAISED BABY ARTICHOKES
SPAGHETTI WITH MEATBALLS
PISTACHIO ICE CREAM

[BEEF GOULASH]
BEET BORSCHT
BEEF GOULASH
SPAETZLE WITH WILTED SPINACH
CHOCOLATE PUDDING WITH WHIPPED CREAM

[BEER-BRAISED BRISKET]
RADISH AND CUCUMBER SALAD WITH YOGURT DRESSING
BEER-BRAISED BRISKET WITH CARAMELIZED ROOT VEGETABLES
MASHED POTATOES, FINALLY REVEALED
DEVIL'S FOOD LAYER CAKE WITH WHITE MOUNTAIN FROSTING

[SANTA MARIA BARBECUE]
SWEET PEA SOUP WITH WALNUT CROUTONS
SANTA MARIA BARBECUE
GRILLED CORN WITH HERB BUTTER
CAMPANILE BEANS
STRAWBERRY ICE CREAM

[MACARONI AND CHEESE]
BEEFSTEAK TOMATOES WITH CUMIN-OREGANO
VINAIGRETTE AND FETA
MACARONI AND CHEESE WITH WILD MUSHROOMS
CONCORD GRAPE SORBET